A Civic Revolution

Modern Municipal Government & its establishment at Ballarat 1855-1857

Graeme S Cartledge

First published in Australia in 2024 by Local Research Publishers
Winter Valley Victoria 3358
graemescartledge@outlook.com

Copyright © Graeme S Cartledge 2024 All rights reserved

ISBN 978-0-6458362-3-3

Abstract

This book contends that modern municipal government was an important nineteenth-century initiative to address social and political change. Focusing on British origins, it argues that it performed a vital role in integrating the population into the modern state while establishing rational civic order. It argues that it also became necessary for the Ballarat goldfields due to the failure of the government to adapt to the changing nature of gold mining, regional communities, and colonial society. The book thus shows how this occurred due to the miners' movement through 1853 and 1854, which culminated in the Eureka Rebellion and the removal of the Goldfields Commission. Previously quarantined from colonial society by government policy, and hindered in exploiting the local gold resources, it shows how the diggers were then able to revolutionise the administration of the local community and integrate themselves into the civic framework of the colony. Moreover, it tells the remarkable story of how the first elected councillors achieved this in just one year for Ballarat, establishing modern administrative systems and infrastructure, bringing order and progress to a community emerging from tyranny and turmoil.

ACKNOWLEDGEMENTS

This book is based on my 2018 master's thesis which owes a great deal to the kindness, patience, and consideration of many people and organisations. I would like to express my appreciation for the guidance and support of my principal thesis supervisor Anne Beggs-Sunter whose love of Ballarat's history and heritage is truly inspiring. Professor Weston Bate who passed away during this project also has my gratitude for inspiring this thesis through his iconic contribution to the history of Ballarat.

I would also like to thank the HDR team at Federation University and their professionalism which made it possible to gain the necessary skills to complete the research project. The staff of the E J Barker Library also are very deserving of praise for their high degree of efficiency and expertise in obtaining and providing many of the resources relevant to this thesis.

My gratitude and thanks are also extended to the staff at the Public Record Office, Victoria at Ballarat and North Melbourne, the Ballarat and Prahran Mechanics Institute, The Geoffrey Blainey Research Centre at Federation University and the staff at the City of Ballarat Library and the Australiana Research Collection. The completion of this book also owes a great deal to the resources available through Trove and the National Library of Australia and its digitized resources, many of which before its existence, would have been beyond the resources of time and travel to obtain.

This research has been supported by an Australian Government Research Training Program (RTP) Scholarship.

Contents

Illustrations ix
Introduction 1
PART 1 8
A 'system of life constructed on a wholly new principle' 8
1. Urbanization of British Society... 9
   The New Towns & Cities.. 9
2. Aliens & Enlightened Immigrants 19
   Anomie & the Industrial Society.. 19
   Respectable Migrants.. 22
   Colonial Aliens... 29
3. Historiography 33
   Before the 1856 Colonial Franchise... 33
   Historical Perceptions of Municipal Government 44
   Local Histories and Local Government History 49
4. Local Government in Transition.. 57
   British Local Government... 57
      The Old Tory Order & the Need for Change 57
   Victorian Local Government 64
      Regional Victoria to 1856 66
5. Creating Modern Municipalities 71
   Re-integrating and Re-ordering Society...................................... 71
   Basic Themes.. 76
   1.   *Order from Chaos*.. 76
        British Towns and Cities... 76

  Ballarat Goldfields 79
 2. A Struggle for Recognition 83
  The British Experience 83
  The Ballarat Goldfield 86
 3. *A First Taste of Democracy* 88

PART 2 92

The Goldfields & Civic Society 92

6. Social & Political Dilemmas of Gold 93
 NSW Gold Discovery & the Government 93
 Containing the Gold Rushes 104

7. The Victorian Gold Rush 117
 Implications of a Regional Population Boom 117
 Victoria 1851: Anticipating Social Change 119
 Gold Legislation: 'a field for crude experiments' 121

8. Victorian Regional Government 1851-1855 131
 Local Government Policy 1851-1854 134

9. Ending Local Government by Commission 141
 1853: Ballarat Miners and Local Government 145
 1854 and the Commission of Inquiry 147

PART 3 150

Creating Civil Administration at Ballarat 1855-1857 150

10. Local Consolidation after Eureka 151
 To preserve the liberties and institutions of their fatherland ... 151
 Victorian Reform League & Local Leadership 156
 The Law & Order Crisis 161

Ballarat vs the Miners *167*

11. 1856 Ballarat West: Fit and Proper Persons 184
The First Election *184*
Inaugural Chairman James Oddie *190*
Robert Muir *193*
Creating Local Institutions *196*
Creating a Modern Society: Liberals and Old-fogeyism *199*

12. Establishing Local Authority 209
A Town Hall & Local Opposition *209*
The District Roads Board *211*
Land & Council Jurisdiction *213*
Starting With Nothing *221*
Main Road & the Municipality Streets *227*
Income & Expenses First Half Year *230*

13. Challenges and Achievements 1856-1857 233
Bylaws & Enforcement *233*
Water Supply *238*
Accounting & the Streets *244*
Political Factions and Market Square *246*
Ballarat East Link Road & Telegraph *256*

Conclusion 260

BIBLIOGRAPHY 268
Primary Sources *268*
   Newspapers *268*
   Public Records *268*

 Government Reports and Gazettes 269
 Secondary Sources 270
  Theses 276
  Periodicals 276
  Pamphlets 278
INDEX 279
APPENDIX 307
 Appendix I 307
  Rated property in Ballarat West 1856 307
 Appendix II 309
  Frenchman's & Whitehorse Leads mining 1856 309
 Appendix III 316
  April 1855 Public rally on Law & Order 316
 Appendix IV 318
  The Municipality Petitions 1855 318
 Appendix V 320
  Petition Proclamation 320
 Appendix VI 321
  List of Petitioners 321
 Appendix VII 325
  Offer of Land by Government Surveyor 325
 Appendix VIII 327
  Valuator's First Report: 327

Illustrations

1. *Portrait of Alexander Thomson*, 1st Geelong Mayor by Frederick Grosse 1866, State Library of Victoria, 49196700 P.36
2. Serle Percival, *Dictionary of Australian Biography* Angus & Robertson, J T Smith Mayor of Melbourne entry & portrait P.39
3. Ballarat Gold Diggers' Petition, *Geelong Advertiser* 24 Sept 1851 P.40
4. Bendigo Miners letter of appreciation to Melbourne Mayor J T Smith for support in 1853 Protests, Argus (Melbourne), Saturday 6 August 1853 P.41
5. Letter of appreciation of support from Tasmanian Legislature regarding protests against Dept of Prisons to Melbourne mayor J T Smith October 1855, *The Argus* (Melbourne) 22 October 1855, p5, Tasmania P. 42
6. Mike Nevell – Housing in 19th century Manchester, photograph of Ancoats 1870, Marple Local History Society 2024 P.76
7. Daintree, Richard, 1832-1878, photographer [ca. 1861] *Ballarat East gold workings and miners' cottages also Bricklayers Arms Hotel & Canadian Creek.* P.80
8. *Ballarat First Survey 1852* P.137
9. *Letters from the Chief Commissioner of the Goldfields*, cost estimate for gold escort Mt Alexander to Melbourne for 1853, p.142
10. Monthly return for officers employed at the various gold fields of the colony of Victoria 29 September 1853 P.143
11. Design for the Military Barracks at the Commissioners Camp Ballarat 1853 P.144
12. Copy of a parchment map of the Township, possibly late 1854, certainly dated between 1853 and 1855 without Drummond, Errard, Lyons, and Raglan streets, very likely the one referred to by the Age 28/6/1855 *Township of Ballarat [cartographic Material]*. Vale Collection 1851, P.152
13. Cr Robert Muir: from the collection of The Ballarat Historical Society, section of B/W photo of *Ballarat's first Council 1856, Cr Dr J. Stewart, Cr J Oddie, Cr A B Rankin, Cr R Muir, Cr W Tulloch, Cr J S Carver.* Catalogue No 106.81, P166
14. *The Hon John Basson Humffray*, pastel on brown paper by Thomas Flintoff, 10 August 1859. State Library of Victoria catalogue No H325, P.166
15. *Cobb & Co Leviathan Coach arriving at Bath's Corner ca 1860.* The booking office was on the corner of Sturt and Lydiard and Bath's Hotel was next door with a 'right of way' approved in 1856 by the council, separating the two buildings. Note the front entrance to the hotel on Bath's Lane.

Deutsch, H. Cobb & Cos. *Leviathan Coach Carrying 89 Passengers, Running between Ballarat & Geelong* [Vic.] H. Deutsch., 1862, P170

16. *1857 Plan detailing surveyed lots for Main Street (now Bridge Street) Ballarat East and Bakery Hill.* P.172
17. *1857 Plan detailing surveyed lots for Main Road to Peel Street Ballarat East and Bakery Hill.* P173
18. *Rows of dots indicating shafts sunk along leads leading to the Township 1855* P176
19. *Enlargement of Township -shown on Ballarat First Survey 1852, with 1856 proposed sites of Telegraph, Patents Office, and new Post Office on Lydiard Street.* P178
20. *Black and white photo of Ballarat's first Council 1856, Cr Dr J. Stewart, Cr J Oddie, Cr A B Rankin, Cr R Muir, Cr W Tulloch, Cr J S Carver.* From the collection of The Ballarat Historical Society P183
21. *Golden Fleece Hotel in Lydiard Street where the first meeting took place to discuss the formation of the council in 1855. From the collection of the Ballarat Historical Society, Ballarat Victoria, catalogue No 248.81* P186
22. Chairman James Oddie From the Collection of Federation University Australia Historical Collection (Geoffrey Blainey Research Centre) Federation University P.191
23. 1856 *Survey map with details of companies, claims, and relative positions on the Whitehorse, and Frenchman's Leads to the South of Ballarat located in present-day Sebastopol and Magpie:* Lithographed at the Surveyor General's Office, January. 29th 1857, by J. Jones P. 203
24. *Proposed Ballarat South Extension 1857 with surveyed lots detailing terrain, mining activity, and occupation Ballarat South Extension* P.216
25. *An 1860's black and white photograph, showing 1860s Ballarat South from the Ballarat Benevolent Asylum. Evident in the photos are houses, gardens, shingle roofs, fences, St Patrick's Cathedral, Black Hill, Ballarat West Fire Brigade tower, mine dumps, mullock heap, and large chimneys.* From the collection of Federation University Australia Historical Collection P .217
26. *1859 Plan of Soldiers Hill Ballarat with eastern boundary with Ballarat East on Havelock Street,* Historic Plan Collection CN94: VPRS 8168 P0005 P. 218
27. *Copy of extract from Council Minutes noting personal guarantees for initial commencement loan & extended overdraft 15 February 1856* P. 222 & 223
28. *Advertisement placed in the Ballarat Star Saturday 4 October 1856 offering a reward for signatures for a petition against Ballarat East wine & Spirit licenses* P. 228
29. *Extract from Council Minutes 6 June 1856 on clarification from Colonial Government on the jurisdiction of the Council regarding mining and integrity of the streets and private property* P. 229
30. *Extract of the half-yearly report as published in the Ballarat Star 14 August 1856* P. 230
31. *letter by Chairman James Oddie dated March 28, 1856, to the Surveyor General regarding the site for the manure dump on the northeast boundary of the Municipality* P.235

32. *Sketch of manure dump location that accompanied the letter by James Oddie to the Surveyor General June 28, 1856*, P. 236
33. *lithograph of the north side of the swamp with the perimeter road (now fairyland?) 1856-1859 with established businesses nearby* P. 237
34. *Extract from the Ballarat Star Saturday 30 August 1856 showing part of the Water Supply report by Town Surveyor Samuel Baird* P. 240
35. *Lydiard Street 1855*, from the collection of the Ballarat Historical Society Catalogue 232.80 P. 247
36. *Lydiard Street North 1857*: Photo/coloured line engraving: S T Gill 1857 and J Tingle se: titled *Ballarat Post office & Township from Government enclosure*. Ballarat Historical Society Collection Images Catalogue No 321.79 P. 247
37. Lydiard Street South looking north 1858, after two years under municipal government, From the collection of the Ballarat Historical Society, B/W lithograph by S. T. Gill titled *Township of Ballarat from Bath's Hotel*, Catalogue No 531.81 P.248
38. *Advertisement in The Ballarat Star Monday 9 March 1857 with the location of Market Square and weighbridge* P. 250
39. *the marketplace on the corner of Mair and Doveton Streets in 1866 with the Borough Weighbridge Centre and the recently completed railway station in the background*: State Library Victoria, Series / Collection A.V. Smith photographs of Ballarat and district.: Market Square ca 1866 P. 254
40. *1860's Panoramic view of Lydiard Street South in Ballarat. The view shows the former Ballarat Supreme Court (later the Ballarat School of Mines), the Lydiard Street Wesleyan Church (later the Ballarat School of Mines Museum), the site of the Ballarat School of Mines Botanical Gardens, George Smith's Nursery, Ballarat Gaol.* From the collection of Federation University Australia Historical Collection (Geoffrey Blainey Research Centre) Federation University E J Barker Library, Mount Helen Victoria, Object Registration 04258 P. 255
41. *1856 plan of township and extension before the Yarrowee River bridge – note reserved land in blue – churches left and right on Dana Street and court & Gaol precinct on LHS of Grant Street* P. 257
42. *1870 photograph with a view of Eyre Street extension to Golden Point and bridge over the Yarrowee top left with School of Mines, courthouse and Gaol centre top and immediately right.* The bridge over the Yarrowee top left with the School of Mines, courthouse and Gaol centre top and immediately right. P. 258

Introduction

In an obituary for J B. Humffray on his death in 1891, a newspaper correspondent recounts an anecdote on the relationship between Humffray and the other leader in the Eureka Rebellion, Peter Lalor. Drawing on the widely known and occasionally bitter rivalry between them, the story takes place in Melbourne in their later years where they both lived in Portland Street in Richmond. When the weather was fine, like many others, they both liked to walk to the city. However, they never walked together and never on the same side of the street. It was a relatively short distance and passed through 'the paddock' at Richmond, a fenced-off park with a turnstile entrance. The correspondent writes that occasionally their paths would merge at the turnstile. In more than one instance it was noted, with each having a hand on the turnstile, they paused and glared at each other. Then Lalor, would stoop and proceed to climb through the rails of the fence rather than concede. At the same time, Humffray followed suit on the other side of the turnstile forcing his gout-ridden body through the fence choosing also not to commit to a possible confrontation. Once on the other side they both paused for a moment and burst out laughing, then proceeded on their separate ways into town.[1]

As a feud that was never mended, it encapsulates quite well the state of Ballarat society from the time of the Goldfields administration until the establishment of the first Municipality. Humffray represented the possibilities attainable in a world free of old traditions while Lalor, although acting as the nemesis of the Goldfields Commission, nevertheless epitomised the past they all had left behind in Britain. It was a fundamental difference in outlook that was part of a collection of cultural and ethnic

---

[1] A Street full of Chests, (From the Bulletin), *The Great Southern Advocate* Korumburra, Vic, Friday 17 April 1891, page 1

allegiances and grievances aggravated by the intense competitiveness of life under the Goldfields Commission.

The Commission and the various local goldfields communities it created were from the beginning, beset by an ugly assortment of problems with many of the ingredients for a social revolution accumulating as time went on. Conceived in haste and implemented with little to no accounting for the needs and variations of human society and existence, its equally dictatorial and *laissez-faire* approach set people against each other and encouraged all sorts of abuses of civil order and corruption of normal administrative processes. Consequently, people tended to band together, making and enforcing their own rules designed to maintain and preserve their shared interests in the quest for success.

This gave birth to a variety of hated practices such as 'shepherding' and 'peacocking' – the practice of taking out multiple claims and paying associates to mind and sometimes working them until they were able to devote more attention to them if they had potential. Thus, more than occasionally, tensions rose over the practice in addition to the usual competition for successful claims. By far, the most intense rivalry was that between the English and the Irish, the two dominant ethnic groups that produced the two leaders of the Ballarat resistance to the Goldfields Commission. Humffray was a Welsh Chartist and the leading proponent of non-violent moral force. Lalor, however, represented the 'physical force' element – an Irishman, old-style liberal and member of the landed gentry and those who agitated for Irish home-rule.

While both supported anti-establishment causes, they couldn't have been further apart when it came to confronting the common enemy on the goldfields. From around 1852 there had been numerous violent exchanges between the two groups with the local police also involved. This was due to the creation of ethnic enclaves that developed because of the failure of the Commission to provide any effective planning for how claims were allocated or for residential occupation. Consequently, the spectacularly rich deposits along the Yarrowee River and Canadian Creek valleys became occupied predominantly by English, Scottish and Welsh miners, while the less lucrative Eureka and Red Hill leads to the east were mostly Irish. Matters had been particularly hot leading up to the Eureka rebellion as impoverished Irishmen, many of whose claims had dried up, had turned to crime as a way to remain on the goldfields. The fundamentally flawed policy of extracting fees from the successful as well as the unsuccessful had finally run its course with the dwindling alluvial resources close to the surface. This added to an accumulation of grievances against the Goldfields Commission as the local governing body and a growing sense of a failure of government concerning the people living on the goldfields.

By the end of 1854, matters in Ballarat, once a model example of the apparent success of La Trobe's goldfields policy, had boiled over, resulting in the burning of the Eureka Hotel and the Eureka Rebellion, all occurring in the impoverished Irish sector of Ballarat East. The local population had had enough and demanded the removal of the Goldfields Commission and the old administrative apparatus. Being administered as a quasi-police state, where all were assumed to be hostile to the government, was viewed as detrimental to mining communities such as Ballarat with its vast deposits, and large permanent population. It was the final act in a long campaign for comprehensive change to the goldfields administration that had begun from the commencement of the gold rushes.

However, notwithstanding the apparent solidarity among the diggers, old divisions re-opened, and new ones formed, threatening communal harmony once the furore surrounding the Eureka rebellion had subsided. Humffray, as the anecdote indicates, alluded to these problems and divisions as he made his pitch for political support in later elections to the Legislative Assembly. With many Eureka diggers still around at the time, he reminded them of how he stood for common sense, order and the best interests of the community as he resisted the violent elements of the 'physical force' faction that triggered the Eureka massacre. He made no bones about the fact that he had been threatened at gunpoint to cease his call for reason and common sense and to continue the negotiation with the authorities. He also reminded them of how he stood for the advancement of the Ballarat community and would support anyone, even those who were not part of his constituency. This was a fact confirmed many times during the first few years of the Ballarat West municipality, where he was approached by those who were unable to succeed with Lalor, their local member. This most likely is what contributed to the ongoing feud between them.

Insofar as Peter Lalor is concerned, after the rebellion, his image as the miners' leader began to tarnish. His family connection to the Irish independence cause and his partisan support of his Irish colleagues at Eureka placed his role into a more complex political and self-interested context. Thus, despite his stand against goldfields tyranny, his political beliefs, which he later defiantly defended at Ballarat after Eureka, suffered because of his opposition to democracy and his support of the 'fourth clause' giving a political advantage to landowners. But it was his apparent lack of interest in healing the effects of the Eureka rebellion and promoting the progress of the Ballarat district that raises historical eyebrows. Thus, in the quest for the heart and soul of the Ballarat community and leading it into the future, it became the task of J B Humffray the 'moral force' champion rather than the man who is given the credit for ending the tyranny.

While not representing the Ballarat Township, which fell within Peter Lalor's electorate from 1856, in almost all the progressive measures for the Ballarat district from 1855-1857 Humffray played a key role. These include Municipal Government, the Miners' Courts, the local magistrates' courts, the restoration of law and order after the Eureka Rebellion, the local water supply, local

Introduction 5

planning and many other initiatives like the telegraph. Almost all of them originated in Peter Lalor's electorate of North Grenville. Moreover, municipal government became Humffray's first major project for Ballarat, announcing to the community in April 1855 the commencement of the petition and pursuing its progress once elected to parliament. However, at Ballarat itself, it would be a vigorously contested process, as much of the old divisive elements that were behind the chaos of Eureka sought to frustrate the process.

By presenting alternative projects for Ballarat East prospectors, they also sought to dominate the petition and influence decision-making once the council was established. However, with powerful allies in Ballarat West, a comprehensive plan to develop the mining resources of Ballarat South in conjunction with a massive extension of the township was launched in 1855. This proved to be far more popular with the bulk of the public who, after spending years in tents, wished to build homes and settle down in the Ballarat district as quickly as they were able. It would prove to be the vision that would enable the community to unite and progress from the chaos, disorder and tyranny of life under the Goldfields Commission. With democratically elected local representatives, it would also be a means to resolve the conflicting issues among partisan groups. By focusing on the needs of the wider community fairly and logically, local leaders maintained a process of civic reconciliation that had already begun by the Ballarat Reform League and later the Humffray-led Victorian Reform League that operated in that capacity at Ballarat immediately after the violence of the stockade and martial law had passed.

Once established, the municipality of Ballarat West rapidly prospered through the support of local ventures like the Whitehorse and Frenchman's Lead project south of Ballarat. It eliminated much of the old ethnic rivalry and the unfair practices that it created, providing business opportunities and employment on a scale that could never be achieved under the old *laissez-faire* regime of the Goldfields Commission. With the commission out of the way, the local Miners' Court was free to innovate and progress the mining industry with equality of opportunity being virtually guaranteed under the 'frontage system' promoted by the members and local engineer James Baker. The establishment of the Ballarat municipality therefore, proved to be the catalyst for this vision as a huge waiting list of expectant diggers for urban land was established as early as 1855 as miners who had put funds aside for the eventuality, applied for surveyed land adjacent to the new mining activity. Within a decade, the district had been transformed through planned development and the creation of civic order and regulation by the application of scientific methodology.

This revolutionary civic development of Ballarat follows a similar trajectory to that of Britain. With the creation of the Municipal Reform Act in 1835, the project of methodically and scientifically transforming British society from one based on centuries-old feudal structures to conform to the demands of a modern commercial society began. By the end of the century, the replacement of the old civic arrangements that dated from feudal times, was mostly complete and many of the problems like disease, high infant mortality rates and haphazard development were being addressed or greatly reduced. This was a much-needed social innovation due to the problems and deep social divisions created in the transition to a modern society. Deeply divided along lines of class and property, since the end of the eighteenth century, fears of revolution gripped the country. This was largely due to a minority of landowners monopolizing the main drivers of society such as the economy and the political systems, local, county and national. However, with the implementation of the new Act in 1835, it was not long before the Tories and landowners were sitting together with their erstwhile tenants and subjects on the new municipal councils. It thus proved to be a successful integrative measure as the modern state evolved. Moreover, large numbers of people, who had no previous civic status, were integrated into the fabric of the modern state. Where many were only registered on a payroll in a large factory, or on the roll of a non-conformist church, they also became members of 'the public' appearing on the municipal rate rolls and registers of public utilities and services that were established under the new municipal councils.

Likewise, in colonial Victoria, without any pre-existing British society, municipal government, using the British model as a template, for a time became *the* primary political institution for the developing colony. It provided social status and a sense of citizenship as a growing and diverse population developed a unified public identity through the purchase and organization of town and city land and shared public assets. Moreover, modern municipal government, particularly in the colony of Victoria without the established institutions and social problems of their homeland, thus provided a welcome and effective platform to realise the creation of a society compatible with the commercializing trends of the past century.

PART 1

A 'system of life constructed on a wholly new principle'

1. Urbanization of British Society

The New Towns & Cities

Philosophers, particularly the Scottish, from the eighteenth century were anticipating dramatic social changes coming with continued commercialization and the urban industrial economy. Adam Smith, the much-published Scottish political economist, and widely acknowledged 'father' of free-market economics, was particularly concerned about the instability it could bring to Scottish society and how people would conduct themselves in a system based on self-interest. Writing from the mid-1700s, he warned of a bleak future where the foundations of agricultural interdependence upon which their towns and villages were based, would be under threat. Smith's greatest fear was that an increase in the influence of urban dealers, merchants, and manufacturers, would work against the interests of the public and the stability of the nation.

He argued that it would result in shifting national wealth from the country to the city and a loss of independence to rural society. An expansion of their kind, he protested, was a threat to liberty as the 'basic principle of the mercantile system is monopoly.' And what was even more concerning according to Smith, was that at a fundamental local level, the manipulation of labour, stock and prices in manufacture, and trade by forces often unknown, left everyone at the mercy of uncontrolled market forces driven by unrestrained self-interest. This was because wealth derived from urban manufacturing, he contended, unlike that derived from agriculture 'has no loyalty to any particular nation' or locality as it was not anchored in native soil.[2]

---

[2] David McNally, *Political economy and the rise of capitalism: a reinterpretation*, University of California Press, Los Angeles 1988, p224

Smith believed that land and the industry and lifestyle derived from it offered greater certainty and security to that of larger cities like Glasgow where manufacturing industries were just beginning to appear. For him, he believed that in an agricultural political economy, social and economic systems were self-sustainable and largely kept society in a state of economic and social equilibrium. He maintained that there was a level of social security and independence not experienced in an industrial city. Its high division of labour and commerce, he argued, tended to human decay, loss of skills and stupidity.[3] Smith, as David McNally points out, pictured a stable, idyllic world where landed country gentlemen and lords presided over a contented and decentralized population of towns and villages. Populated by tenant farmers and happy and fulfilled labourers and artisans they derived satisfaction and fulfilment from the utilization of their wide array of skills, close historical affiliations, and culture.

Ignoring the aristocratic monopoly of the existing social system, his was a hoped-for future where commercialized agriculture would continue to be the basis of the national economy and Lords and gentlemen farmers, in a highly regulated society, would continue to rule. However, the historical reality, overlooked by Smith, was that there had been substantial and progressive change to land use, and how society was organized in Britain since the time of Henry V111.[4] The Tudors' 'revolution' that began with the split with Rome, had initiated social political and economic trends that were not originally envisioned. It set in motion, as Rule points out, the progressive restriction of access to common land and the slow redundancy of land agreements, such as ownership, copyholding, leases and commons rights. This all came with significant social and political impact on local communities over the following

---

[3] David McNally, *Political economy and the rise of capitalism, a reinterpretation*, p228-229
[4] John Rule, *The vital century: England's developing economy, 1714-1815*, Longman, Harlow, Essex UK 1992, p. 68-100

centuries as the Elizabethan regime instituted poor laws to ameliorate the loss of church influence and growing unemployment due to the commercialization of agriculture. What was evolving, as John Rule explains, was a 'capitalist and individualist conception of property rights.'[5] Smith, writing at the threshold of the nineteenth century therefore could see even more rapid change coming with industrialization and a greater division of labour as technology and mass manufacturing techniques suggested the coming of machines and factories bringing a new type of world that nobody could clearly conceptualise.

In his native Scotland, it was approaching in a hurry gathering pace after the final defeat of feudalism in 1746. Its effects on towns and local communities were dramatic, with rapidly diminishing commons and the local mill and the local market no longer prioritizing the local community. Instead, just as it was in England, their produce was quickly transformed by the new overlords into a commercial commodity. Rather than being allocated the first fruits, they found, as Smith predicted, that it had all been prioritized by contract to unknown middlemen from outside for sale on an open market. This was often the root cause of social unrest, sparking violent and widespread protests well into the nineteenth century as never-before-experienced shortages and price increases came with the predominance of large-scale contracts and export markets.[6]

As land and harvests became even more rationalized, the people themselves were displaced with whole villages on occasion, particularly in the Scottish Highlands, given the 'option' to leave or emigrate as the pace of change accelerated. It would touch all

---

[5] J L Hammond and Barbara Hammond, *The village labourer, 1760-1832*, Longman Group London, 1911, p. 26-42 John Rule, *The vital century: England's developing economy, 1714-1815*, p. 79

[6] See E P Thompson, the moral authority of the English crowd, in the eighteenth century, in *Past and Present* No 50 1971, Christopher Whatley, *Scottish society 1707-1830: beyond Jacobitism toward industrialization*, Manchester University Press Manchester, 2000, p286-293

sectors, as Smith's much-feared future arrived with heavy industry, factories and new technologies feeding growing urban population centres all over Britain a generation after he died in 1790. The mass market it created, reshaped society bringing new trades, and making others redundant, creating winners and losers in a commercialized world. By the nineteenth century, as the Hammonds show, the changes had become largely implemented with farms becoming much larger by many degrees and the small village and town subsistence plots and the life, occupations and culture that went with it mostly gone.[7]

The passing of the old ways was lamented particularly in Scotland where commercialization had been relatively sudden, largely implemented by decree in accordance with the terms of the English victory at Culloden in 1746.[8] Thus, just a few generations later writers such as James Hogg, the Ettrick Shepherd, himself a tenant farmer, lamented that commercialization was decimating the towns, villages, and country areas. Believing the old culture was dying, he conducted a one-man crusade throughout Scotland to revitalize the culture with traditional song, dance, stories, poetry and sporting events. Eventually, he conceded, with the massive rates of immigration that were occurring, that 'the best are all leaving' and society was being replaced by 'something less personal, meaner and less respectful.'[9]

This was an enduring theme as J L and Barbara Hammond, writing over a century after Adam Smith, also painted a bleak picture of a world in transition to modernity from the seventeenth century to the 1830s. With the spread of factories and industry from the end of the 1700s, it was not unusual, as the Hammonds

---

[7] J L Hammond and Barbara Hammond, *The village labourer, 1760-1832*,
[8] Niel Davidson, The Scottish path to capitalist agriculture 2: the capitalist offensive (1747-1815), *Journal of Agricultural change*, Vol. 4 October 2004
[9] The Ettrick Shepherd (James Hogg), To the Editor of the Quarterly Journal of Agriculture, on the habits, amusements, and condition of the Scottish Peasantry, *The Quarterly Journal of Agriculture*, Vol 111, February 1831, September 1832, William Blackwood, Edinburgh, p256-263

point out, to see the rapid transformation of villages into cities or the creation of totally new towns to cater to the labour needs of the factory. Well-known towns like Leeds, Preston, Sheffield, and Birmingham which had been in existence for centuries, were overwhelmed with the onset of the Industrial Revolution. Factories needed labour and often by the thousands. A typical advertisement in a Macclesfield paper in 1825 called for 'between 4000 and 5000 persons between the ages of 7 and 21 years as many large and new factories were built, particularly in the north of England.[10] With Manchester as an example, the Hammonds contend, that unlike its mediaeval counterpart, the industrial city, as Smith had feared, had become a place without a history, not a refuge but 'the barracks of industry' where people lost their skills and independence.[11] It represented a substantial change to the lived experiences enjoyed just a few decades after Smith's groundbreaking work.

Obtaining such a large and ready workforce at the turn of the 19th century was not that difficult due to the demographic changes brought by the dramatic reduction in the rural labour force. The displaced from the rural areas, therefore, found new family occupations in the emerging textile and ceramics industries from the early part of the 19th century. With many traditional agricultural workers chronically dependent on poor relief from the local parishes, the new factories were, not surprisingly, seen as a better option than the more draconian workhouse where many may have ended up. As Rule explains, the industrialization of manufacturing thus came in conjunction with a dramatic increase in population as families working in manufacturing in many cases viewed it as a family enterprise, much like they did in the agricultural industry. Marriages, consequently, were occurring at an earlier age and

---

[10] J L Hammond and Barbara Hammond, *The town labourer, 1760-1832*, 1917, p. 41-43
[11] J L Hammond and Barbara Hammond, *The town labourer*, p. 41-42

couples were having more children.[12] However, as more were displaced and moved into the towns and cities, these largely unregulated factory precincts became the inspiration for Engel's depressing but widely acknowledged writings describing the bleak existence of workers under free-market capitalism during his visit to Manchester in the 1840s.

Here, like many other places, commons and meadows had been enclosed almost a century earlier. The pristine air of the countryside had been replaced by factories belching smoke and other noxious fumes into the air, destroying the health and happiness of all who lived there. The smoke was often so thick during the day that people, depending on the wind direction, had to grope their way through the streets.[13] Without sanitation or building regulation, people were accommodated in back-to-back hovels without toilets, damp and poorly ventilated and rife with diseases such as consumption, cholera and typhus. Often, these terraces were constructed on land owned by a local squire, or lord who held or controlled the county position of the Lord Lieutenant or Chief Constable with little idea of public need beyond the value of the rent return on his land. Manchester, for example, as late as 1838, continued, as William Cobden complained, to be run from Rolleston Hall in Staffordshire, where the Lord of the Manor controlled the ancient Court Leet responsible for fines, permits and law and order, and his henchman Nadin brutally controlled the city for many years.[14]

Britain thus represented a society that appeared well organized at a county and national level with its lordly representatives and wealthy commoners and their landed monopoly. Under the surface, however, in the towns and the cities, it no longer functioned effectively under old established administration

---

[12] John Rule, *The vital century: England's developing economy 1714-1815*, p. 16-27
[13] J L Hammond and Barbara Hammond, *The town labourer, 1760-1832*, 1917, p. 45-46
[14] Ibid, p. 47

systems. Most of the population remained virtually unintegrated in a civic society where chaos and *laissez-faire* often ruled. Many only existed on the payroll of the local factory or the dwindling books of the local established parish church – a body, in many localities that had been largely eclipsed by the non-conformist expansion of the past century. This paralysis of leadership was graphically portrayed in the Mike Lee documentary 'Peterloo' where the city management of Manchester had long ceased to effectively function. With decision-making in the hands of an avaricious local Lord, his local enforcer, and inept local magistrates, their attempts at containing 60,000 social activists at St Peter's field in 1819, led to the deaths of nine and the injury of hundreds of others. It served as an ongoing reminder of the failures of a divided society and became a catalyst for some of Britain's most comprehensive social and economic reforms.[15]

Thus, the changes wrought over the past century were finally knocking on the door of the last Tory bastion, the civic governing bodies. Manchester, like many of the new urban centres across Britain, was symptomatic of the failure of the old feudal local government system in the modern commercial society. On its last legs, it was incapable of addressing the mounting civic needs of a modern industrial urban population. Most, having been incorporated under the old feudal system were finally given notice by the Municipal Reform Act of 1835 which was quickly and eagerly adopted by lower class radicals and liberals in most towns and cities across Britain.

For the newly urbanized multitudes, therefore, the adoption of modern municipal government provided an initial integrative measure into the modern commercial society. The 1835 Act provided the means for creating the legal and physical framework for what came later – the utilities and amenities, the parks, the

---

[15] Lee Mike, *"Peterloo". Venice International Film Festival 2018. Venice Biennale.* 16 July 2018. Retrieved 27 July 2018.

clubs, churches and many other social organizations. The Act was so successful in its integrative role, that as the century progressed, even the Tories, after a period of aloofness, were absorbed into the new civic society and its common leadership. As the mounting problems of urbanization such as disease and mortality began to affect even the most elite of society, the Tories took a leading role having no choice but to invest their vast wealth to help solve them. Thus, a common need brought them to sit at the same table as many of the lower classes on the new municipal councils.

However, it was also more than self-preservation, for as David Cannadine points out, the upper classes could not remain apart and aloof for long, especially with the investment opportunities that were being presented with the Industrial Revolution and new technologies. With the shifts in society and culture as the modern age developed, many of the upper classes reinvented themselves and their roles in society embracing modernity, and using their land as collateral for railways and other industrial and civic enterprises.[16] With a growing number of industrialists joining their ranks, the elite also supplied jobs, housing, social activities and new skills to a new, dependent and often grateful generation, so restoring significant public support over the course of the nineteenth century.[17] This was despite the growing power of liberal non-conformists during the Victorian era and politicians acting more as delegates, as movements such as Chartism, free trade, and an increasingly independent fourth estate, brought pressure to bear.[18]

---

[16] David Cannadine, *Class in Britain*, Penguin Books London 2000, p65; David Spring, 'English Landowners and Nineteenth Century Industrialism', in *Land and Industry: the landed estate and the industrial revolution*, a symposium edited by J T Ward and R G Wilson, David & Charles, Newton Abbott, 1971, pp15-62

[17] Patrick Joyce, 'The factory Politics of Lancashire in the Later Nineteenth Century', in: *The Historical Journal, Vol. 18, No. 3 (Sept. 1975)*, pp 525-553

[18] Alan Sykes, *The rise and fall of British Liberalism 1776-1988*, Addison Wesley Longman, Edinburgh Gate, 1997, pp 46-68; Cheryl Schonhardt-Bailey, *From the Corn-laws to free trade: interests, ideas and institutions in historical perspective*, The MIT Press, London 2006; Brown Lucy, "Chartists and the anti-corn law league", in

The liberal storm was weathered, helped to a large extent by the emigration of many of the 'troublemakers' and the displaced both occupationally and residentially. Thus, power continued to be based on the traditional pillars of land ownership and occupancy and the established church rather than natural rights.[19]

However, among the landless lower classes whose adaptive options were always very limited, strong anti-establishment attitudes simmered over the property and political monopolies enjoyed by the social elites. While freehold opportunities and commensurate political representation were not unusual in places like Leeds, Birmingham and Manchester for example, the aristocracy continued to maintain ownership over large parts of the country as the towns and cities expanded into their estates.[20] In some cases, whole suburbs of London and towns like Barrow, Bath, Brighton, Eastbourne, and Edgbaston were owned and developed by Lords of the Realm who exercised a significant influence in industry and development and the residential constituency both local and national.[21] This was the 'old fogeyism'

Asa Briggs ed., *Chartist studies*, Macmillan, London, 1959; James A Epstein, *Radical expression: ritual and symbol in England 1790-1850*, Oxford, University Press, New York, 1994.

[19] F M L Thompson, 'Land and Politics in England in the Nineteenth Century', in: *Transactions of the Royal Historical Society*, Vol 15 (1965) pp 23-44, J V Beckett, 'The Pattern of Land Ownership in England and Wales, 1660-1880', in *The Economic History Review, Vol. 37, No.1, (Feb 1984)* pp 1-12, David Cannadine, *Class in Britain*, 73, also W D Rubenstein, 'Elites and the Class Structure of Modern Britain', in: *Past & Present*, No.76 (Aug. 1977), pp. 99-126 for a statistical analysis that shows the overwhelming number of million and half-millionaires among the land-owning elites, and pp73-103

[20] David Cannadine, 'Urban development in England and America in the nineteenth century: some comparisons and contrasts', in *The Economic History Review, New Series, Vol 33, No 3 (Aug. 1980)* pp 309-325; Derek Sayer, 1992, p1410

[21] David Cannadine, *Lords and landlords: the aristocracy and the towns 1774-1967*, Leicester University Press, 1980, F M L Thompson, *English landed society: in the nineteenth century*, Routledge & Keegan Paul Ltd, London, 1963, J T Ward and R G Wilson (eds.), *Land and industry: the landed estate and the industrial revolution*, David & Charles, Newton Abbot, Devon, 1971

as many described it, that immigrants to the Australian colonies came to escape. It had for many of them, despite commercialization that had transformed the fabric of society, resulted in loss of status, position and place in society, while the monopolists of the old pre-commercial world enjoyed all the perks and benefits of the new conditions.

2. Aliens & Enlightened Immigrants

Anomie & the Industrial Society

It is no surprise, therefore, that studies of society that began to proliferate later in the century, identified social integration as *the* major issue in the development of the modern commercialized and industrialized state. For Marx, it applied at the even more fundamental level of work, where, unlike life in an agricultural subsistence economy, a person's labour and the products they created in a commercialized political economy were no longer their own. And for Durkheim, at a sociological level, a pervasive level of anomie or loss of social connections underpinned the often violent actions of individuals and the masses in the transition to a modern commercial society.[22]

For many in the lower classes, therefore, society appeared to be less secure and even hostile with no stake or influence over the changing conditions which rendered many merely as 'surplus' labour. This was a salient issue discussed at length by people like E G Wakefield whose schemes sought to provide for the establishment of a commercialized British agricultural society in South Australia and New Zealand. It would, he argued, resolve the issue of 'excess labour', lack of local investment, and British social instability.[23] This coincided with other measures on the other side of the globe in Australia, for similar reasons. Anticipating an increasing population and a diversifying economy, Australian reformers such as J D Lang were seeking skilled immigrants to

---

[22] Durkheim, Émile. *The Division of Labor in Society*. Free Press, [1893] 1964,
[23] See Onur Ulas Ince, *Colonial capitalism and the dilemmas of liberalism, (capitalism, colonization, & contractual dispossession: Wakefield's Letters from Sydney)* Oxford University Press New York 2018, pp2-21

establish a modern Australian liberal democratic and protestant regime throughout the 1840s.

It was a vision sold to and expected to be realized by early pioneers who were part of the great transition into the modern state. They were constantly changing times built on the concept of modernity, which, as Stuart Hall explains, is 'the belief that everything is destined to be speeded up, dissolved, displaced, transformed, reshaped – a reinterpretation of the famous epigram coined by Marx in the 1850's – 'All that is solid melts into air'.[24] This is certainly a process that the British working population was only too well aware of as technology and scientific advancement were forcing redundancy and displacement amongst many traditional skills and occupations.[25] Studies such as I. J. Prothero's into the 'respectable trades' and Chartism and Jennifer Bennett's study of the London Democratic Society, reveal a process of disintegration and reconstruction with the arrival of 'big capital,' the increasing division of labour and the coming of the factories.[26]

Artisans, sole traders, and mechanics who for centuries had enjoyed the protection and patronage of the guilds, the old municipal corporations and the independence of self-employment, from the mid-1700s, were with succeeding generations, no longer passing their businesses, skills and crafts onto their descendants. Their children no longer followed the family occupations nor were they rotated and absorbed within the local or wider society in the traditional ways. Instead, by the 1800s, most were reduced to permanent journeyman status by the high division of labour in the

---

[24] Stuart Hall, 'Introduction', in Stuart Hall and Bram Geiben eds., *Formations of modernity*, Polity Press Cambridge 1992, p15

[25] Richard Broome, *The Victorians: Arriving*, Fairfax, Syme & Weldon Associates, McMahon's Point NSW, 1984, pp 69-70

[26] I. J. Prothero, 'London Chartism and the trades', in *The Economic History Review*, Vol, 24 No. 2 (May 1971), pp 202-219; Jennifer Bennett, 'The London Democratic Association 1837-41, a study in London radicalism', in: James Epstein & Dorothy Thompson (Eds.,) *The chartist experience, studies in working class radicalism and culture, 1830-1860*, MacMillan, London, 1982, pp55-60

factory system. Overtaken by the proliferation of specialist, less-skilled factory hands and lower-paid outworkers, these pillars of the local community had lost touch with the fabric of society.[27]

Having lost their independent social status through the economics of mass production, many of this category had turned to the radical politics of Tom Paine, the cooperative theories of Robert Owen and the radical politics of Chartism. Many, as James Epstein shows, invested their savings and labours into newspapers and publishing establishing a vibrant fourth estate and voices of protest.[28] As time elapsed, their numbers swelled with agricultural workers, small farmers and yeomen losing access to land through continued enclosures, farm rationalization and modernisation of agricultural practices and famine – all having lost out to economic forces and technological improvement.[29] An intergenerational surplus of labour in the 'corn heartland' of the southern counties of England where wages had been depressed for at least forty years since the Napoleonic wars[30] as well as dispossessed agricultural workers and tenants in Scotland and Ireland in the 1850s thus, saw many emigrating.[31] From the 1830s societies like the Petworth Emigration Society in southern England worked to assist their

---

[27] John Rule, *Albion's people: English Society 1714-1815*, Longman New York 1992 p. 7

[28] I. J. Prothero, 'London Chartism and the trades', in *The Economic History Review*, Vol, 24 No. 2 (May 1971), pp 202-219; Jennifer Bennett, 'The London Democratic Association 1837-41, a study in London radicalism', in: James Epstein & Dorothy Thompson (Eds.,) *The chartist experience, studies in working class radicalism and culture, 1830-1860*, MacMillan, London, 1982, pp55-60

[29] J D Chambers & G E Mingay eds., *The Agricultural revolution 1750-1880*, B T Batsford London 1966, pp 137-147

[30] ibid

[31] Croggan Janice, *Strangers in a Strange Land*, Phd. Thesis, Federation University Ballarat, 2002, Richard Broome, *The Victorians: Arriving*, pp 69-81, Erickson Charlotte, *Invisible immigrants: the adaption of English and Scottish immigrants in 19th century America*, first published Cornell Paperbacks, Cornell University Press, New York 1990

fellows in re-establishing themselves in the colonies along with philanthropists like Caroline Chisholm. [32]

Respectable Migrants

Charlotte Erickson's study on British emigration in the mid-19th century, thus reveals a growing tradition from the late eighteenth century among the 'respectable' lower classes towards emigration. Many of these were successful tenant farmers and artisans of small independent capital seeking to preserve status and maximize opportunities, especially in land that was unavailable in Britain. The economic depression of the late 1840s and the repeal of corn laws only accelerated the flood of people leaving.[33] Many of these 'casualties' of modernity came to Australia endowed with long memories and a strong sense of injustice over commercialization that had preserved and increased the fortunes of the aristocracy and the social elites often at the expense of their own and their families. They were the 'respectable' gold-seekers of the early gold rushes who, with sufficient resources, were able to purchase the necessary supplies and equipment to travel to the interior and remain there for lengthy periods. There they were able to quickly capitalize on land releases, establish enterprises and later man the local government engine rooms of the great liberal economic and political expansion in the following half-century.

James Oddie, the first Chairman of the Ballarat West Council and Robert Muir, a founding councillor were typical of those respectable immigrants. Oddie, the first chairman of the Ballarat municipality along with his fellow pioneers were committed to the establishment of a better society based on social justice without the

---

[32] J D Chambers & G E Mingay eds., *The Agricultural revolution 1750-1880*, p146
[33] Charlotte Erickson, *Invisible immigrants: the adaptation of English and Scottish immigrants in 19th century America*, p23-39, William Van Vugt, Running from ruin? The emigration of British farmers in the wake of the repeal of Corn Laws, *Economic History Review*, 2nd ser XLI 3 1988, D Morier-Evans, *The commercial crisis 1847-1848*, Letts & Son & Steer, London 1849

corrosive effects of monopolies on the fabric of society. Holding to an undiminished reverence for its casualties, he also declared many years later, that the Eureka rebellion was a pivotal moment of cultural change for the Ballarat goldfields and for Ballarat itself. The demise of the Goldfields Commission at Eureka, Oddie claimed, resulted in the creation of the first municipality at Ballarat. While in advanced years by 1906, and at times prone to exaggeration of events in the past, on this occasion, there is much to corroborate his memories of the Eureka era and what came after for Ballarat. For him and most of his class, they were memories coloured by their experiences from their old homes in Britain where they and their forebears, also had existed as people without status in a society that had fundamentally changed. This forced many of them, as they had in Britain, to agitate and fight for their place in the colonies.

As a resident of Manchester and London and a young man working in manufacturing, he was an active member of trade associations like the Moulders' Club and well-versed in the contemporary struggles for political and civic status.[34] Therefore, he would have expected life on the goldfields to, at the very least, once the population began to increase towards the end of 1851, to have experienced the introduction of the basic elements of a civilized society. But as time went on, from his first foray onto the Ballarat Goldfields, nothing remotely like that was developing. The small township founded in January 1852 merely existed as an enclave of alienated land within the goldfield, a region along with the diggings described by W B Withers in 1870, as existing 'outside the mystic circle of government' without any social or political

---

[34] G A Oddie, Oddie, James 1824-1911, *Australian Dictionary of Biography*, Centre of Biography, Australian National University, Anne Beggs-Sunter, An eminent Victorian: James Oddie and his contribution to Ballarat, *Victorian Historical Journal*, Vol 72 1-2, Sept 2001 p. 105-116

status.³⁵ This ran counter to the values held by most local diggers like himself leaving them in the same position as they were back in Britain, with little option for political engagement on civic and social matters apart from street protests and direct petition to the government.

Likewise, in the 1840s Robert Muir, also a key figure in the establishment of the Ballarat West municipality, had experienced the breakup of his family through the loss of the family farm, a casualty of the economic chaos of the late 1840s and the consolidation of lordly estates. His misfortunes continued with the great railway and economic collapse of 1847-1848 which, as a qualified engineer, forced him to look for opportunities in Canada, the United States, and the Caribbean on the sugar estates. It provided him with a unique insight into the inner workings of privilege and monopolies both political and economic. It also inspired a campaign in later life against the sugar monopoly of CSR and other large capitalists in Queensland and Northern New South Wales.³⁶

Like James Oddie and Robert Muir, many of this class and station came to seek their fortunes, acquire land, which was out of reach in Britain and regain their lost independence. This was all part of a shared aspirational package. As their writings, speeches and actions often demonstrated, it was to lay the foundations of what they believed was a society that embodied the ideals and values that were heralded and applauded by the educated and political elite but unrealizable to most of the others. Statistics presented by Geoffrey Serle are indicative: from 1854 to 1860 unassisted migration shows 62,310 adult males with declared occupations as commerce, professional, skilled trades and

---

[35] W B Withers, *History of Ballarat and some reminiscences, first published 1870*, published in Ballarat by Ballarat Heritage Services 1999

[36] Graeme S Cartledge, *A nineteenth century Scot in colonial Australia: the adventures, misadventures and enterprises of an entrepreneur and pioneer in the eastern Australian colonies*, Local Research Publishers, Winter Valley Australia 2022

agriculture out of a total number of 100,000 with the significantly higher number of artisans in this period noted. For assisted migrants however, the effect of displacement on the unskilled is shown to be even more drastic with a total of about 90,000 from the United Kingdom in the decade from 1851-1861 made up of 45,000 domestic servants, 30,000 agricultural labourers, 9000 mechanics and a fewer number of tradespeople.[37]

From 1855 to 1857 in Ballarat West, as more town land began to be released for sale, growing numbers of these immigrants attained their goals of land ownership and creating a fairer society. This is borne out by an examination of the rate records for that year where this is indicated with over 90% private ownership and the low figure of 0.08% for private rentals from a population of largely lower middle-class artisans, successful miners, farmers, and small businesspeople.[38] This was a significant achievement that did not come without vigilance and a struggle as attempts to recreate monopolies of all kinds were strenuously resisted. The way forward for this new society therefore was viewed as the unhindered adoption of modern, liberal and progressive ideals derived from the enlightenment period that had emerged over the earlier two centuries.

Without an impenetrable class system [39] highlighted so eloquently by Samuel Smiles in his 1859 best seller *Self Help*[40] it was a belief held by many in the 1850's that despite its shortcomings, the British social and political system with its tamed monarchy and more liberal character, was superior to those in the rest of Europe.

---

[37] Richard Broome, *The Victorians: Arriving*, p72
[38] Appendix I, page 187-8, and VPRS 7260 P0002 Rate Assessment Books 1856-1857
[39] See: Julia Smith, 'Land Ownership and Social Change in Late Nineteenth-Century Britain' in: *The Economic History Review, New Series*, Vol. 53, No.4 (Nov 2000) pp 767-776 Smith's statistical analysis shows a strong correlation between new money and growing numbers of landed elite during the nineteenth century.
[40] Samuel Smiles, LLD., *Self Help, with illustrations of conduct and perseverance*, First Published 1859, Popular Edition, John Murray, London, 1897

This was a view held and espoused by future Prime Minister Lord Alfred Cecil after he toured the goldfields where he was highly impressed by the orderly and self-regulatory behaviour of the predominantly British population.[41] It was also a belief that did not dissipate over time as the virtues of the British system were extolled and toasted in 1872 at the inaugural meeting of the Ballarat Pioneers Association. The success of founding a liberal society was viewed by all as the outcome of the 'liberties and laws of that glorious old land that most of the pioneers were proud to call their fatherland'.[42]

Thus, by the 1840s immigration, which had been just a trickle, began to gather momentum through the efforts of Australian agents like J D Lang and British activists like Edward Gibbon Wakefield. Proposing immigration as the solution for a large unemployed and displaced population, Lang particularly targeted the highly skilled sons and daughters of tenant farmers in a shrinking agricultural sector and the mechanical and technical trades. Aimed at fulfilling his vision for a diversified and self-sustaining Australian society, he sold a vision of freehold land and ground-breaking opportunities available without the aristocratic monopoly over land, the economy, and a political system as the realization of the promise of a liberal commercialized society. His Cooksland campaign in Scotland in the 1840s, created an expectation among people like Robert Muir of Ayr, that the modern, liberal, and independent society was just waiting to be created in a land with untapped potential and unlimited resources.[43]

---

[41] *Lord Robert Cecil's Gold Field's Diary, with Introduction and notes by Professor Ernest Scott*, Melbourne University Press, Melbourne, 1935

[42] *The Ballarat Star* Tuesday, August 27, 1872, The Ballarat Pioneers, page 2

[43] John Dunmore Lang, *Cooksland in North-Eastern Australia; the future cotton field of Great Britain: its characteristics and capabilities for European colonization, with a disquisition on the manners and customs of the aborigines*, Longman Brown Green and Longmans, London, 1847, Jack Harrington, Edward Gibbon Wakefield, the liberal political subject and the settler state, in *Journal of Political Ideologies*, 20 (3), pp333-351, Michael Radzevicius, *Edward Gibbon Wakefield and an Imperial utopian dream*, Ph.D., University of Adelaide, 2011, P106-7

However, arriving in Melbourne, they viewed with dismay scenes little different from those they had left, the chaotic wharves, the crowds widespread squalor and the politics. One thing they all discovered, however, was that there were, as Lang had told them, no aristocrats in the Australian colonies. The monopoly that they enjoyed did not extend to the other side of the globe. The closest equivalent was in New South Wales, an old military elite who served their masters in Britain. In Victoria however, the small pastoral cliques of Batman and Fawkner of the 1830s, who had dominated the early evolution of the colony, were witnessing their eclipse with a steady increase of a liberal-minded urban and commercial population.

With the commencement of the 1850s, Victorian society had undergone a significant change. New industries were being proposed, and small existing ventures greatly expanded such as Henry Langlands's iron foundry which supported a vibrant building industry with castings and ornate décor. Other heavy industries manufactured farming equipment while many others also were doing well with coach building, bakeries, tanneries, and those associated with the pastoral industry.[44] Society, therefore, had become diverse enough to support a growing civil infrastructure, workers' movements, and a political opposition that effectively echoed the same social issues in the home countries – the availability of land and a political voice for large and growing numbers of unenfranchised and unintegrated citizens.

With the discovery of gold, the mood changed considerably as unimagined numbers of new arrivals, and the political makeup of the colony began to take on an even more liberal outlook. This was creating headaches for the first and inexperienced government of Victoria, just over six months old at the commencement of the goldrushes. As most of the population remained unenfranchised and in the case of the diggers virtually unintegrated into colonial

---

[44] Geoffrey Serle, *The golden age*, p125

civic society, talk of tyranny was increasingly in the air. It had never really abated after the vigorous campaign for independence from the 'tyranny' of New South Wales. Begun in 1840 from amongst a population of only 10,000, and fed enthusiastically by J D Lang, then an administrator of Port Phillip, it grew in proportion with the growing immigrant population fresh from the British Chartist and associated political campaigns for the electoral franchise. By November 1850 with a population that had reached 77,000, separation was achieved and an even more vigorous debate commenced, raging over the founding constitution and a new electoral and political system. [45] By the middle of 1853, the population had passed the 200,000 mark with a third of them on the goldfields. This very quickly created a social crisis over an issue that began as an assimilation problem regarding gold-seekers that the new government was unwilling and unequipped to deal with. [46]

Unlike the old masters who controlled British society, in the colonies, the ruling pastoral elite's grip on colonial Victorian society had become much less secure with the onset of the gold rushes. As they continued, it placed increasing amounts of political power and leverage into the hands of a public sector's increasing awareness of their political potential. This was an inverse position to that of Britain, where the offloading of the excess population largely had solved a pressing problem for the ruling upper classes and enabled them to consolidate. Their immense reserves of uninvested wealth, ownership of most of the land and control of the political system, thus enabled them after the defeat of the chartists in 1848, to take a leading role in the transition into a modern industrialized society. However, in colonial Victoria, large numbers of newcomers in the gold rush era discovered many like minds and a rapidly maturing culture of opposition to an

---

[45] Geoffrey Serle, *The golden age*, p 1-5
[46] See Serle's mining population table based on Commissioners reports, *The Golden Age*, p 388

establishment with any semblance of similarity to the culture they had left behind.

Colonial Aliens

For them, without any aristocrats and primogeniture laws, having large swathes of landlocked away under pastoral leases and virtually nothing available for purchase, was both illogical and unreasonable. With land ownership and occupation as the basis of prevailing British political theory, it was, as the increasing population protested, part of a system of tyranny that appeared even worse than that which they had left behind. That, as well as many other issues such as ending transportation, were high on the agenda of a new generation that wanted to see the colony progress beyond its penal roots and pastoralism towards a modern liberal democracy with a diverse economy that offered a fair go for all. However, while much of the political agitation themes had origins in Britain, there was also for colonial Victoria, a strong lead supplied by a similar trend in New South Wales. From the 1830s, following the campaign by British Chartists and democratic activists, a vigorous movement based on similar principles had been steadily evolving. Emerging from a slowly diversifying economy, growing numbers of organizing tradespeople and a working class were demanding recognition often with rowdy and violent protests.[47] By 1848, Henry Parkes declared, on the election of Robert Lowe with the support of large numbers of workingmen to the limited parliamentary system of New South Wales, that it was the birth of Australian democracy.[48]

This movement merged with other equally radical initiatives, particularly the anti-transportation campaign which sought to transition the Australian colonies beyond the convict colony era

---

[47] Terry Irving, *The southern tree of liberty: the democratic movement in New South Wales before 1856*, The Federation Press Sydney NSW 2007
[48] Terry Irving, *The southern tree of liberty*, p 251

and create a modern secular and self-determinate society. Prominent in this along with Parkes and others, was John Dunmore Lang, Presbyterian minister, and New South Wales politician. As a leading advocate of immigration rather than transportation from the 1840s, he was also the leading campaigner for the establishment of an Australian nation and independence from Britain. It was Lang also an administrator of the Port Phillip colony who advocated for the separation of the Port Phillip settlement from New South Wales. In Victoria surrounded by a pastoral majority, John Pascoe Fawkner also was often a lone voice against monopoly and tyranny from its beginning. As one of the founders of the new settlement of Melbourne, while not a democrat, he provided a voice of social conscience standing for the protection of the poor, against tyranny and exploitation, the squatter monopoly and religious tolerance.[49]

With the discovery of gold, the monopoly was challenged even more vigorously as a rapidly developing commercial sector, the nouveau-rich merchants, and multitudes of successful miners, a fair percentage of them rich enough to exert political influence, entered the political fray. All were forcing noisy a transition to a liberal-democratic society. Prominent in the political agitation, as it was in Britain, were the Municipal governments of Melbourne and Geelong. Their mayors and councillors were often instigators of social action, chairing meetings and commenting and leading on the issues of the day like land, transportation and the goldfields.
But like their aristocratic counterparts in Britain, the pastoralists were the conservatives trying to hold back the democratic tsunami that threatened to engulf them. So, they came up with a master plan that they hoped would settle things down until the gold ran out, the gold fever abated and the huge and threatening population of gold-seekers would go back to where they came from. It certainly didn't include local government or any sort of regional

---

[49] Geoffrey Serle, *The golden age*, p 7

self-determination. For them, the solution was a short-term policy as nobody really thought the gold would last as long as it did, or that the diggers would settle down in the regions and so demand civic institutions like everyone else.

Thus, in 1851, one of the most creative ideas put forward by the pastoralists and their political representatives was the Goldfields Commission. But unlike their British counterparts, their hold on society was tenuous and soon to be exposed by the sudden and ongoing influx of indiscriminate wealth from gold. Their plans designed to slow, contain and direct the pace of change were blown apart within the space of a few years. Their creation, which many believed would protect their privileged positions, became instead a millstone around their necks; a most controversial measure that, at one point, had most of them fearing that the colony of Victoria would erupt into a full-blown revolution.

However, as they already knew, a revolution was never going to happen as the aim of the diggers was never about overthrowing the government. What they were interested in was getting the government off their backs and setting the conditions for local justice and achieving the same level of self-administration that was enjoyed elsewhere in the colony. For them, many of whom had come from towns and cities where modern municipal government and civic society had been established for at least a decade, conditions had regressed significantly. Under the Goldfields administration, it had become even worse than what they had experienced back home.

Thus, within a few short years, the goldfields and the cities of Melbourne and Geelong became hotbeds of activism. As the population increased and the nature of the mining evolved from simply picking it up off the ground to more sophisticated underground methods, so also did the social circumstances. By 1854, most people were no longer roaming from one location to another but staying put, and as a government inquiry in October 1853 conceded, the conditions for 'normal society' and industry were beginning to appear. This demanded a change in administration, something diggers had been calling for with municipal government proposed by Ballarat miners' delegates that same year. However, achieving this would not be easy as they faced a regime that was just as recalcitrant as the one that they had left behind in Britain. It stood before them fully entrenched with all the political backing of the colonial government with its police and military resources.

However, just as it was in Britain, the presence of liberal men with foresight, regardless of their motives, envisioned a future where tyranny could not exist in a commercialized world if all citizens were obliged to take part. In Britain, it resulted in political action by Whigs and other non-conformist groups within the system to push for reasonable improvements considering their large and growing constituencies. This resulted in the Great Reform Act of 1832 followed soon after by the Municipal Reform Act of 1835 which allowed for greater representation at a national and local level while integrating the working and middle classes into a national cohesive society. The British initiatives would initiate a dramatic change in the makeup of society, admitting many middle-class representatives into the House of Commons and in the towns initiating a complete change in how most of them were administered. It would initiate a tumultuous transition process that for Britons would reign for most of the nineteenth century. Likewise in the colony of Victoria, similar visionaries in the government as well as diggers representatives also sought to capitalize on the growing numbers in the regional areas for similar reasons. In Victoria, however, it would be compressed in an even shorter timeframe with even more revolutionary outcomes.

3. Historiography

Before the 1856 Colonial Franchise

Before the separation of New South Wales and Victoria in 1850, the creation of separate constitutions, and a popular voter franchise, Municipal Government was the only form of government that most people related to. It was particularly the case in colonial Victoria where the population was overwhelmingly based in the two urban centres of Melbourne and Geelong. Thus, early municipal leaders like John Thomas Smith of Melbourne, and Dr Thompson of Geelong often acted as *the Government*, regularly exceeding their roles and dabbling in colonial politics and locally based political movements. In fact, Thompson was acknowledged in the press as being far more effective at representing the interests of the people of Geelong at a colonial level after a colonial government was installed, than their existing representative James McArthur.[50]

From the early 1840s, municipal government had become a fiercely contested political arena, developing a popular platform for the political views of liberals and radicals unable to participate at a colonial level. It was also the first experience both colonies had with electing a government free of nominated representatives. Functioning alone in this capacity for over a decade, the municipal corporations therefore were able to establish a great deal of credibility and kudos among the public with the ability to enact local laws and create infrastructure such as roads, sanitation, bridges, and public buildings and parks. During this period, due to their close affinity with their constituents, it became an established

---

[50] Geelong, *Geelong Advertiser*, 15 March 1852, p2

practice for the public to approach their local aldermen and the mayor as an effective way to resolve their problems.

It is no surprise therefore, that it was also an effective channel for public organizations participating in the drafting of the New Constitutions of New South Wales and Victoria after the 1850 separation. With strong and widespread public involvement in the process, there were many well-organized groups such as the diggers and anti-transportation leagues, all with their own charters and lists of demands. These were widely published and presented to the press and the government and often sponsored by municipal corporations and their mayors. It all began in an intensely political mood driven by the same issues that had led many of them to emigrate to Australia – the monopoly over the political and economic systems by minority interests such as the nobility and the squatters.

However, with wages in the Australian colonies much higher than they were in Britain, it meant that the rules that kept most of the lower classes out of politics were less of a barrier. Thus, as the first popular democratic election held in Australia, the Sydney Municipal Council election held on 1 November 1842, attracted large crowds on what was declared a public holiday. In a carnival atmosphere, they were all feted with free drinks and festivities. The low franchise qualification ensured a victory for liberals and a defeat for the old established elite. The *Colonial Observer* thus reported 'O long may the Tories of Sydney remember with sorrow and sighing the first of November' while Governor Gipps lamented that it was a victory for the lower classes of the city.[51] And indeed it was, with a majority of 'plain practical men' elected who, as Terry Irving reminds us, would be able to maintain the local infrastructure.[52] They were members of a rapidly growing class of unenfranchised workers and professionals – solicitors,

---

[51] The *Colonial Observer* 5 Nov 1842, in Terry Irving, *The southern tree of liberty* p81, 86
[52] *ibid*

Historiography 35

doctors, tradesmen, and small businessmen such as shopkeepers and merchants.[53]

Once established in the 1840s, the municipal councils, true to their word, became a springboard for major political reforms, supporting the New South Wales Anti-transportation movement in 1848 which became a catalyst for other popular political activity. Formed after attempts by Lord Grey to have it reinstated after its 1840 abolition, the fires of independence and autonomy were fuelled by J D Lang, Henry Parkes and growing numbers of like-minded people. The mayors of Sydney, Melbourne and Geelong were actively involved, providing leadership and often chairing meetings. A monster meeting of over 4000 in Sydney in June 1849 addressed by Lang was supported by members of the Sydney local council. Ex-mayor Edward Flood was one of the speakers reinforcing their demands with the suggestion of using physical force.[54]

In Victoria, much the same class of people were also growing in number and increasingly invested in a future where they could exert political influence locally and at a colonial level. They were given a great deal of encouragement by Lang as a representative for the District of Port Phillip from 1843. Most were echoing New South Wales reformers, advocating for separation, fair representation and an Australian republic from 1851 and ending transportation to all the Australian colonies. The Australasian League, an umbrella organization formed in New South Wales, was well represented by Victorians, with the Mayor of Melbourne William Nicholson appointed just as the gold rushes began in earnest in 1851.[55] Prominent also was Geelong's first mayor, Dr Alexander Thompson who also served as a Victorian delegate along with succeeding mayors of both cities. He was also

---

[53] Terry Irving, *The southern tree of liberty*, p87
[54] Terry Irving, *The southern tree of liberty*, p187-190
[55] Australasian League, *The Argus*, 25 Feb 1851, p2

controversially nominated as a delegate to represent the league's interest in London, a position that came with a £600 salary.[56]

Thompson,[57] who served several terms during the 1850s was also a member and prominent supporter of the local Anti-transportation League. Along with the long-serving Melbourne mayor J T Smith. Thompson particularly, was heavily invested in the formation of the new constitution chairing the Geelong District Constitutional Committee and serving as president.

Their reach, on occasion, also extended directly to London, bypassing the existing colonial government. In March 1851 along with other local leaders 'a respectful address' by the Geelong Municipal Council was transmitted directly to Lord Grey in an attempt to circumvent the influence of squatters over proposed district councils. Reminding Lord Grey of provisions in the original draft of an Australian colonial union, the imposition of intercolonial customs duties was also requested to be repealed. At a later meeting, it was also resolved that a memorial be approved for printing on the settling of electoral districts and how it would affect the interests of the public. Copies would then be presented to the Legislative Council and the press.[58] The districting issue, however, continued to be a bone of contention, with Thompson

---

[56] Anti-transportation banquet in Sydney, *South Australian Register*, 8 May 1851, p2, Geelong, *Geelong Advertiser*, 20 March 1851, p2
[57] *Portrait of Alexander Thomson*, by Frederick Grosse 1866, State Library of Victoria, 49196700
[58] The Geelong and District Constitutional Committee, *Geelong Advertiser*, 6 March 1851, p 2

Historiography

continuing to fight against the influence of Government nominees and squatters over the final draft over the course of 1851. A further petition was drafted and sent to the New South Wales Legislative Council a month later, accusing them of deception and violating British constitutional principles by favouring squatters and increasing their numbers in the legislature. It was signed in the absence of Thompson, by James Cowie, saddler and Geelong Mayor 1852-3.[59]

Complementing the actions of the mayors were also those of the local commercial interests and Chambers of Commerce. As the establishment of Ballarat West municipality illustrates, these bodies worked closely with the municipal councils often interchanging members.[60] Thus, in Geelong, one of the most vocal of the public bodies created was the People's Association with prominent local members who also served on the Chamber of Commerce established in 1853 and later in the municipal council.[61] Like the Anti-transportation League, the aims of its 3-400 artisan and business members were, like the diggers with their charter in November 1854, directed at influencing the application of the New Constitution under discussion for the benefit of the large numbers of unenfranchised citizens of Victoria.

They were led by Capt. John Harrison, a leader in the Bendigo Diggers movement in 1853, and C J Dennys, the founder of well-known Geelong firm C J Dennys & Co wool brokers and Dennys Lascelles. Their aims, as the *Geelong Advertiser* reported, were considering the recent separation from New South Wales, to promote 'the moral, social and political advancement of the people. Dennys was particularly focused on the reduction of protection for the squatting interests and the encouragement of

---

[59] Electoral Bill, *Geelong Advertiser*, 11 April 1851, page 2
[60] See list of founding members of Geelong Chamber of Commerce which includes aldermen & Mayor & ex-Mayors, Chamber of Commerce, *Geelong Advertiser & Intelligencer* 13 June 1853 page 2
[61] The People's Association, *Geelong Advertiser*, 30 July 1851, page 2

general commerce.[62] An important role they expected to play was to ensure the integrity of voting districts, voter rolls, and the election of fitting members for all classes in the colony.[63] Harrison in a later meeting, declared that the time for a 'universal ballot' was not far distant and with the discovery of gold, the railway and electric telegraph would ensure the power of the aristocratic class would be a thing of the past.[64]

At the meeting were other notable leaders of the Geelong community, such as well-known businessman and later burgess auditor T C Riddle, Chartist Robert Booley and medical pioneer and activist Dr Mingay Syder. Riddle, in a speech to the Association, declared he also believed that a universal ballot was a cure for many social evils and would have prevented much of the troubles that Ireland was experiencing. With the upcoming election in mind, he also put forward a case for public education and increased immigration.[65]

However, the role of local governments extended beyond the new constitution. During the gold rush era from 1851 – 1854, it was the municipal councils and their mayors that often provided a mediating and sometimes supporting role in the miners' fight with the colonial government for status and recognition. It was the mayor and municipal council of Melbourne that organized a gold committee, in response to the discovery of large gold deposits in New South Wales in May 1851. At what was described as one of the largest daytime meetings ever held in Melbourne, it was resolved to call on the colonial government to do its duty and provide a land grant and a cash reward for similar results in

---

[62] *Geelong Advertiser* 28 August 1851 p 2 People's Association, The People's Association, *Geelong Advertiser* 31 July 1851 p2, Geoffrey Serle, The golden age, p17
[63] The People's Association, *Geelong Advertiser*, 30 July 1851, page 2
[64] People's Association, *Geelong Advertiser*, 12 Sept 1851 page 2
[65] *Ibid*, the Argus (Melbourne) 4 March 1856 p5

Victoria.⁶⁶ The Mayor J T Smith and the councillors who led the meeting believed that it was necessary to avert a social and economic crisis for the new colony as people left for the New South Wales goldfields.⁶⁷

Shortly after, with their own gold rush commencing the mayor and the council remained closely involved.⁶⁸ In the early days of the Ballarat gold rush, the high cost of the gold license and the failure of the government to honour its word on protection and fees had ignited a great deal of disaffection with the colonial government and the Lt. Governor. A mail robbery and the staking of unauthorised but later sanctioned claims had gotten the 600 miners outraged. This came in addition to the original outrage at the Government for breaking its promise of not imposing the license fee until November. Meetings led by Herbert Swindells and James Oddie, the first chairman of the Ballarat Municipality, were held in September 1851 where the government was accused of imposing tyranny on the diggers by extracting taxes but not providing adequate services. The familiar cry heard all over the goldfields of 'taxation without representation is tyranny' was raised. Petitions were then organized on the matter and sent to the only government they had any faith in, the Municipal Council of Geelong, to advocate on their behalf.⁶⁹

---

⁶⁶ Mineral Discoveries, *Geelong Advertiser*, 5 June 1851 p2, Gold Again, *Geelong Advertiser*, 21 June 1851 p2

⁶⁷ Meeting to offer a reward for finding a gold mine, *The Argus*, 11 June 1851 p4

⁶⁸ Serle Percival, *Dictionary of Australian Biography* Angus & Robertson, J T Smith entry & portrait

⁶⁹ Ballarat Diggings, *Geelong Advertiser* 23 Sept 1851, p2, The Gold Diggers' Petition, *Geelong Advertiser* 24 Sept 1851, p2, see petition next page

With the relationship between the diggers and the Government off to a bad start, matters only deteriorated through 1852 and into 1853. As the campaign to lower the license fee was in full swing from the middle of 1853, the diggers found a sympathetic and supportive ear in the Melbourne City Council and its notorious mayor, J T Smith. As the Mayor of the City of Melbourne, Smith was making a powerful statement to Governor La Trobe, who also attended, that he was there as the presiding official representing the interests of the people of the colony and especially a most vital class – the miners. With a petition of 7000 signatures and representing the interests of 30,000 miners, it was not an insignificant matter.

It was an important forum that diffused the elements that were threatening violence by giving all parties a chance to make their cases in the presence of the public

Historiography

> To the Editor of the Argus
>
> TO THE RIGHT WORSHIPFUL JOHN THOMAS SMITH, ESQUIRE, MAYOR OF MELBOURNE.
>
> Sir,
>
> We desire, on the part of the gold-digging community, to return you our sincere thanks for the very courteous manner in which you received us, as well as for your kindness in presiding over last evening's meeting. We shall not fail to inform the diggers, on our return to Bendigo, that the citizens of Melbourne, by their Chief Magistrate, sympathise with the digging community in the efforts now being made to destroy, constitutionally, an obnoxious law, as well for honouring, for the important class whose interest we represent, those political and social rights to which they are entitled.
>
> We have the honour to be, Right Worshipful Sir,
>
> Your very faithful servants,
>
> (Signed) D. G. JONES,
>
> G. R. BROWN,
>
> E. G. THOMPSON,
>
> Delegates from the Gold-Fields,
>
> Melbourne, August 5, 1853.

as well as the Government and the Lt. Governor. That they believed they were taken seriously is confirmed by a letter of appreciation published two days after the meeting.[70] It was a role that would be played again in the wake of the Eureka rebellion a year later. Once again, it was the actions of the mayor and the City Council that harnessed the rage of the diggers and the people.

While Hull, the mayor during the Eureka rebellion who appeared to be somewhat less of an interventionist than Smith, nevertheless also called a public meeting on the issue.

With J T Smith once again at the helm in 1855, his penchant for speaking on behalf of the people of Victoria continued unabated. A political crisis was looming in Tasmania in September and October 1855 after the discovery of the deaths of 227 children of convict parents had ignited public outrage against the Government and the Convict

---

[70] *Argus* (Melbourne), Saturday 6 August 1853, page 7
See letter next page

> **VICTORIAN SYMPATHY WITH THE TASMANIAN LEGISLATURE,**
>
> His Worship the Mayor has handed to me for publication the following letter-
>
> New Norfolk, Tasmania, Oct 1855
>
> Sir-1 have much pleasure in forwarding a resolution passed at a meeting held here today on the privilege question and trust you will take time to convey the sentiments contained therein to the people of Victoria.
>
> I have the honour to be, Sir,
>
> Your obedient servant,
>
> J Turnbull Chairman
>
> John Thomas Smith, Esq, M.L.C., Mayor of Melbourne
>
> Third Resolution. - "That this meeting offers our thanks to the people of Victoria for their sympathy' for the cause, and that the Chairman of this meeting be requested to convey these thanks to the Mayor of Melbourne.
>
> "This meeting, moreover, desires to express their acknowledgment of the strenuous support which the Legislative Council of Tasmania has received in its momentous struggle from the press of Victoria, New South Wales, and South Australia.
>
> Carried unanimously

Department. With the executive and the legislature at odds over establishing an official inquiry over that and other mounting constitutional matters, the dispute spilled over into the public arena.

In a public mood reminiscent of the Eureka rebellion, rallies were held, and the police and the military were mobilized. Matters quickly escalated as large numbers of the gathered working classes were violently disrupted by supporters of the Convict Department leading to injuries and extensive property damage. It did not take long for the Mayor of Melbourne to show his hand, sending a letter of support to the beleaguered Councillors as they pressed for an inquiry.[71]

Thus, as these few examples illustrate, modern municipal governments, in the early history of Australia, as they were also in nineteenth-century Britain, were champions of democracy, justice and many social and political causes. In Australia, particularly, in the absence of a universal voter franchise and separate constitutions, they were the only government body that welcomed lower-class participation. Moreover, it was also viewed as a powerful means to create a social environment that reflected their political ideals both locally and at a colonial level.

Moreover, as this book illustrates, modern municipalities also played a crucial and primary role in establishing the scientific, modern methods of organizing society that have prevailed for the last 170 years. This early history of Australian Local Government, however, covers a relatively tiny space in the history of Australia, and the key role it played in founding a network of towns and cities across the continent. It's a memory that has been largely lost in the history of the establishment of the modern Australian state and the different levels of government. Instead, what seems to have happened, is that historical research on the topic has largely focussed on where municipal government, conceived as a relatively powerless body, fits within the social and governmental system as a whole.

---

[71] Tasmania, *Adelaide Advertiser*, 20 October 1855, p7, Tasmania, *The Argus* (Melbourne) 22 October 1855, p5, Tasmania, *The Argus* (Melbourne), Monday 29 October 1855, page 4

Historical Perceptions of Municipal Government

The late eighteenth century and a greater part of the nineteenth century, according to historians, is identified as a period of *revolutionary* change. Historians have identified the Agricultural Revolution,[72] the Industrial Revolution, a Consumer Revolution,[73] while local government historians Beatrice and Sidney Webb suggest that Britain also experienced a local government revolution. However, historians generally have not viewed local representative municipal government as a significant element of the fundamental social changes during that period. Similarly, sociology places little emphasis on modern municipal governments as a key implementor of the establishment of rational and scientific reorganization of society as the 'project of modernity' gathered momentum from the nineteenth century.

Rather, local government is allocated an ancillary role within the history of politics and society with an emphasis on its often-troubled relationship with higher levels of government. Considered to be the 'lowest' level of government it is viewed, like many of the old British municipal corporations, as existing merely to implement the schemes of local enterprise and those of colonial, state, and federal politicians. Thus, the many interventions from state governments over persistent reports of corruption, collusion with politicians and other issues to do with planning etc continue to dominate the news. However, despite this bad rap as a relatively powerless and often corrupt political body, once again, social change is in the air and local governments are poised to play a significant role. New technology and changing environmental circumstances once again threaten old hierarchies. Federal national

---

[72] J D Chambers & G E Mingay, *The agricultural Revolution, 1750-1880*, B T Batsford Ltd London, 1966,
[73] Neil McKendrick, John Brewer and J H Plumb, *The birth of a consumer society: the commercialization of Eighteenth-century England*, Bloomington: Indiana University Press 1982

governments and old established political parties are viewed with increasing suspicion and hostility due to their captivity to global economic interests.

At a local level, however, people in many and varied ways, are increasingly exerting an influence over their social and natural environment. Household power independence and the internet-connected world offer local business opportunities as well as the ability for many to work from home in new industries as the old fossil fuel economy is phased out. Environmental concerns also increasingly result in towns and cities opting for their own solutions rather than waiting for a politician based in a faraway capital to make a decision. This places the focus once again on the local community and local self-determination as the place where 'the rubber meets the road' and where changes are most observable and experienced just as it did in the early 1800s. Global climate change is also placing a higher importance on local resource sustainability just as it was before the onset of commercialization and a globalized economy. Thus, with all this now becoming a reality, local government is ripe to become a topic of contemporary and historical interest.

For the most part at present, the historical focus continues to be on how local governments operate within the existing political system – whether through measures of local autonomous action, as dispensers of the policies of higher levels of government or a combination of both. Thus, as Bligh Grant and Joseph Drew in their 2017 study argue, histories of local government in Australia are dominated by the opposing perspectives of voluntarism and centralization.[74] Australia-wide, however, a centralist historical view appears to predominate overshadowing the spontaneous

---

[74] Bligh Grant & Joseph Drew, *Local government in Australia: history, theory and public policy*, Springer Nature Singapore, 2017, pp 1-26, 64-65

actions of local and municipal leaders.[75] Margaret Bowman, who was prolific on the topic during the 1980s, thus argues that in Australia 'local government has never been more than ancillary, first to colonial and then to state governments.'[76] Bowman like Judith O'Neill[77] argues that the primary reason for municipalities was to defray expensive infrastructure costs by the colonial governments. This approach is dominant in studies by Grant Rootes[78] (2006), Wettenhall (1981)[79] and E R Ruzicka's, (2016)[80] in the generally troubled history of Tasmanian local government. The emphasis here is on poor funding from the central government and the persistence of British cultural influences while also noting the rarity of subsequent rigorous intellectual study.

The Tasmanian local government system of the nineteenth century is one of our oldest and most closely resembles its British early nineteenth-century counterpart. It has been described by Rootes as 'chaotic' without system and without adequate services relying heavily on the central government treasury due largely to the sparse and widely dispersed population. Similarly, Ruzicka

---

[75] R J K Chapman & Michael Wood, *Australian local government: the federal dimension*: George Allen & Unwin, Sydney; 1984, Bowman, Margaret, *Local Government in the Australian States*, Australian Government Publishing Service, Canberra, 1976, 'Local Government in Australia' in: *Local democracies: a study in comparative local government*, Margaret Bowman & William Hampton eds, Longman Cheshire, Melbourne, 1983; D M Purdie, *Local government in Australia: reformation or regression*, The Law Book Company, Sydney, 1976; R J K Chapman & Michael Wood, *Australian local government: the federal dimension*:1984, p19

[76] Margaret Bowman, 'Local Government in Australia' in: *Local democracies: a study in comparative local government*, Margaret Bowman & William Hampton eds., Longman Cheshire, Melbourne 1983, p165

[77] Judy Mc Neill, 'Local Government in the Australian Federal System, in: Brian Dollery & Niell Marshall eds. *Australian local government: reform and renewal*, MacMillan Education Australia, South Melbourne, 1997, p18-19

[78] Grant Rootes, *A chaotic state of affairs: the permissive system of local government in rural Tasmania 1840 – 1907*, Phd Thesis, University of Tasmania, Hobart, 2008, 1

[79] R L Wettenhall, 'Towards a reinterpretation of Tasmania's local government history', *Journal of the Royal Australian History*, 67 1981-2 102-118

[80] E R Ruzicka, '*A political history of Tasmanian local government: seeking explanations for decline*' Phd., Thesis, University of Tasmania, 2016

argues that it bears a strong resemblance to their British counterparts before the adoption of the 1835 Municipal Reform Act, with the domination of local land-owning 'squire-aucracies' proving to be an impediment to the effective creation and operation of modern facilities such as roads and bridges. This 'chaotic' situation contrasts with the establishment of Victorian local government and the relatively rapid establishment of roads, bridges, paving, sanitation and other services especially in Melbourne from the 1840s and Ballarat West from 1856. It also contrasts with the British counterpart which was built on a strong basis of local action stemming from strong local initiatives to take advantage of the central government's encouragement to incorporate under the new Act of 1835.

As pointed out in a 1981 government study, there are notable exceptions where some municipal corporations were established independent of the central government initiatives.[81] Obvious early examples in Victoria are Melbourne and Geelong which existed before the separation of Victoria from New South Wales. Added to this are examples of other communities in regional Victoria such as Portland, Ballarat West, Castlemaine, and Bendigo, founding successful municipalities by taking advantage of the 'permissive' legislation of 1854. This was almost completely due, as it was in many cases in Great Britain, to the voluntary actions of local activists playing leading roles in establishing Municipal Corporations in their existing localities.[82] It led, as Fraser points out, to an emerging tradition of participation primarily in local *British* municipal politics for many disqualified under the £10 franchise and the property qualification. It also led to facilitating

---

[81] John Power, Roger Wettenhall and John Halligan, 'Overview of local government in Australia, in: *Local government systems of Australia (Advisory Council for Inter-Governmental Relations Information Paper No 7)* Australian Government Publishing service Canberra, 1981, p9-10

[82] Derek Fraser, *Power and authority in the Victorian city*, Basil Blackwell Oxford, 1979, p. 151

the development of the idea of active citizenship and political action for the renter of the lowest status. It led to many of the previously silent masses acting against the oppressive policies of their erstwhile feudal overlords who had become accustomed to exerting unquestioned power and influence in the towns and their local politics.[83]

Likewise, for the diggers on the goldfields, the idea of attaining respect, legal status and citizenship was equally important in their ongoing campaign for rights, local self-determination and the franchise at a colonial level. Thus, as it is argued by Grant and in this book, in regional Victoria the specific conditions on the goldfields facilitated a strong 'commitment of the early Victorian settlers to the voluntarist principle of social action' which came about for a variety of social, political, and economic reasons.[84] Moreover, once established, the municipality became a springboard for the launching of a plethora of commercial, social and political initiatives not only associated with the mining industry but also with other commercial ventures along with social schemes for housing, welfare, and education.

Therefore, as Power et al (1981) argue, the role of local government should be conceived to be wider than mere service delivery and to defray the costs of a colonial or state budget. It should also include locally conceived and driven initiatives for technological and economic development and any discussion of specific functions should take place within this general framework.[85] Unfortunately, a voluntarist local perspective in Victorian Local Government history has suffered from being

---

[83] Derek Fraser, *Power and authority in the Victorian City*, p. 161-162
[84] Bligh Grant & Joseph Drew, *Local government in Australia: history, theory and public policy*, Springer Nature Singapore, 2017, pp 1-26, David Dunstan, 'A long time coming' in Brian Galligan ed., *Local government reform in Victoria*, State Library of Victoria Melbourne 1998, p11-14
[85] Power et al, Overview of local government in Australia, in: *Local government systems of Australia (Advisory Council for Inter-Governmental Relations Information Paper No 7)* 1981, p96

generally overlooked particularly as a response to modernity and rapid modernization in nineteenth-century Colonial Victoria. Except for David Dunstan's account of Victorian Local Government history and that of Melbourne specifically, and Bernard Barrett's account of the establishment of the Victorian system, most historians largely ignore the fundamental influences of modernity and a progressive local mindset in local government during the nineteenth century in the creation of modern and rationalized urban living conditions.[86] Unfortunately, this mindset also extends to the voluminous numbers of local histories that highlight the actions of local leaders, companies, and other organizations where the role of the municipal government as the engine driving most of it is generally ignored.

Local Histories and Local Government History

The most comprehensive works of the early history of Ballarat are W B Withers' *History of Ballarat*[87] and Weston Bate's *Lucky City*.[88] Both histories have strong political themes that elaborate to some extent on the motivating influence of progressive British political movements such as Chartism on the leaders of early Ballarat. They also proclaim the contribution of civic-minded, commercial pioneers and their enterprises that built Ballarat into a great regional population centre. However, little credit for it has been attributed to the vision of the foundation members of the Ballarat West municipality, the first in the region.

Noticeably absent are any references as to how or why the Municipality of Ballarat West was formed. Instead, Weston Bate

---

[86] David Dunstan, *Governing the metropolis: politics, technology and social change in a Victorian city: Melbourne 1850-1891*, Melbourne University Press, Melbourne 1994, Bernard Barrett, *The civic frontier: the origin of local communities and local government in Victoria*, Melbourne University Press, 1979

[87] W B Withers, *History of Ballarat and some Ballarat reminiscences*, First Published 1870, Published in Ballarat by Ballarat Heritage Services, 1999

[88] Weston Bate, *Lucky City: the first generation at Ballarat 1851-1901*, Melbourne University Press, Melbourne, 1978

places a puzzling emphasis on the establishment of the Ballarat East municipality in 1857. However, as the record shows, it was Ballarat West where the first land lots were alienated, and the first actions were taken to establish a municipal council. While generally noted, the work of people responsible for its inauguration such as J B Humffray and Robert Muir, is largely ignored by both Withers and Weston Bate. Conspicuously absent from most local government histories is any credit given to the Government's policy of regional development and the role played in this by the encouragement of municipalities. In comparison, Frank Cusack, in his history of Bendigo, attributes much of the progress to civic society with the 'red ribbon' movement linking the need for local services with the neglect of the Goldfields Commission.[89]

This compares with the call for progress in matters of enfranchisement, local government, and human rights in Britain. It also explains the actions of the highly motivated generation that arrived in Victoria during the mid-nineteenth century gold rush era. However, few histories of the time and even fewer relating to local government provide any real background of the motivating 'push and pull factors' driving those displaced by changing circumstances at home. While there were many cashed-up opportunists, many were, as Serle shows, in Victoria in the mid-1850s because they had been displaced and disconnected from the emerging commercial society and the related social and political system. With their livelihoods decimated by the factory system and industrialization and their once-respected social status under threat or extinguished, emigration became an attractive option.

Thus, despite popular movements in Britain such as Chartism, Owenism and the Anti-Corn Law League, there was limited success in achieving similar rates of progress for the bulk of the

---

[89] Frank Cusack, *Bendigo: a history*. Heinemann, Melbourne, 1973

Historiography

population both locally and nationally.[90] Land ownership, despite the urging of Scottish social and economic theorists like Adam Smith, Henry Home, Hume et. al. land as a widely available commodity, proved to be the one obstacle that commercial and political idealism failed to traverse. Limited by law and custom throughout Britain to the aristocratic class and the very wealthy, as the basis of political representation, it prevented the lower classes from gaining access to political power at a national level. Although some farmers and greater proportions of the upper middle class were beginning to acquire small plots of land, there were insufficient numbers to support a wide base of electors or rate-payers independent of the dominant aristocratic landowner class.

This situation would persist into the twentieth century as many large estates that were expansive enough to contain local towns and villages, remained locked by restrictive laws of entail and primogeniture. With the gold rushes and a booming economy, therefore, it would offer a perfect opportunity to find fulfilment for the ideals that they and their forbears had espoused during the long half a century of campaigning against the injustices of the transition to a modern commercial society. They came armed with a body of knowledge that fuelled expectations of a better world or at least one that could have been more justly structured as the commercialization of society picked up speed from the end of the eighteenth century.

In so far as Ballarat is concerned, therefore, with this mindset also prevailing amongst the local mining population, direct links to the Eureka rebellion can be made. As a very early activist from the very start of gold discovery at Ballarat, its first municipal chairman James Oddie stands as a prime example. His long-forgotten

---

[90] Briggs, Asa (1963), *Victorian cities*, Penguin Books, Harmondsworth (1968), Gurney, Peter (2015), *Wanting and having*, Oxford, Manchester University Press, especially chapter 4, also see Dorothy Thompson *The Chartists: Popular politics in the Industrial revolution* (Aldershot 1984) pp 341-68, thirty-eight such associations are listed (a conservative estimate)

declaration in 1906 that municipal government was a consequence of the Eureka Rebellion, however, seems to have escaped the notice of researchers and historians. Bernard Barrett's history of local government in Victoria, for example, is dominated by his well-documented recounting of the evolution of the city of Melbourne and the suburbs and the progress of legislative solutions to urban growth. But as Barrett emphasised, this was not without its issues, particularly with the controversial origins of Emerald Hill (now South Melbourne) where staunch resistance to being rated by Melbourne City Council was met with cries of 'no extravagant taxation' and 'no taxation for which value for money is not given.'[91] However, in his brief description of the transition of the goldfield districts to municipalities, there is no suggestion that similar resistance to an unfair tax and administration may have also led to a change in governance.

Barrett presents Castlemaine as a 'central example' of how the goldfield communities made the transition to civil government.[92] Although this is problematic when applied to Ballarat, Frank Cusack, in his history of Bendigo, argues that generic problems with the Goldfields Commission were shared across the goldfields as he writes, 'common grievances cut more sharply on the southern field' where physical differences in mining made for greater hardship. And as he also points out there were no level heads at Ballarat like Sandhurst's Panton to maintain order and good relations with the miners.[93] As he also shows, despite the success of the Red Ribbon protests in forcing a reduction to the license fee in the latter part of 1853, new leaders such as Dr Owens, Dr Wall and William Denovan quickly emerged for the total abolition of the license fee which resonated loudly twelve months later at

---

[91] Bernard Barrett, *The civic frontier: the origin of local communities and local government in Victoria*, Melbourne University Press, 1979, p152
[92] Bernard Barrett, *The civic frontier* p159-174
[93] Frank Cusack, *Bendigo, a history*, p105

Eureka amongst the unsuccessful miners on Ballarat East.[94] As Cusack also shows, the new movement or 'Diggers' Congress' stood for a much more comprehensive agenda. This was made clear to the Sandhurst survey party, led by the Colonial Secretary and Clarke the Surveyor General in January 1854, by local elder Angus Mackay's declaration that constant unrest on the goldfields would continue until the franchise was extended to the miners as well as all the privileges enjoyed by the other members of the community.[95]

Marjorie Theobald's recent work 'The Accidental Town' as another example thus portrays the creation of Castlemaine and its transition from the arbitrary rule of the Goldfields Commission to civil government.[96] Theobald argues that a sense of civic consciousness emerged from a curious event in May 1853 that involved a temperance agitator, sly grog sellers and an over-zealous camp Commissioner.[97] Perjury and counterclaims make it difficult to determine what really happened amongst all the competing local factions with an interest in the matter. However, this episode, like Ballarat, and in many others all over the goldfields, illustrates the confused state of many mining communities without any civil administration under the rule of the commissioners. It is also a story about the major issues of the nineteenth century, the problems of re-establishing a sense of civic order that had been lost in the transition and the social re-integration of the many millions of people placed in a virtual state of non-status as British and colonial society was commercialized and made the transition to a modern, urban, industrial society.

---

[94] *The Argus* (Melbourne) Saturday 7 January 1854, p5 Bendigo
[95] Frank Cusack, *Bendigo, a history*, p99, *The Argus* (Melbourne), Thursday 19 January 1854, p5 Bendigo
[96] Marjorie Theobald, *The accidental town: Castlemaine, 1851-1861*, Australian Scholarly Publishing, North Melbourne, 2020
[97] *Ibid*, p48, the whole story is in a large file at PROV *VPRS1189/P0000/86 Letters from the Chief Commissioner of the Goldfields*, Inward Registered Correspondence, 53/5701

Likewise, the significance of Ballarat activists such as Carr and Sylvester during 1853 highlights the importance the Ballarat diggers places on developing civic institutions and making the goldfields part of the civic framework of the colony. Withers, Ballarat's first historian, like Cusack, attributes the Eureka Uprising to 'social *and* political' (italics mine) grievances. Like Sir George Verdon, he describes the original status of the miners under the Goldfields Commission as being 'outside the mystic circle of governing power … treated … like felons and were too often abetted by their superiors in this treatment of men practically deprived of two centuries of political progress.'[98]

This situation was becoming increasingly untenable for a growing community as Weston Bate in *his* history of Ballarat, *Lucky City*, highlights the emergence of Ballarat as a rapidly urbanising market town early in 1854. The anticipated release of large tracts of farming land to the west therefore was most likely accounting for the early advocacy for and adoption of municipal government as commercial interests began positioning for the realisation of its future economic potential much earlier than the Eureka crisis. The location he points out, perfectly catered to all interests with a township centrally located high on the escarpment relatively free from mining, flooding and other geographical impediments.[99] This contrasts with Bendigo where local government was ridiculed and resisted and in Castlemaine where boundaries and rates were thorny issues for both localities based around geographical obstacles and the scattered groups of miners.[100]

Bate, nevertheless takes the 'social' rather than the political position against an out-of-touch Goldfields Commission where

---

[98] W B Withers, *History of Ballarat and some reminiscences, first published 1870*, published in Ballarat by Ballarat Heritage Services 1999
[99] Weston Bate, *Lucky City: the first generation at Ballarat: 1851-1901*, Melbourne University Press 1978, Melbourne Vic, p41-42
[100] Marjorie Theobald, *The accidental town: Castlemaine, 1851-1861*, p56-57, Frank Cusack, *Bendigo, a history*, p110

Historiography

desperate elements were pushed to extreme and out-of-character measures. Eureka is described as 'more of a vehement last-ditch protest than a rebellion,' a theme reinforced and expanded upon in his article published in 2004.[101] However, unlike Oddie, the Royal Commission of 1854-55 and the Melbourne and Geelong press, he fails to clearly link the need for effective local government and services and the miners' protest movement which was evident over many social issues well before Eureka. Overlooked also is the fact that local government became a priority early in 1855 at Ballarat by the newly formed Victorian Reform League that declared 'we would gain a local self-governing power of unquestionable advantage.' The intervening period in Bate's history of Ballarat that should document this important transition between Eureka and the first elected local government remains strangely absent.[102]

What *is* acknowledged by some, is the fractured nature of colonial Victorian society from 1851 to 1855 and the need to incorporate the goldfields. Contemporary historian and politician, William Westgarth thus argues that the diggers at Eureka were making a case to become an integral part of the newly created Colony of Victoria.[103] This is also the conclusion drawn by Weston Bate in *Lucky City* as he argues: the removal of the Goldfields Commission 'achieved at last by Eureka, simply freed the goldfields to join the rest of the colony.'[104]

The social division caused by the continued operation of the Goldfields Commission was highlighted by many public figures from within its ranks and from outside confirming the validity of the ongoing protests by the diggers. Sir George Frederick Verdon, a prominent leader in the municipal movement in the 1850s and

---

[101] Weston Bate, *Lucky City*, p68, Weston Bate, 'Perceptions of Eureka', in *Victorian Historical Journal*, Volume 75, No.2, September 2004
[102] *The Colonial Times* (Hobart) Wednesday 21 March 1855, Victoria, p2
[103] William Westgarth, *The Colony of Victoria, its history, commerce and gold mining; its social and political institutions; down to the end of 1863*, Sampson, Low, Son and Marston, London, 1864, p149
[104] Weston Bate, *Lucky City*, p73

Historiography

1860s and Goldfields Commissioners J R Hardy, the first Chief Commissioner for NSW, and R H Horne of the Waranga goldfield were among the many attributing the causes of the Eureka uprising to the failure to spend the mining taxes on the mining communities and too much power in the hands of a centralized administrative regime.[105] These were the types of flaws in local government existing before the 1835 Act that had failed in an urbanizing British society. Thus, while existing centuries before and acting as a community leadership body with dignitaries and established customs, they were not answerable to the public, existing primarily to preserve its commercial interests and those of its exclusive members. Nevertheless, despite these indictments and obvious shortcomings, the Goldfields Commission, for several years, did function as a form of local government until it was restructured in June 1855 after the findings of the 1854-55 Royal Commission.

---

[105] Sir George Frederick Verdon, *The present and future of municipal government in Victoria*, Melbourne, W. Fairfax & Co. 1858, page 4, J R Hardy, *Squatters and gold diggers, their claims and rights*, Sydney, Piddington, George Street, 1855, Commissioner Horne in *The Age*, Melbourne, 28 May 1855

4. Local Government in Transition

British Local Government

The Old Tory Order & the Need for Change

The transitions to modern representative local government in Britain and the colony of Victoria, both follow a similar troubled path. In Britain, as Derek Fraser explains, local government before the Act of 1835 while infinitely variable could be broadly categorised as incorporated or unincorporated towns and cities. Initially, as the act suggests, it targeted the existing corporations due to their close affiliation with the established Tory order – the church and the landowning politicians.[106] As society progressively changed around them, by the early 1800s many had become little more than clubs peopled and run by loyalists from the church, old families, and those whose connections harked back to the days when guilds predominated and nominated freemen artisans did the bidding of their political masters. The unincorporated town, however, eludes such a simple definition. This was where threats to traditional Tory hegemony were more noticeable - the larger towns and cities where factory manufacturing in new industries like textiles had become established. In many such places dissenter factory owners and entrepreneurs were taking an active interest in local government as a more progressive mood was emerging. Measures like Sunday Schools, denominational schools, home construction for their workers, workers clubs and societies were permanently altering the

---

[106] Derek Fraser, *Power and authority in the Victorian city*, Basil Blackwell Oxford 1979, p. 1-21, V A C Gattrell, Incorporation and the pursuit of Liberal hegemony in Manchester 1790-1839, in Derek Fraser, *Power and authority in the Victorian city* p. 16-53

social fabric. The more radical Factory owners like Owen who implemented strict alternative social measures to poor law and other government systems, thus exposed the ancient close corporations and vestry-run towns and parishes that were ill-equipped for the task of meeting the modern world and its social and civic requirements.[107]

For Britons however, before the 1835 Act, the concept of local government being a provider of public services and facilities was a significant departure from the historical understanding of its role in society. From the time of Elizabeth 1 until the British Municipal Corporations Act of 1835, the only experience many Britons had with local government was the ancient model with its centuries of culture derived from the feudal system. Such local corporations did not exist primarily for the residents but to further the aims of the corporation in the management and control of local trades, manufacturing, and commerce. In effect, they existed to prevent disruption to local trade and commerce keeping it all within local hands through the maintenance of local customs and traditions. They were the very antithesis of free trade that was becoming the norm from the middle of the eighteenth century.

As the towns expanded, they were the organizations that facilitated local infrastructure as private commercial enterprises that they owned and controlled exclusively such as water supply, sewerage, ports, roads and turnpikes and other mandated affairs such as poor relief. As public health became a pressing issue in the eighteenth century, the inadequacy of these 'enterprises' in providing any public benefit to the increasing numbers of lower and working classes became exposed. Their sense of entitlement, however, was, in many cases, based on centuries of tradition where communities were relatively stable and not subject to the rapid changes that a commercial and industrial society generated.

---

[107] Bernard Barrett, *The civic frontier*, pp84-90, pp123-125

Local Government in Transition

Surviving with many and varied unique customs and practices during a long history of conquest and re-conquest dating back to Roman times, many towns and villages across Britain had maintained a continuing tradition of self-governing independence offering fealty to a local warlord or king whose army kept order. As regimes changed, the outside appearance of local governments did as well, taking on legal mandates of the new overlords while preserving much of the pre-existing culture and traditions. Thus, with the coming of the Normans, and the later regimes of the competing royals to the present Westminster system, the legal structure of the ruling regime was superimposed many times across the realm. Absorbing a collection of traditions that were generally based on land ownership and protection of specific interests they were controlled by the appointment of various officials that deferred to the higher levels of authority such as the county seat and the crown.[108]

While the traditional circumstances varied considerably in such a confusing system, by the eighteenth century, as J A Chandler writes, local government can be understood as having three basic strains. The oldest were those controlled by local landowners through a local magistrate who was usually the legal official, those controlled by the church or parish which became more common after the Elizabethan poor laws, and the Improvement Commissions which became common in the eighteenth century as expanding towns created problems that could not be solved by existing town governments. The first of these was formed in 1662 through a Private Act of Parliament for the City of London for street cleaning and sewer construction.[109]

Many towns such as Manchester also defied such definitions or involved elements of them all but primarily evolved because of

---

[108] J A Chandler, *Explaining local government: local government in Britain since 1800*, Manchester University Press 2007, p. 2
[109] J A Chandler, *Explaining local government: local government in Britain since 1800*, p. 14

commercial activity and the increased population that they attracted. It was possible, therefore, to have all three styles of local government bodies operating around an old core organization that existed as a cultural nod to old traditions having had long lost any real relevance. For such towns and cities with a corporation charter, and despite their irrelevance, a long and strongly held sense of self-determination prevailed. Many continued the maintenance of customary displays with parades led by a mayor and other officials and traditions reinforcing a sense of local identity. Having existed for centuries with no overlord, their only obligation was paying an annual sum or *firma burgi* to the King to guarantee freedom from all other claims. They were then left to conduct their own (usually commercial) affairs with their unique conditions but subject to the law of the land through a local magistrate.[110] A peer usually held this office, which was incorporated into the county and national legal system legislating permits, licenses and other related matters.

Over time this system had grown in number and complexity to include 246 towns and cities by 1835 when the new Municipal Corporations Act was passed. Invariably linked to the national party-political system, it was a necessary change, designed to address the political reality of middle-class urban existence and to correct a system moulded or corrupted as Jenks explains, by royal dynasties and the parliament as they vied for effective control of the country.[111]

For many old corporations in urban centres like Bristol for example, the 1835 reform act was essentially a threat to their existence as power was effectively given to residents to elect representatives to manage the city. As owners and administrators of its assets for centuries, however, municipal corporations pre-1835 had not been answerable to the local population. The attitude

---

[110] Edward Jenks, *An outline of English local government*, Methuen & Co, London, 1894, p189
[111] ibid

Local Government in Transition

of the Bristol corporation in the words of its council members, is described by Bush, a local historian:

> As an essentially private body, our first charge is to administer our inherited assets and affairs as we deem fit, not subject to outside scrutiny or external direction … the public have no legitimate access to either our deliberation or our funds … But … provided our rights are not at risk, we will endeavour to promote the city's interests. It must be expressly understood that we reject the notion of being answerable to any body of people except than ourselves. [112]

Much of the revenue in question, collected and administered by pre-reform corporations, related to tolls and charges from other infrastructure assets like dockings, harbours, bond stores, turnpikes and canals etc with the profits supporting the poorhouse system and other private enterprises like gas and water supply companies related to the corporation.

While those loyal to the traditional ways attempted to cling to their old privileges, the transition into modernity during this period was facilitated largely by an expanding middle class and nonconformist businessmen. They represented a new type of liberal-minded civic leaders with a new-found sense of public consciousness. Birmingham, for example, is credited as an important origin of the movement that delivered many iconic public buildings and facilities through the work of prominent citizens not connected to the old order. Well-educated and well-connected, unitarian George Dawson of Birmingham is particularly remembered for his community work in this era and was honoured with a statue in the centre of the city for his municipal achievements.[113]

---

[112] Derek Fraser, *Power and authority in the Victorian city*, St martin's Press, New York, 1978, P113
[113] Andrew Reekes & Stephen Roberts, *George Dawson & his circle: the civic gospel in Victorian Birmingham*, The Merlin Press Dagenham UK, 2021

Dawson, while active locally, was instrumental at a national level as a lobbyist for civic amenities and as a public speaker in high demand promoting the spread of public facilities like schools, libraries and other public services as a religious as well as a civic duty.[114] Statistics gathered by Hennock for 1851 show that the extent of non-conformist affiliation ranged from 18.3% in Liverpool to 45.5% in the manufacturing town of Bradford indicating a huge nationwide drop in support for the old church-state power nexus that had prevailed for centuries.[115] This new urban and often non-conformist approach to civic life was also supported locally by a growing liberal outlook during the mid-nineteenth century leading to the rise of the Liberal Party to compete with the old aristocratic landowning parties of the Whigs and Tories. For example, the Birmingham Municipal Council's composition reflects this with an increasing diversity of middle-class occupations such as solicitors, lawyers, doctors, accountants and small business proprietors who in most cases during the 1850s held a majority.[116]

However, this was not without its problems. For a large part of the 1850's, after legitimisation was won in the courts by the new corporations, many large landowners and their supporters withdrew into projects of their own making choosing to develop separate estates and townships like Lord Calthorpe's Edgbaston in Birmingham and the Dukes of Devonshire and Brighton for example. This then provided an opportunity for small business proprietors such as Joseph Allday, a Chartist and radical who ran an 'economist faction' in Birmingham from 1853 to 1859.[117] While keeping rates and costs low, Allday and his followers also reflect

---

[114] E P Hennock, *Fit and proper persons: ideal and reality in nineteenth century urban government*, 1973 pp 61-79 and Derek Fraser, *Power and authority in the Victorian city*, p 102-106
[115] Hennock, *Fit and Proper Persons*, p357
[116] *Ibid*, table 15 Leeds Town Council 1852-76 selected occupations
[117] Hennock, *Fit and Proper Persons* page 31-34

the lack of individual landowners and ratepayers with sufficient wealth to fund vital public works for water supplies and sanitation for crowded working-class tenements. This had the effect of delaying the fundamental changes to meet the needs of expanding populations. Instead, it continued the practice of resorting to the national government through Improvement Commissions using the local members for separate acts of parliament for facilities management until further reforms at the end of the nineteenth century.

This then led to questions on local government autonomy during the mid-nineteenth century as its role in modern society was seriously questioned. Rather than incorporate the services under separate acts into local government, a 'modern and scientific' approach advocated by early Utilitarians such as Jeremy Bentham and his followers sought to have these functions centralised. The case for a decentralized 'modern' local government was taken up by lawyers such as Joshua Toulmin-Smith who took the fight to centralizers like Edwin Chadwick in the 1840s and 1850s. [118]

Chronicled by Beatrice and Sydney Webb in their early twentieth-century series on English local government the reader becomes increasingly aware of the need for fundamental reform and rationalization of functions particularly in the regional areas of

---

[118] Ben Weinstein, "Local Self-Government is true socialism: Joshua Toulmin-Smith, the state and character formation", *The English Historical Review*, Vol. 123, No. 504 (Oct.2008) pp 1193-1228.
Joshua Toulmin-Smith, *Local Self-Government and centralization: the characteristics of each; and its practical tendencies, as affecting social moral and political welfare and progress, including comprehensive outlines of the English Constitution*, John Chapman, London, 1851; Joshua Toulmin-Smith, *Local Self-Government un-mystified, a vindication of common sense, human nature and practical improvement, against the manifesto of centralism put forth at the Social Science Association*, London, 1857; Lewis R A, 'Edwin Chadwick and the public health movement 1832-1854', PhD. Thesis unpublished, University of Birmingham, 1949, Anon, *Engineers and officials: an historical sketch of the progress of "health of towns works" (between 1838 and 1856) in London and the provinces: with biographical notes on Lord Palmerston, the Earl of Shaftesbury, Lord Ebrington, Edwin Chadwick, C.B., F.O. Ward*, John Thwaites. 1856. London: E. Stanford

England where autonomy was long-standing and highly valued.[119] Polarised debates such as this highlight the difficulties involved in establishing modern municipalities in Britain after the Municipal Corporations Act of 1835. However, the new law, as the Webbs argue, was nevertheless, nothing short of a revolution, becoming well-established over the next half-century. Thus, as Mackenzie reminds us, the Municipal Corporations Act of 1882 also granted powers to form byelaws and acquire public property.[120]

Victorian Local Government

In Australia however, local government began without a pre-existing network of autonomous towns and cities – an inverse process to that of Great Britain. But as the population expanded into the interior, tension between local and central administration developed, especially in Victoria with the gold rushes of the 1850s. Ordained from the central government for many years in NSW and Van Diemen's Land, the local authority rested with the police magistrate, usually a local landowner of independent means, who oversaw all the legal and criminal arrangements within a prescribed district.[121] This situation existed, particularly in NSW until the NSW Municipalities Act of 1858 and beyond, as many towns and localities preferred to continue the funding for works from the NSW treasury and its indirect but guaranteed stream of indirect taxation.[122] The resistance against the imposition of rates in NSW was very widespread and because the central government had no army at war, funds were much more readily available for local

---

[119] Webb, Sidney and Beatrice & Ponsonby, G. J., *English local government. Vol. 5: The story of the King's highway*. Cass, London, 1963
[120] Albert Shaw, "Municipal Government in Great Britain". *Political Science Quarterly*. The Academy of Social Science. 4 (2) 197-229, J P D Dunbabin, "British Local Government Reform: The Nineteenth Century and After", *The English Historical Review*, Vol. 92, No. 365, (Oct 1977) pp 777-805, WJM Mackenzie, *Explorations in government, collected papers*, p71
[121] John Hirst, *The strange birth of colonial democracy*, 244-246
[122] John Hirst, *The strange birth of colonial democracy*, 262

works than they were in Britain. Hence, as Hirst explains, the central government of NSW rather than local councils, was able to initiate and control services such as education and law enforcement, maintaining this system until well into the 1860s. [123]

In Victoria, before the gold rushes, official local government began in September 1836. This occurred after the acceptance of the illegal settlement at Port Philip by the Port Philip Company in 1834. It was legitimised by Governor Burke who sent a detachment of troops from Sydney under the command of Captain William Lonsdale. Legally endowed as the first police magistrate for the district, one of his first tasks was to conduct a survey and formulate a plan for selling the land. Within three years the settlement had been named Melbourne and covered almost ten square miles and a multitude of surveyed and privately owned plots of land.

It exemplified the uniqueness of Australian communities. Beginning with the notion of private ownership of land, the imposition of land taxes as the most effective and lucrative means of revenue quickly led to the establishment of a democratic local government. This was a logical development with the growing public need for roads, sanitation water supply and other services and regulations.[124] It thus avoided many of the problems with the transition to responsible local government in Britain where property was in the hands of the few and facilities privately owned.

As settlement and commerce increased in the Melbourne area, the first local civic initiative was the establishment of a commission to oversee public markets. It was based on an act for similar local markets in Syndey and Paramatta in 1839. With a population of 9000 by 1841 and 3000 eligible electors, eight commissioners were elected from a division of four wards covering the settlement in November 1841. As Bernard Barrett reminds us, this was Port Phillip's first legally constituted electoral body and the first

---

[123] *The strange birth of colonial democracy*, 264
[124] Bernard Barrett, *The civic frontier*, p. 1-17

opportunity to exert political control independent of the powers based in Sydney. It was announced in the press as a stepping stone to the higher functions of a municipal council and a legislative assembly for the colony.[125]

At the same point in time, legislation passed in Sydney, A New South Wales Police Act, provided for law enforcement over street alignment, nuisances, and sanitation. First applied to Melbourne in 1838 and Geelong in 1841, it was followed shortly after by the Town and Country Police Act and the Management of Towns Act following the model established in NSW and Tasmania.[126] With the passing of the British Municipal Corporations Act in 1835, its merits were extensively debated in New South Wales. Subsequently, legislation was passed in New South Wales in 1842 for the incorporation of Sydney and Melbourne with Sydney designated a city and Melbourne a town. For Melbourne, as Barrett points out, it came with a greater political significance for its residents than those of Sydney, as many saw it as progress towards independence for the Port Phillip district.[127] Incorporating the four wards of the existing Market Commission, the Melbourne Corporation was officially formed with an election held on December 1 of that year. It began with an appropriation of £2000 conditional on the collection of a corresponding amount in rate revenue.

Regional Victoria to 1856

In the regional areas despite the sparse and isolated population and without any regard for the existing Aboriginal designations, vast areas had early on been created on paper as parish and county divisions in preparation for future expansion. Attempts to legitimise them however were unsuccessful as several schemes that attempted to raise revenue for road building and maintenance were

---

[125] Bernard Barrett, *The civic frontier* p. 27-28
[126] Bernard Barrett, *The civic frontier*, p17
[127] Bernard Barrett, *The civic frontier*, p 40

Local Government in Transition

resisted by the few people who lived there. Nevertheless, the relative districts continued to be staffed by a Police Magistrate and a clerk. With relatively undefined and discretionary powers they officiated in much the same way as the early colonial administrators into the gold rush era.[128] Their duties encompassed almost all community activity where legalities or record keeping was required such as census, crimes, licensing, and arbitration and enforcement of regulations such as traffic, sanitation and commerce.[129]

Thus, when the gold rush began in earnest later in 1851, managing the enormous numbers of people from a centralized authority in Melbourne quickly exposed the need for some form of local administration in the regional areas. As such a development had not been a matter of pre-emptive policy and planning, the Government was found wanting due to a lack of consideration for the needs of the miners both on a personal and a civic level. With miners' protests over conditions increasing from the first moment of government involvement in the gold industry, the only real response was the formation of a District Roads Board in 1853. However, control remained firmly in the hands of the Melbourne politicians. It became the main vehicle for establishing main roads throughout the colony with treasury funds and the imposition of tolls replacing the old District Councils that had ceased to function.[130] A compromise, however, was reached in 1856 when local Roads Boards were formed. In the Ballarat district, the first such body was created that year after an election with Robert Muir, a municipal councillor and prominent local businessman, elected as president.

After the Eureka rebellion, the lack of civic services and failure to establish regional autonomy for the increasingly large and permanent regional population was identified by Sir George Frederick Verdon as a major contributing factor. Not alone with

---

[128] Bernard Barrett, *The civic frontier*, p10
[129] *The civic frontier*, p89
[130] *The civic frontier*, pp84-90

this assessment, he echoed similar criticisms of John Hardy, the New South Wales Goldfields Commissioner from 1851 to 1855 of the failings of the goldfields administration in that colony as well. As a prominent Municipal Government activist in the 1850s and member of the Williamstown Council, Verdon was also a municipal magistrate and Chairman of the Conference of Municipal Delegates that sat in 1856 and again in 1858. Verdon was scathing of the practical shortcomings of the government's short-sighted approach that had led to so much violence and social unrest. His pamphlet published in 1858 links the events of Eureka and protests elsewhere on the goldfields to the lack of attention of the Government and their regional arm, the Goldfields Commission to the immediate social needs of the diggers.[131]

Verdon thus argued that its Melbourne-based authority which assumed pre-eminent power wherever its officers were placed, failed to consider the day-to-day living conditions of mining localities. As he pointed out, police and other officers who would have ordinarily been deployed in the management of the mining settlements by monitoring and enforcing customs and regulations were employed in goldfield duties such as license collection, claim monitoring and arbitration. This, he declared, effectively nullified the prevailing Town and Police Act and effectively hindered the development of normal civic processes as occurred in Melbourne and Geelong.

In quoting British politician Sir E. Bulwer Lytton, he makes his position on centralization clear:

> ... to true liberty and permanent order Centralization is deadly poison. The more the provinces govern their own affairs, the more we find everything, even to roads and post horses are left to the people, the more the municipal spirit pervades every vein

---

[131] Sir George Frederick Verdon, *The present and future of municipal government in Victoria*, p10

of the vast body, the more certain we may be that reform and change must come from universal opinion …[132]

George Verdon thus argues that the 'responsible local governments' established in Melbourne and Geelong were the correct and expected response to the development of the permanent towns of Victoria from 1852. However, on the goldfields, he points out, this process was halted because of large numbers of people, the lack of settled populations and the 'chaotic state into which the community was precipitated …[133]'

This situation, as Verdon explains, led to a return to 'the old system of irresponsible government.' In each district, the Commissioner ruled with almost absolute power 'like a mandarin of the celestial empire.' Unlike the magistrates and their designated districts, the Goldfields Commissioners had to make and administer the laws specific to mining but made no allowances for the 'peculiar requirements of a mining community.'[134] And in conjunction with autocratic methods in conceiving and enforcing the rules and regulations it was no surprise that it ended in disaster. Thus, as Verdon further comments on the failure of the Commission:

> The establishment of local courts and mining boards has been the practical result of experience, obtained in the saddest and most costly way in which it can ever be purchased by a people.[135]

For the miners and the associated commercial interests, most of their problems were more practical rather than constitutional in nature. The inability to exercise any control over issues that affected day-to-day living like law and order, access to the

---

[132] *Ibid*, 4
[133] *Ibid*
[134] Sir George Frederick Verdon, *The present and future of municipal government in Victoria*, p 10-11
[135] *Ibid*

goldfields, the regulation of liquor, accommodation, prices etc were a significant aspect of the miners' protests. It was this that concerned the majority 'moral force' position led by J B Humffray who could be considered the unacknowledged representative of those who did not directly participate in the Eureka conflict. Many of these were the storekeepers and their city suppliers, successful miners and those who had purchased land and had a vested interest in settling down at Ballarat. They represented the very class of people that the pastoralists and their political backers mostly feared would alter forever their pastoral domain in regional Victoria. They were the very same types of people that had wrought so much change in Britain through the vehicle of the Municipal Corporations Act of 1835.

Local Government reform was made in the interests of private property and a free market economy'. W J M Mackenzie 1961

5. Creating Modern Municipalities

Re-integrating and Re-ordering Society

Local municipal government is a curious creature that has a history as long as human settlement in towns and cities around the world. Like a chameleon, it has survived the tests of time under many different ideologies and regimes. Currently, it exists as a major development in the transition of Western societies from feudalism into modernity as the modern democratic municipality. It may yet evolve again as we move beyond the post-modern world. Created for British residents in the nineteenth century, it began with the British Municipal Corporations Act of 1835. This provided a template for the Australian counterpart that was established soon after in Sydney, Melbourne and Geelong in colonial Australia. Conceived as a replacement for local government corporations and commissions that hark back to feudal and pre-modern eras, it is one of the first social and political institutions created specifically for modern British society. Initially devised as a scheme to shore up anti-Tory political power in the early 1800s, as some historians argue, it emerged over the century as *the* primary body for local government achieving consolidation of most other existing local bodies while adopting modern scientific and rational concepts in solving the problems of the growing urban existence.

As Marx observed, over the eighteenth and nineteenth centuries, older social structures perceived as impediments to social progress began to melt away under the onslaught of commercialization and a scientific and rational worldview. Thus, by the early nineteenth century, Whig government reforms provided an avenue for nonconformist entrepreneurs to bypass the local monopolies of the old Tory establishment over local government and commerce. Employing the clever device of a Royal Commission in 1832, the exclusive interests of Tories and their supporters were effectively exposed and neutralized paving the way for local government reform and providing a social and political platform for many excluded by the old monopoly. This became one of the Whigs' most significant achievements establishing local democracies for many excluded from the national franchise in the form of democratic municipal governments.[136]

While a political ploy designed to increase Whig representation on the backs of radical influence, as prominent Tories protested, the proposed Municipal Corporations Act also strongly reflected the views of those *without* pure political motives. Benthamites like J A Roebuck and particularly Francis Place believed that 'municipal government was created by the people to promote their common welfare.' Their vision encompassed the assumption and maintenance of all infrastructure within the town boundaries, including schools, hospitals and charities and the power to create laws for their regulation, assessment of taxes and to employ and manage personnel.[137]

This came on a wave of theoretical development driven by a more secular and utilitarian view of society by mentors like Jeremy Bentham, whose relativist views produced the famous quip, 'pushpin is as good as poetry'. Advocating a methodological and scientific approach to identify causes and improvements to social problems, thus provided powerful and reasonable justifications for overriding political and cultural objections. Offering solutions to the many problems to do with health, access, and order as the populations of the towns and cities underwent dramatic increases,

---

[136] Derek Fraser, *Power and authority in the Victorian city*, Basil Blackwell, Oxford UK, p 1-11
[137] *Ibid*, p 16-21

he was a man in many ways ahead of his time. Evidence of his influence on the modern and utilitarian approach can be seen in the proliferation of institutions designed for the efficient serving of the needs of a mass society. This is a long list - hospitals, sanitation works, water supply, bridges and roadworks, prisons, power supply, public and administration buildings and private land ownership and town planning as well as the systems to control and manage them. All were evidence of the transformative application of science and the positivist ideals that derived from two centuries of enlightenment.[138]

However, this transformation was not always a smooth and planned process. For almost a century, as modern British industrial towns and cities were created or expanded, urban society appeared to be in a state of chaos. Streets that wound in and around smoke-belching factories; uncontrolled waste, haphazard residential construction, and the remnants of engulfed villages and towns created a mishmash of environments. Gone were the open fields and the blue skies of the agricultural world that most were raised and worked in, later to be nostalgically commemorated by the proliferation of public and municipal parks and gardens. Thus, as the modern world developed, it was the creation of modern representative municipal governments that created modern order and mass regulation as the older cooperative feudal entities and organizations became redundant and ineffectual. Their pre-modern thinking resulted in a lack of foresight and the inability to conceptualise the functioning of a modern urban society. It was invariably therefore, the work of a publicly run local council often in conjunction with, engineers and scientists, that urban populations were able to break the monopoly of vestries, Improvement Commissions, and old chartered corporations, and solve their many problems. However, as a basic pillar of modern

---

[138] Stuart Hall and Bram Gieben eds., *Formations of modernity*, Polity Press 1992, Cambridge UK, p, 14

society, there has been, unlike the higher levels of government, comparatively little historical or theoretical discussion on what it is or what is its function. This was the point made by W J M Mackenzie on British Local Government in the 1960s.

Arguing in a series of lectures, that there is no theory of modern local government, Mackenzie pointed out that 'it evolved to satisfy the emerging interests of private and public property and the free market economy during rapid urbanisation in the nineteenth century'.[139] A decade later, social historian Derek Fraser of the University of Bradford on the topic of municipal government, also argued that 'what had no philosophy could hardly be deemed ideological yet paradoxically it became so.'[140] According to Fraser, the arrival of municipal government after the 1835 Act ignited conflicts and debates between collectivists and socialists, proponents of *laissez-faire* capitalism and followers of Benthamite utilitarianism. At the heart of the matter, however, was the increasing importance of the 'public' and the breaking down of the old structures that had no or little public accountability. It involved the recasting of concepts about public space and public welfare through the application of reasonable, scientific, and legal measures. The creation of new and modern urban spaces thus became the basis for several important cases launched by newly formed municipal corporations for control of local privately owned utilities and services during the 1840s.

The theoretical argument underpinning it all owed a great deal to Benthamite concern for social utility and the pursuit of happiness as a fundamental human instinct. As one of the earliest modern social theories, it incorporated the belief that the state should provide a decent liveable space for the large masses of people congregating in the cities from the late eighteenth century. Prominent proponents were political theorist John Stuart Mill and

---

[139] W J M Mackenzie, *Explorations in Government, collected papers: 1951-1968*, The Macmillan Press London 1975, pp 68-75
[140] Derek Fraser, *Municipal authority in Victorian cities*, p. 170

the earlier Utilitarian Edwin Chadwick and his scheme for a national sanitary body to manage and improve public health. However, while a sound concept and well-intended and supported at a national level, his concept of social utility and happiness was challenged over its lack of political empathy. It was not long therefore before his tyrannical approach to imposing a 'happiness' quotient on towns and cities across the realm was steadfastly resisted. Most viewed it as a loss of their long-held local autonomy to national bodies based in London. At a local and county level, however, the 'centralization' debate was seized upon as a means of driving wedges between the various local public factions enthusiastic about the new Municipal Corporations Act. However, these attempts ultimately failed due to the strong independent local identities of the largely decentralized British society. Local municipal government adopted and driven by locals thus emerged as a powerful force for urban development and the implementation of many solutions for urban populations during the nineteenth century.

Thus, while local government has always been with us, *modern municipal government*, therefore, can be understood as a level of government created to transition British and colonial society into the modern world. Its genius is that it exists to integrate and reconcile competing interests and political philosophies for the betterment of a liveable urban and town existence. With a local focus and power base, unlike its federal counterpart which often gets bogged down in ideological debates, its practical emphasis is largely due to local leaders fulfilling a progressive vision and unlike a national politician, it is directly for their neighbourhood public. However, achieving this did not come easily as powerful elements of the old order taking advantage of the opportunities capitalism and technology, often took little interest in paying for or considering modern urban living conditions. With their mindset and culture based on the old ways, it took a period of struggle before the modern municipality became established by residents and their visionary champions. This was a shared experience by many British towns and cities as well as those in the Australian colonies particularly concerning this history, the Victorian goldfields. It became a process that generally followed a similar path that could be summed up by the following themes: creating order from chaos, fighting for recognition, and the first form of democracy for the unenfranchised.

Basic Themes

1. Order from Chaos

British Towns and Cities

Addressing the uniquely modern problems of population growth and the challenges of urban living, was effective when people utilized the newfound authority of modern municipal governments. In places like Manchester in the 1840s, results speak for themselves[141]. As an unincorporated town not subject to the compulsory dictates of the 1835 Act, Manchester, like many others, remained untouched and beset by all sorts of problems. Free trade campaigner Richard Cobden, commemorated in many street names and a town in Victoria, was convinced that replacing the old order would solve most of them. The underlying problem was essentially the same as the Eureka miners - a large underclass with no official status or political voice. The exorbitant price of bread dictated by the price of grain, high rents, and poor living and working conditions were existential matters over which they had no control. Like Eureka on the goldfields of Victoria three decades later, it was only after mass demonstrations and loss of life at Peterloo in 1819, that the Tory overlords began to seriously entertain the explosive issue of corn laws and other local issues.[142]

Beatrice and Sidney Webb thus describe scenarios under the Tory system like Manchester where Cobden lived where the *laissez-faire* administration of the manufacturers and the aristocrats had produced poet William Blake's 'dark satanic mills' so described by communist social theorist Frederick Engels. The town in 1819 was well on the way to becoming the city he later described with a depressing vista of smoke-belching chimneys and disease-ridden ghettos of poorly constructed hovels, the outcome of the unregulated expansion on properties owned and managed by the ruling landowner class. Achieving any sort of local change, however, invariably aroused contests between those vested in maintaining their centralized power over local affairs and the ever-growing numbers of local activists.

---

[141] Mike Nevell – Housing in 19th century Manchester, photograph of Ancoats 1870, Marple Local History Society 2024

[142] Richard Cobden, 'Incorporate your Borough' in Ralph Roth & Robert Beachy, *Who ran the cities: city elites and urban power structures in Europe and North America 1750-1940*, Ashgate Publishing, Aldersgate UK, 2007 p. 47, V A C Gattrell, 'Incorporation and the pursuit of liberal hegemony', in Derek Fraser ed., *Municipal reform and the industrial city*, Leicester University Press, 1982, p. 31

The Peterloo massacre was, like Eureka on the goldfields, a watershed event that highlighted the deep social problems and the need for change. Asa Briggs, like many contemporaries, thus describes the growing metropolis of the first half of the nineteenth century as a place of lawlessness, and disorder. It was, he wrote, 'with no adequate police, no effective machinery of modern local government, a disturbed social system which lacked the benevolent influence of natural gradations.'[143] As time progressed, other leading figures like Heywood, a radical publisher, and small businessman, along with Cobden, a local manufacturer and free trade advocate, took on the task of solving the many problems. At Cobden's urging, taking the path of incorporation in 1839 led to progress with local infrastructure, living conditions and prosperity over the course of the century.[144] Thus, Heywood, as an aldermanic candidate in 1853 could proudly proclaim that as head of the Highways, Paving and Sewerage Committee after incorporation, the results of his work were obvious for all to see. Of particular importance, he declared with some exaggeration, was that the health of the residents of the township of Manchester had never been better, due to there being 'scarcely a street within the walls of that neighbourhood which had not a good pavement over its surface and a sewer underneath.'[145] Nevertheless, compared to what was before, it was a trend toward cohesive improvement that progressed as the century unfolded.

Such dramatic early progress was patchy and often dependent on federal funding as many new municipalities fought for

---

[143] Asa Briggs, *Victorian cities*, Penguin Books, Harmondsworth England, 1963, p. 92

[144] Joanna M Williams, *Manchester's radical Mayor, Abel Heywood, the man who built the town hall*, The History Press, Port Stroud, Gloucestershire UK, 2017, Richard Cobden, 'Incorporate your Borough' in Ralph Roth & Robert Beachy, *Who ran the cities: city elites and urban power structures in Europe and North America 1750-1940*, Ashgate Publishing, Aldersgate UK, 2007 p. 47

[145] Joanna M Williams, *Manchester's radical Mayor, Abel Heywood, the man who built the town hall*, p 84

recognition and the assumption of utilities owned by the old corporations. Taxpayers and ratepayers initially were few and generally belonged to an elite club dominated by landowners. As the primary source of taxation and the funding for much-needed amenities, overcoming the collusive protection of the old corporate bodies was a major task. Prominent citizens like the local parliamentarian, the landed Justice of the Peace at the county level, ensured in many cases, that the real power in local affairs was based in London or the county seat for much longer than it should have. This alliance allowed them to delay the march of municipalization by maintaining control of how decisions were made and where the money was spent. This extended the lives of statutory authorities created for sewerage, drainage and other services in a diminishing number of towns and cities, for decades but eventually, most were incorporated under the municipal umbrella by the end of the Victorian era.[146]

Ballarat Goldfields

On the goldfields of Victoria, however, the process of creating order from chaos occurred in a great deal less time but with a great deal more drama due to the Eureka Rebellion. As the final act in the campaign for the removal of the Goldfields Commission, it resulted in relatively sudden and unexpected success. This allowed for the incorporation of Ballarat West into the social and civic framework of the colony just a year later. Municipalization became the means to providing local self-determination and satisfied the demands for revenue raised locally to be spent locally. With many diggers buying up the increasingly alienated land as soon as it was made available, the township in the space of a year, expanded dramatically, emerging as a social and economic powerhouse setting a precedent for Ballarat East which followed in 1857. The

---

[146] Webb, Sidney & Beatrice, and G J Ponsonby, *English local government. Vol. 5: The story of the King's highway*. Cass, London, 1963

Creating Modern Municipalities 80

rate book compiled during 1856 illustrates the popularity of Ballarat West with the local diggers displaying more pages allocated to prospective ratepayers on a greatly expanded town development for the next year than those already existing!

This was an overwhelming endorsement of the results of the political agitation as the tent-dwelling diggers finally were able to

147

settle down, build homes and create a future for themselves and their families. It began the process of creating order and social cohesion in the chaotic situation on the Ballarat goldfields. More importantly, it provided a powerful link to local and outside investment opportunities that had been previously monopolised by the old regime of the Goldfields Commission and their acolytes.

---

[147] Daintree, Richard, 1832-1878, photographer [ca. 1861] *Ballarat East gold workings and miners' cottages also Bricklayers Arms Hote*l & Canadian Creek. Compare with Ballarat West & South in same period see p 256, 259

Wracked by jobbery and corruption, which became exemplified in the burning of the Eureka hotel, the new council represented a new beginning based on fairness rather than fealty. Uniformity and upgrades quickly came to the streets, and fairness and regulation to commerce. Numerous infrastructure programs like water supply, marketplace, rail and telegraph all projects not considered by the Commission, also were launched in the first twelve months by members of the new Municipal Council. Additionally, the new councillors were prominent and enthusiastic sponsors and initiators of social, commercial, and mining projects. Thus, in much the same manner the municipal corporation as a powerful new agency available to disparate groups of people, became the engine of unity, progress, modernity, and prosperity for urban populations. It is a common narrative that reveals how modern municipal governments became *the* pivot point for resolving the pressing issues of urban living in the relatively new commercialized and industrial world of the nineteenth century.

The contrast after twelve months of operation of the municipality with the diggings under Goldfields Commission administration was stark. There, just across the river, with little to no regulation, traders continued to fight for space as close as possible to the mining activity on a first come first come first served basis. The outcome, not surprisingly, had resulted in many unsafe buildings and shopfronts encroaching into agreed thoroughfares sometimes leaving barely enough space for traffic. In other cases, premises, and the lots they occupied were not secure and could be taken away on the whim of the commissioner or because of an anonymous complaint. And, as the Eureka Hotel affair of 1854 suggests one could never be sure of anything due to an entrenched network of patronage and insider knowledge. It was an ongoing problem, despite the removal of the Goldfields Commission in 1855, where corruption continued to raise its head in areas under administration by the Gold Department, its replacement body. One of the most audacious was the explosive issue of the Ballarat North land development and Gold Warden Sherrard throughout 1855 to 1857.

Likewise, in Ballarat East on the old diggings after incorporation, it took a considerable amount of time to restore any semblance of order that even approached that of Ballarat West, as the above 1860 photograph indicates. This was largely due to the haphazard approach of the Goldfields Commission which had never conceptualised any sort of urban or township environment existing in the future. Residential areas situated close to the mining activity, usually in an elevated location, were also never planned. Newcomers could simply obtain a ticket for a tent site in a generally designated area. Sewerage also was unplanned and open at the rear of the buildings, as the sketch shows, generating a dank stench of grey water and human excrement mixed with silt from the Yarrowee – a murky miasma of disease that ran downhill towards Buninyong. It all resulted in a generally chaotic situation that was unhealthy with no provision for thoroughfares, sanitation, or drainage. The road to improvement only began with the creation of the second local municipality of Ballarat East in 1857 that went to work on tackling the many issues of the diggings making it liveable over the following half-century. Occurring in conjunction with a campaign to alienate many of the haphazard shopfronts along the main thoroughfares, the powers endowed on the new council enabled the leaders of Ballarat East to begin the long process of introducing uniform regulations such as planning and sanitation through the imposition of by-laws and local rates and taxes.

2. A Struggle for Recognition

The British Experience
Enacting a democratic Municipal Government and its authority, however, did not occur simply as a matter of course – in many cases, it was achieved after a struggle with the old established powers. For Britons, the aristocrats and landowners suddenly, after the Act of 1835, found themselves answerable to their erstwhile subjects for civic matters. Generally, these up-and-coming locals were the diverse and growing group of middle-class manufacturers, commercial proprietors, professionals, and artisans featuring in the rise of the liberals from the 1850s.[148] Based in the 'consumer revolution' which had taken off from the eighteenth century, they were driven by the values of the free market, innovation, and the 'logic' of capitalism rather than class and local protectionism. They were led by a diverse group of shopkeepers, publishers, manufacturers, and consumers in many old, new, and developing sectors. Existing outside of the old guild-controlled system that had dominated trade in towns across the realm, these new classes of people were staking their claim as an essential part of a new commercial society speaking the non-discriminatory language of money and shared humanity. This growing class of people, many of whom were prominent in the early to mid-century Chartist and free-trade movements, announced their arrival through sponsored merchandise, souvenirs, public speaking and a plethora of newspapers.[149]

---

[148] Alan Sykes, *The rise and fall of British Liberalism 1776-1988*, Longman London 1997, p. 1-19, see also E. P. Hennock, *Fit and proper persons: ideal and reality in nineteenth century urban government*, Edward Arnold Publishers London 1973

[149] Grant McCracken, *Culture and consumption*, p. 16-22, see also Peter Gurney, *Wanting and having: popular politics and liberal consumerism in England 1830-1870*, Manchester University Press, 2015, see also James A Epstein, *Radical expression: political language, ritual and symbol in England 1790-1850*, Oxford New York, 1994

For the old order, the impending social changes coming with municipal government represented a revolutionary loss of status. The concept of 'the public' especially with rights and legitimate needs that had to be met by an administrative body operating on their behalf, remained a foreign concept and was steadfastly resisted. For them, the transfer of private corporate assets to the public represented socialism by stealth with the Municipal Corporation often being called a 'Fabian Trojan Horse.'[150] However, the threats and fears of socialism were soon quelled by the pressing need for effective sanitary measures to deal with mounting mortality rates, widespread disease and poor or non-existent building regulations.

With most of the early sanitary works in the hands of old local municipal corporations that operated on an individual fee for service, the service that they were supplying was viewed as a primary cause. Dirty water supply, haphazard sewage works and connections, and stormwater that was installed in selected areas, all exposed the total inadequacy of user-paying capitalist monopolies. As Adam Smith had warned half a century earlier, if not regulated, the capitalist system always tends to private monopoly at the expense of the public interest. Thus, for the municipal newcomers, there was no other alternative but to assert their legitimacy through the courts in response to legal challenges to deal with the pressing problems of urban expansion. The famous Manchester case of *Rutter v. Chapman* thus affirmed the legitimacy of the new municipal charters while confirming others under a cloud like Birmingham and Bolton.[151] While providing a valuable precedent, however, skirmishes such as the drawn-out legal battles for the creation of

---

[150] Ibid, p. 172
[151] Derek Fraser ed., Municipal reform in historical perspective, in *Municipal reform and the industrial city*, Leicester University Press New York, 1982, p. 6

Creating Modern Municipalities

utilities like water supply in large towns like Bradford continued over the rest of the nineteenth century.[152]

Another and more relevant example of the fight for recognition occurred at Leeds. With a well-established municipal corporation originally granted in 1626, it existed primarily to preserve the interests of its members – an 'oligarchy of gentleman merchants' in the wool trade. Having admitted a few textile and other manufacturers with the onset of the industrial revolution, it remained, as Derek Fraser outlines on the passing of the 1835 Act, a Tory Anglican preserve. Even more exclusively, it functioned within a tightly knit circle where all positions were guaranteed and passed down to family members.[153] With the first popular election, one of the earliest under the 1835 Act taking place in December, liberals were unanimously elected. However, they found on assuming their new positions, that all the funds of the old council had been alienated, leaving them to commence with nothing.

With the public funds given to the Anglican Church and its various arms in direct contravention of the Act, a legal battle ensued for their recovery. After a long process of resistance by the Tories, the case was eventually won five years later in December 1840. Like *Chapman V Rutter,* this case, as it related to the assets of old corporations provided a clear picture of the legal standing of the new corporations. Furthermore, with Improvement Commissions also recently democratized after an equally bitter legal fight with Tory obstructionists, vacancies also were won by increasing numbers of chartists and liberals. This led to the amalgamation of Improvement Commission functions with the Municipal Council under a new Act in 1842. This, Fraser argues, was more important than the 1835 Act itself as it represented for Leeds and other British councils, one of the first acts of municipalization of most public utilities and services. It contained,

---

[152] Adrian Elliott, Municipal government in Bradford in the mid-nineteenth century, in Derek Feser ed. *Municipal reform and the industrial city,* p. 117- 124
[153] Derek Fraser, *Power and authority in the victorian city,* p51-77

he points out, 392 clauses empowering the council with most of the regulatory functions that modern councils now embody.[154]

This establishment phase from 1835, provided a proving ground for the new municipal concept as a public and not private body and its applicability to other long-held concepts surrounding property rights and the rights of the public. Thus, in an era where people at the lowest level of society were increasingly consumers, taxpayers, property owners, ratepayers, and users of services, it was established that precedents had long been set by social change and technological progress. As the corporate and private owners of the facilities in towns and cities across the realm discovered in the courts of law, utilities such as water, sanitation, gas, and roads had become as essential as housing and food for the urbanized public and so had become more than simply private assets. Thus, in Britain from the late 1840s until the end of the century, many of the privately owned local utilities and services were municipalised.[155]

The Ballarat Goldfield

Similarly, in the colony of Victoria, the new municipality of Ballarat West was founded by many of the same class of people prominent in the creation of British municipal governments under the new Act. Resourceful non-conformists, many espoused the values and beliefs of the Anti-corn Law movement and the Chartists. Thus, early Ballarat witnessed the construction of Presbyterian and Methodist houses of worship appearing alongside, Anglican, and Catholic. With strong liberal values, they believed in equal opportunity and a fair go. These were the same ideals that were shared by those that populated the first municipal council which

---

[154] Derek Fraser, *Power and authority in the victorian city*, p62-63
[155] For example, see Adrian Elliott, 'Municipal Government in Bradford in the mid-nineteenth century', in Derek Fraser ed., *Municipal reform and the industrial city*, p. 117-124, J A Chandler, *Explaining local government: local government in Britain since 1800*, p., 78-80

contained merchants, hoteliers, doctors, and lawyers reflecting similar trends to that of the councils of Melbourne and Geelong. Such a climate of diversity and liberality was not welcomed with open arms by those who had previously wielded local authority either officially or unofficially through the Goldfields Commission. Therefore, for a time after its removal, elements used to dealing with an organization with a single and inflexible charter – the administration of the exploitation of the gold resources, continued to assert themselves and resist the new local government administration.

In the leadup to the granting of the petition for the municipality of Ballarat West, a strong play was made by those under the Goldfields administration to influence the boundaries of the proposed municipality and present acceptable representatives as candidates. An example of this was Councillor Carver, who represented the interests of diggers under Gold Department administration on the eastern side of the river. He served an acrimonious one-year tenure opposing many township initiatives and regularly locking horns with Councillor Muir and Chairman James Oddie. Likewise, H. R. Nicholls, having tempered his violent rhetoric, attempted to mount an opposing petition for incorporation representing a large cohort of eastern diggers hoping to benefit from his large mining and flood mitigation project on the Yarrowee River boundary of the proposed municipality. Additionally, Peter Lalor, the hero of Eureka, whose prospective 1856 Legislative Assembly seat covered Ballarat West, did little to promote the establishment of the municipality. It was only the insistence of J B Humffray later in 1856, as the Eastern diggers representative, that the petition was expedited. Startup funding also was not provided by the colonial government, thus forcing the new councillors to take out loans under their own guarantees to commence operations. Unlike their British counterparts, their independence was curtailed due to the refusal of the Colonial

Government to allow local control over policing and later, the water supply.

Once operations commenced, in January 1856, there were many more instances of overt and passive resistance that the new council had to overcome. Issues like rubbish dumping, water supply, mining, and the respect for the sanctity of the street network against mining interests were all contested during the first year of operation by a few influential but recalcitrant locals used to the *laissez-faire* approach of the Goldfields Commission. Other government bodies like the Department of Works also initially refused to work with the new council, setting up roadblocks to progress in various diabolical ways. However, as time elapsed, these obstacles were overcome by the new councillors who acted with the confidence and the collective power of the local population that had elected them. Establishing civic society on the goldfields was viewed as a solemn duty by the new office holders as well as their electors many of whom considered this a first taste of democracy that had been denied them for over three years under the boots of the Goldfields Commissioners.

3. A First Taste of Democracy

Colony-wide elections that included the gold districts were conducted six months after the establishment of the Ballarat West municipality. For the colony, it was a momentous occasion conducted with a lot of fanfare but as G R Quaife's study shows, for various reasons, the level of interest and participation was disappointing. For people in the township of Ballarat West, however, the arrival of democratically elected local councillors was far more engaging having more to do with how their businesses and daily lives were conducted. As Quaife pointed out, by 1856, the wandering diggers had become more interested in roads and bridges and the only body that could be seen doing anything about it in 1856 were the new municipal councils. The presence of the council was always immanent and unavoidable, particularly with the appointment of the town inspector Alexander Dimant, an enthusiastic and meticulous enforcer of the new rules and regulations. This was an esteemed role for which he was honoured at the jubilee celebrations in 1906. Significantly in 1855, with limited opportunity available for standing for election in the colonial legislatures, the prospective councillors of Ballarat West and local members of the Victorian Reform League, as they declared in the press, saw the extension of local government as an opportunity to gain valuable political experience for the first upcoming general election in 1856 under the new constitution.[156]

This mirrored earlier developments elsewhere in the colony before the separation of Victoria from New South Wales and the establishment of the Legislative Council. Arriving with the establishment of representative bodies for markets and the creation of the Municipalities for the towns of Melbourne as well as for Geelong, effective local democracy had been operating for decades before a colony-wide democratic franchise was established. In this case, it was established with little resistance but rather was enthusiastically welcomed. And, as outlined in chapter two, for the public, the mayors and the local municipal government functioned as an effective mediatory agency in dealing with the colonial government and even the British government on a wide range of issues.

Similarly, in Britain, despite significant electoral reform in 1832, most of the working classes and lower middle classes remained effectively excluded from the national electoral franchise. Notwithstanding the emerging commercial juggernaut of the Victorian era that had swept all classes before it, the political

---

[156] Domestic Intelligence, *The Argus*, (Melbourne) Thursday 15 March 1855, p 6, Municipal Elections, *Tasmanian Daily News* Hobart, Saturday 16 February 1856, p 4

dimensions of the commercial society remained out of reach for the landless and the lower classes. Chartism, the predominantly working and lower middle-class movement had by 1848, failed in its bid for a seat at the political table. Betrayed by their wealthier free-trade colleagues who had largely achieved their agenda, local government, therefore, was the one place where many could make their mark. While generally excluded from political representation in national politics by the property qualification, it was not the case in local government under the Municipal Reform Act of 1835. Owners of small properties or renters of modest means were able to represent the public. This is reflected in cities and towns like Bradford where in the 1850s the municipal electorate outnumbered the parliamentary by almost five times.[157] Thus, small businessmen, professionals like lawyers and doctors, as well as many idealogues from the waning free-trade and chartist movements, were all enthusiastically invested in the new Act with many standing for municipal elections from the 1840s.

In Leeds, with its particularly strong Chartist movement, the failure of repeated efforts to achieve political endorsement of the People's Charter also resulted in many prominent activists turning to local government. With enough small business proprietors able to satisfy the £40 qualification, it was not long before the first, John Jackson, a miller, was elected to one of Leed's Improvement Commissions in 1840. This precipitated a torrent of successful candidates standing for election to any local body in the newly incorporated city and elsewhere in all available positions. Subsequently, but not as successfully, the eyes of the Chartists turned to the upcoming municipal elections at the urging of the

---

[157] Adrian Elliott, Municipal government in Bradford in the mid-nineteenth century, in Derek Fraser ed., *Municipal reform and the industrial city*, p136

Chartist newspaper the *Northern Star* declaring that 'local power is the key to general power.'[158]

In the Australian colonies in the same period of the late 1840s and early 1850s, however, a far different mindset prevailed. Their enfranchisement was always within reach in a society where the aristocratic monopoly was absent. Theirs was a civic problem to do with assimilating the rapid population increase occurring with the goldrushes. A ruling elite of pastoralists and military men assumed a level of authority over the unpopulated interior they believed would never be threatened. With the discovery of gold, however, their authority was questioned as the population increased dramatically and conditions that required the organization of civil society evolved far more rapidly than they were prepared for.

---

[158] Brian Barber, Municipal Government in Leeds, 1835-1914, in Derek Fraser Ed., *Municipal reform and the industrial city*, Leicester University Press, New York, 1982, p. 62-110, J F C Harrison, 'Chartism in Leeds' in Asa Briggs ed., *Chartist studies*, McMillan London 1959, p 85-88

PART 2

The Goldfields & Civic Society

6. Social & Political Dilemmas of Gold

NSW Gold Discovery & the Government

The history of local government in regional Victoria effectively begins with the discovery of gold in the middle of 1851. For the next few years after that, it became the history of the Goldfields Commission which controlled, directed and administered all matters to do with gold. While not a democratically elected body like the municipal corporations that followed it, most of the towns and on the Victorian goldfields were established within its jurisdiction. Bendigo, Ballarat, Castlemaine, and Maryborough, to name the most populous, all began as mining settlements founded and administered by the Goldfields Commission. By 1853 many permanent buildings had been or were in the process of being constructed. As far as the diggers were concerned, the commission was *the government* at all the established camps and townships during its administration.

However, despite being appointed by Lieutenant Governor Latrobe, the commission had dubious constitutional powers that were often questioned by the diggers and even by the police. Many police had strong opinions on the matter questioning the legality of following the orders of a Goldfields commissioner rather than a police commissioner. This, particularly, was an issue that arose as conflict between miners and the Government increased in intensity from 1853. A police strike at the height of the 'Red Ribbon' protests from July to September 1853, thus brought the authority of the Goldfields Commission into question. However, a circular dated 19 September 1853 confirms that the Goldfields Commissioner had precedence over the police, establishing the absolute status of the Commission in goldfield districts.[159] This effectively negated the authority of the magistrates and the legal system itself, about matters relating to the administration of the Goldfields Commission and the territory it administered. It effectively created a separate zone of government in places where the Goldfields Commission were based. People in those zones were not afforded the same status as those living outside of it as the urban populations of Melbourne and Geelong. The miners called it tyranny and resisted it.

The accusations of tyranny began from the commencement of the gold rushes in 1851 and continued to the end in June 1855. The tyranny exercised against the diggers in Both New South Wales and later Victoria was not an explicit government policy or part of the Acts for managing the gold resources. Rather, its evil was in the omission of any provision for the gold seekers' civic needs. The diggers were always of less importance than the product they were extracting from the ground and the tax they paid for the privilege. This, therefore, was the basis for imposing the yoke of tyranny – the absence of any acknowledgement of the diggers' existence and their rights as citizens in arbitrarily defined and governed regions that existed outside of normal society. Thus, in the gold districts, the potential for the abuse of the Commission's discretionary powers was always present depending on the individual in authority.

The gold districts, as one commentator described it, became little kingdoms, not unlike the nineteenth-century social system of China where the emperor enjoyed absolute authority over large territories managed by local mandarins endowed by him with similar powers. As a fluid system, gold districts could be proclaimed once a discovery was made. A local bureaucracy was

---

[159] *Chief Commissioner of Police Melbourne sends a copy of circular H6971 addressed by him to all the officers in charge of police on the goldfields respecting their position in relation to the Resident Commissioners*, 19 September 1853, VPRS 1189 P0000, unit 00091, 53/150, PROV.

then appointed led by a local commissioner along with a supporting clerical and general staff. This operated in conjunction with an ever-expanding police force, many of them of a lower class than the gold-seekers, often from the ranks of Vandemonians, and other emancipated convicts. By the same token, the whole apparatus could be delisted and disbanded once the gold had been worked out. It became a separate and unique social and political system following rules different to the rest of society. Unlike the established towns of Melbourne, Geelong and Portland, civil society did not exist allowing for the narrow definition of law defined under the Gold Acts to be arbitrarily and often brutally enforced. Reminiscent of the earlier era where a convict population existed outside of the confines of decent society, the goldfields and the people populating them were thus viewed as places to be kept apart from decent society.

However, in a world that was becoming more complex and diverse, the Goldfields Commission began to be increasingly viewed by a growing majority as out of sync with modern social trends. Conveniently, therefore, the goldfields, with its liberal-minded population could be the one place where the pastoralist Government could contain liberalizing trends thereby preventing potential social disruptions to the established pastoral order. This was the government's intention from the first official discovery of gold. Unlike the American gold rushes, the Australian discoveries would be tightly controlled. It was justified by social panics such as the idea of convicts, Chartists, and revolutionary elements from various sources upsetting the social order.

The 1851 discovery of gold in Australia is credited to William Hargreaves, a recently returned California digger. This he established during a six-month tour in February of that year through the central and southern regions of New South Wales.[160]

---

[160] *The Maitland mercury and Hunter River general Advertiser*, Wednesday 7 May 1851, page 5, The Gold Discovery

His optimism was based on the unconfirmed reports and impressions from his travels in the district sixteen years before his gold-digging exploits in California.[161] The tour also confirmed the growing body of intelligence based on the reports of Count Strzelecki, Geologist Rev W B Clarke, and stories of local gold finders such as Macgregor, a local shepherd who had become mysteriously wealthy. With these stories beginning to gain public attention, he made recommendations to the government on the gold-bearing nature of the country which was subsequently verified by the Government geologist, Mr Stutchbury by the second week of May 1851.[162]

Within a few days of the information being received by the NSW Government, a proclamation had been prepared for the press by Saturday 17th and was published in the Government Gazette dated 22nd May 1851 by the Governor, Sir Charles Fitzroy. The delay declared the *Sydney Morning Herald* on Wednesday 21, in a matter of such urgency was lamentable and worthy of censure.[163] However, there was little need for concern on the part of the public as a survey party under the leadership of Sir Thomas Mitchell was despatched on Monday 26 May to conduct 'a minute survey' of the proposed gold districts. This would offer the public information on where their efforts would be best directed.[164] Notices were then posted widely in the press on the same day, asserting the pre-emptive right of the Crown to the gold with conditions for the occupation and use of Crown land along with instructions on becoming licensed to dig and search for gold.[165]

---

[161] *The Empire*, Saturday 31 May 1851, page 2, Discovery of the Gold Field, The Sydney Morning Herald, Friday 30 May 1851, page 2, Gold
[162] *The Empire*, Saturday 31 May 1851, page 2, Discovery of the Gold Field
[163] *The Sydney Morning Herald*, Wednesday 21 May 1851, page 2, The Gold
[164] *The Sydney Morning Herald*, Saturday 24 May 1851, page 2, The Gold Districts
[165] *The People's Advocate and New South Wales Vindicator*, May 24, 1851, page 2, The Bathurst Gold Field, Proclamation, Licenses to dig and Search for Gold, *The Goulburn Herald and County of Argyle Advertiser*, Saturday May 31, page 2, Licenses to Dig and Search for Gold

Thus, the discovery and extraction of gold in Australia in the 1850s, unlike elsewhere in the world, was conducted under the careful and active sanction and oversight of the Government. Their role became more sophisticated throughout 1851 following wide public interest and involvement. Adopting a methodical approach, the government, once a substantial gold discovery was confirmed, allocated officers of the Crown to follow the diggers and provide a highly visible presence with police, military and Commission clerks and officers.[166] This became accepted practice for the duration of the early gold rushes in 1851 until more permanent regional centres of administration were established the following year. The land, the workings and the transmission of the gold were also under careful Government supervision, and this provided a relatively secure, safe, and generally orderly process and environment.

The goldrushes began in earnest when the discovery of viable quantities was dramatically announced to the Sydney public by displays of gold nuggets. One was so large, it was named 'Goliath' and exhibited in the window of Jewellers Brush & McDonnell on Wednesday 28 May 1851.[167] The stir and excitement that it caused immediately brought to the fore the issue of law and order as many began preparing to take advantage of the prospect of free money that could be simply dug out of the ground. This was informed by the widely held impression of the recent Californian gold rush being beset with anarchy, lynch law, and a failure of Government control. *Bell's Life* thus reported on Saturday 17 May 1851,

> Confirmation of the astounding intelligence of a gold field of unknown extent in the vicinity of Bathurst has reached the city, and excited a ferment immeasurably exceeding that occasioned

---

[166] J B Hirst, *The strange birth of colonial democracy*, p. 202-210, see also David Goodman, *Gold seeking: Victoria and California in the 1850s*, Allen and Unwin St Leonards NSW 1994, p. 64-104

[167] *The Empire* Saturday 31 May 1851, page 3

by the announcement of the Californian discovery ... whether does the local Government possess the power to restrain within just bounds the popular appetite for gold; or whether the fearful violations of law and order ... in the cities of California are to be emulated in this colony? These are the vital questions that we confess ourselves unable to answer.[168]

However, important differences between the Australian and Californian gold rushes were recognized from the beginning.[169] What set Australia apart was that in Australia there were well-established central and local Government agencies within a short distance from the goldfields in NSW and Victoria. In NSW diggings were established within a day's ride from Orange (12 miles) and the larger town of Bathurst (35 miles) and 8 miles from the village of Cornish Town and just two day's ride from Sydney itself.[170] In Victoria, the first discovery was just 2 day's ride from both Melbourne and Geelong and less than one hour from the village of Buninyong. Thus, Government oversight capability was there from the start. It was also what the community expected at that time, as the *Sydney Morning Herald* indicated, publishing a flood of letters to the paper advising on licensing and law and order. One typical letter to the *Sydney Morning Herald* exhorted:

> You have lately conferred a crown of immortality on the President of the Australasian League; I trust you have a spare one for the Inspector-General of Police or the Attorney General, or some other person. ... The demon of insatiate Greed rides the Colony, and in a few days will be joined by rampant Robbery and grim murder. ...We are a civilized community – law and order are established – we can count our dead and buried – we are not like the Californian Gulf Stream,

---

[168] *Bell's Life in Sydney and Sporting Reviewer*, Saturday 17 May 1851, page 2, Our Yellow Fever

[169] For a comprehensive discussion on historiographical differences between Victorian Goldfields and California see David Goodman, *Gold Seeking: Victoria and California in the 1850s*, Allen & Unwin, St Leonards NSW 1994

[170] *The Maitland Mercury and Hunter River General Advertiser*, Saturday 24 May 1851, page 1, Sydney news

where those carried down were to each other unknown.[171]

This was also the opinion of leading figures such as Sydney solicitor William Redman who later served as an alderman on the Glebe Council, as he thus wrote to the press advocating police oversight as well as recruiting special constables from the miners themselves:

> It must be conceded by all that a powerful protective force is absolutely essential for our actual peace and safety. It will also be granted that the Government must necessarily incur great expense to ensure this protection.[172]

With the same sense of urgency, the Government's assertion of ownership of the gold deposits was followed soon after by an extensive recruitment and establishment of an expanded police force in the NSW Gazette from 22 May 1851.[173] Adequate to deal with the large crowds expected to descend on the countryside, it was an expected response to concerned public and business interests. There were many letters to the press from that sector reminding everyone of the need to counter an anticipated breakdown of law and order such as occurred 'at the Sacramento' in California.[174] Thus with public blessing, Mr John Hardy the Parramatta Police Commissioner, who later was promoted to the position of NSW Gold Commissioner, along with eighteen mounted officers from Sydney, was immediately deployed on the road from Parramatta to the Ophir diggings in the same week of

---

[171] *The Sydney Morning Herald*, Friday 23 May 1851, page 3 Letter to the Editors from "Caution"

[172] *The Sydney Morning Herald*, Friday 23 May 1851, page 3 Letter to the Editor from William Redman

[173] *NSW Government Gazette*, 22 May 1851

[174] *Bathurst Free press and Mining Journal*, Wednesday 28 May 1851, page 2, The Gold Appointments,

the Government's gold notice in the press.[175] In the meantime, it was reported that the District Inspector of Police, C H Green, the district's Commissioner of Crown land and Major Wentworth, accompanied by the local Chief Constable and a Constable McClure, had gone to the diggings to order a halt to proceedings until licenses were issued from June 1 as per the Governor's proclamation. More likely, however, as no arrests or notices were served, the *Goulburn Herald* correspondent believed the real reason was to assert the rights of the Crown and to make their own observations.[176]

At much the same time in Victoria, similar protective expectations of Governmental oversight and control prevailed as the editor of *Geelong Advertiser*, whose opinion changed dramatically as the Victorian gold rush developed, presented his analysis on 31 May 1851

> From the judicious and timely arrangements of the Government, we do not anticipate either outrages in the field or extensive desertion of other occupations. By the issue of a few thousand licenses, a force interested in the maintenance of law and order and in the exclusion of interlopers will be established. The number employed in digging will be completely under the regulation of the commissioner. The number of licenses can from month to month be regulated. ... Thus, during the harvest and shearing seasons, the issue of new licenses can be withheld. The cost of the license too, will restrict the number of applicants. Runaways are usually penniless. People will find out, that between high prices and the Government fee, the diggings will not be very profitable, even if fifteen shillings a day can be picked up. This is a COMMON-SENSE view of the matter and it will be verified.[177]

---

[175] *The Maitland Mercury and Hunter River General Advertiser*, Saturday 24 May 1851, page 1, Sydney News

[176] *The Goulburn Herald and County of Argyle Advertiser*, Saturday May 31, page 2 The Diggins, and page 3, The Gold Mines, and page 4, *The Sydney Morning Herald*, Friday, 23 May 1851, page 3, News from the Interior

[177] *Geelong Advertiser*, Saturday 31 May 1851, page 2, Editorial

With the government in the hands of pastoralists, this ensured that there would be no *laissez-faire* approach, but it would be managed, directed, and controlled as best as possible to protect their interests. As one keen social observer commented, 'we have a government – and have not to make one.'[178] This offered unique opportunities to control and direct developments almost on a day-by-day basis. Thus, as the *Sydney Morning Herald* reports from the commencement of the NSW gold rush:

> A letter has been received by the Magistrates today stating, that an order was issued to the Provincial Inspector of Police to visit the district immediately, and that an augmentation of police would be added to the district. This is highly necessary and as Orange is the most contiguous township, the concentration should take place here. But then, what is the use of a controlling body of police without the controlling and responsible authorities! For our only two magistrates are themselves most active at the diggings. Something must be done in such a case and the remedy lies with the government.[179]

This was typical of early public nervousness informed largely by the still widely held memories and continuing reality, of Australia's penal heritage. Unlike California, this presented unique challenges as well as opportunities for the government legislators to manipulate public opinion. It was *the* issue that caused the most panic. Sharing the country with a large convict population, in transit, under guard and emancipated, made communities very nervous about public safety and security. The *Sydney Morning Herald* stated that it was madness to consider placing convicts in such a place 'where the temptations to abscond would be so irresistible that almost every convict would need a soldier to watch over him

---

[178] *The Empire*, Thursday 29 May 1851, page 4, The Gold Question, *The Empire*, Tuesday 20 May 1851, page 2, Editorial, Intelligence from the Gold Mines
[179] *The Sydney Morning Herald*, Friday, 23 May 1851, page 3, News from the Interior

by night and by day and all year round and this would involve an expense which even Imperial coffers could not afford.'[180]

It was also viewed by the emerging anti-transportation movement as a major reason for the cessation of transportation and the establishment of a greater degree of political independence. An appeal to the Colonial Secretary, in anticipation of a Eureka-style uprising, by the Australasian League thus painted a dire picture of 'criminals of England careering over the waves in prison ships to be bandit chiefs in the gold regions of New South Wales, and eventually Australian Revolutionists.'[181] The *Sydney Morning Herald* itself also joined the protest on the side of the Australasian League arguing to the Australian public,

> No, ministers will be constrained to adopt the unwelcome conclusion, that the sinister scheme of erecting Moreton Bay into a separate colony for penal purposes must be relinquished, and even to send felons to Van Diemen's Land, or even to Swan River, would be no longer expedient or safe. ... Tasmania, which has for so long, and so nobly but so unsuccessfully tried to free herself from the convict abomination, is at last to owe her deliverance to Sydney gold.

It was a theme that underpinned similar social panics in Victoria with its proximity to the convict colonies in Tasmania or Van Dieman's Land. The dreaded 'Vandemonians', (my great, great, Grandfather was one) who, apart from being banned on the goldfields, nevertheless were there in significant numbers. While often prominent in a lot of the unrest as either a cause or apportioned the blame, their presence was the basis for revolutionary concerns that were regularly aired in the press. Alonzo, a regular satirical contributor to the empire, thus expressed the fears of many writing:

---

[180] *The Sydney Morning Herald*, Wednesday 4 June 1851, page 2, What Will Gold do for us in England?

[181] *The Empire* Friday 13 June 1851, page 4, Australasian League

> ... we don't want the devil to become the lessee of Bathurst and open a tragic theatre as that he started in California. Stabbing, shooting and lynching ... firearms, bowie-knives and all other sanguinary weapons should be absolutely prohibited. ... Society must have some tangible framework. Organization is indispensable. ... If supplies are not regularly sent up the country, woe to live mutton, woe to breathing beef! ... What the native dogs leave will be eaten up by the gold diggers.[182]

On the other hand, less sensationalist opinions such as those of 'Moreton Bay Squatter' who declared he was already en route to the diggings, agreed with the measures the Government had put in place. He proposed the establishment of a Commission and the appointment of executive officers to administer the process of searching and digging for gold. As he stated, "I would that even in the gold mania, Englishmen should have the opportunity of showing their attachment to order and their veneration for those laws which have always been so purely administered to them."[183]

Thus, with such strong supportive public opinion for various reasons, the old guard, dependent on its pastoral base, was mainly interested in retaining their half a century of dominance both politically and economically. In Victoria after just three months with much greater yields than NSW, there was growing concern that the gold rush would trigger an economic collapse. In only a couple of months, gold had pressured the rate of exchange which had fallen 6% and was beginning to threaten 'not only those connected with gold interests but the producers of our great staple – wool and tallow.'[184] Additionally, the labour market at the same time was losing workers by the day as many were leaving for the goldfields. This then had a flow-on effect into other sectors as

---

[182] *The Empire*, Sydney, Wednesday 21 May 1851, page 3, 'Gold Properly Controlled'
[183] *The Empire*, Sydney, 29 May 1851, page 4, 'The Gold Question.'
[184] *Geelong Advertiser,* Thursday 20 November 1851, page 2, Legislative Council

wages rose to levels never imagined along with prices for almost everything. By December, Sir Charles Fitzroy as Governor General was forced to act announcing that £69,600 had been raised by Royal Sanction for assisted immigration to increase it to £100,000, specifically to fill the void that gold mining was expected to create in the other industries of the colonies.[185] It was a short-sighted measure that would have unintended consequences a year later on the Ovens and Bendigo goldfields. This time it would be the diggers seeking relief and protection from a social and political system that had not come to terms with including them but rather was designed around a policy of containment and exclusion that effectively shut them outside of normal society.

Containing the Gold Rushes

Fitzroy's measure was a knee-jerk reaction to the threat that gold posed to existing colonial society. Designed to preserve the existing political economy, it was designed to fill an expected gap in the labour market. Underscored by the assumption of a temporary gold rush, however, it failed to account for the social and political significance of the influx of people that were expected to arrive. Issues such as how were they to be accommodated, and what would be their social and political status were never part of the equation. Instead, the focus was on economic regulatory measures that depended on dampening the enthusiasm for gold-seeking through the introduction of a license to dig. It was part of a two-pronged strategy, that along with the licence fee to search for gold, was also designed to maintain social order and economic balance. The license was thus set at a rate to deter those without sufficient means to relocate in large numbers to the goldfields and so be a burden and a problem for lawmakers. The population most in mind were the convicts emancipated or otherwise restricting

---

[185] *The Sydney Morning Herald*, Tuesday 23 December 1851, page 2 Legislative Council 22/12/1851

their ability to move throughout the colonies – a point that was made many times at the beginning of gold discovery in NSW.

> ... the Government is bound to take precautions which may prevent social disorganization and crime – just as it is bound to enforce a quarantine. It is stated that already armed parties in great numbers are on the gold ground; and within six days sail of them are scattered over the colonies, there are more than 50,000 persons who have been transported for various crimes, and a very large number of them within a few hours distance. Should the reports of gold prove true, the excitement, speculation and license, will attract thousands of the worst characters. This no one can doubt and the consequences to the security of life and property without any needless exaggeration are sufficiently appalling. It appears to me that the government should immediately adopt measures of a precautionary kind.[186]

This argument became a central plank in the anti-transportation campaign and local election campaigns from the latter half of 1851. W C Wentworth as a candidate for the city of Sydney thus argued in correspondence to supporters that since the discovery of gold, his opinions on transportation were now decidedly against it and wholeheartedly in support of any measure to have it abolished in all Australian colonies

> the British nation will immediately become aware of the frightful inducement to the commission of crime and of the vast social demoralisation which must at once ensue among large masses of her people, if she were to permit her convicts to be deported to colonise adjacent to our goldfields ... that if transportation is still to be part and parcel of her system of secondary punishment – some new settlement must be formed by her for this purpose in some part of the earth so remote from these shores as to render it next to impossible that any of her criminals, even after the expiration of their sentences, can work their way to any of

---

[186] *The Sydney Morning Herald* Friday 16 May 1851, page 2, 'The Gold Country.'

these colonies.[187]

On this, there was widespread public support both on the goldfields and in the cities. For Victoria, unlike NSW, the possibility of large numbers of ex-convicts presented ominous portents of social instability and crime. In a colony whose only experience with transportation had been a failed colony on Port Phillip Bay, they were proud of their free settler origins. This was also an issue from the very outset of gold discovery in Victoria, raised at the 2 July 1851 meeting of the Australasian League. With most of the local dignitaries present, a protest letter with the endorsement of the Melbourne City Council to Secretary of State Earl Grey was drawn up with specific reference to the recent arrival of the convict ship Lady Kenneway. It was thus resolved by the League that the discovery of gold made it even more imperative that the practice must cease and in the letter of protest it was made clear that while the colonies were desirous of maintaining the link with Britain, if the practice continues the connection may be severed.[188] This was a measure that reflected a number of social, political and economic ends, providing the perfect justification for the gold legislation that followed. However, while not specifically mentioned, the legislation really had only one end in sight and that was the preservation of the established Pastoral political order.

There is no doubt that Victorian Lieutenant-Governor La Trobe was convinced that the Fitzroy government's creation of the license fee and the Goldfields Commission to enforce it, was a piece of creative legislation that would achieve its multiple ends. Making it clear that the goldfields were to be conceived as a separate system distinct from normal society, they would also be governed accordingly. Thus, amid the calls for its abolition two

---

[187] *Bell's Life in Sydney and Sporting Reviewer*, Saturday 13 September 1851, page 4, *The Sydney Morning Herald*, Saturday 24 May 1851, page 2, Mr Wentworth - the Election – the League

[188] *The Argus* (Melbourne), 3 July 1851, page 2

years after its creation and troubled execution he declared in his despatch to Governor General Fitzroy of NSW

> I can never lose sight of an advantage – one far beyond that of a mere increase in revenue, of which it has been productive – that of favouring the maintenance of a steady control over the large mixed and excited population of the goldfields, and of close official connection between the individuals composing it and the constituted authorities. In this respect I am persuaded that it has affected that which no other system could have secured. The time may come when the Colonial Government may find that it may be abandoned with safety, and when the financial and social advantages derived from it may be secured in some other manner; but, for the present, I am quite unable to see on what grounds its total abandonment would be justified.[189]

Thus, from its early introduction in NSW, manipulation of the license fee appeared to confirm that it was also the best way of integrating gold-seeking with the labour market and maintaining a separate social system on the goldfields. Wentworth for example who had permitted mining on his property at Frederick's Valley near Orange NSW, had used this ploy by suspending the issuing of licenses to ensure there was sufficient labour to shear and wash his sheep during the latter half of 1851. Others similarly affected proposed raising the license fee to £5.[190] While in Victoria similar measures were employed to assist the pastoralists, with La Trobe suspending licenses there to support crop harvesting and sheep shearing. Not so fortunate, however, were non-British gold-seekers with a special 'alien clause' inserted in the Act that placed a 100% surcharge per month on the cost of the license fee.

However, resistance to it began from its inception raising concerns expressed later by the diggers, that it would result in

---

[189] *The Argus*, Saturday 27 August 1853, page 4 Council Papers, copy of despatch from His Excellency the Lieutenant Governor of Victoria to His Excellency Sir Charles Fitzroy 1 August 1853
[190] *The Sydney Morning Herald*, Friday 29 August 1851, page 3 'The Wentworth Diggings'

abuses of personal liberty and the revenue it raised would not result in the creation of any regional civic infrastructure or improvement. The *Empire*, from the outset thus warned that the new regulations that accompanied the discovery of gold had multiple intentions not in the interest of miners themselves and warned that abuses of power would certainly follow:

> ... it is not to raise a revenue to be applied to the territorial improvement of the colony; but in the first instance to coerce labourers into their ordinary occupations; and, in the next place, to raise as much as possible, for the service of the Colonial Executive, a fund about which the council can ask no questions. This scheme of making the Commissioner Inquisitor General into the circumstances of every man who comes before him to ask for a gold license is a very dangerous exercise of power which the Crown has become possessed of by extraordinary means, and is liable, under present circumstances to be very greatly abused.[191]

Much of these concerns about an out-of-control system with no public accountability appeared to be confirmed after six months of operation in NSW. The Geelong Advertiser correspondent reporting on Mr Martin MLC's first report on the goldfields thus writes:

> They were now placed in a somewhat strange position, for the power that the Government possessed exclusively over the waste lands has become of importance since this discovery had been made. The Government now had the power to establish a body of police and to hold an uncontrolled patronage for which there was no precedent in the British Constitution. The Council has to consider whether it was wise such an uncontrolled and unconstitutional power should be left in the hands of the Government. One of the returns he asked for was as to the number of police employed by the Government on the goldfields. This number he believed was already very

---

[191] *The Empire* Sydney, Monday 26 May 1851, page 2, 'The Government and the diggers

considerable, and as the discovery extended it must be continually increasing, and thus a small standing army of police would be established which would be entirely beyond the control of the house and which might be applied in a manner dangerous to the liberties of the people.[192]

As they discovered in such a short space of time, the role of the police as agents of law and order and for the maintenance of civil society had been quickly eclipsed by the role of license collectors and enforcers over regions of doubtful constitutional status. This was largely due, unbeknown to the rank and file, to the political role devised by their masters in George Street to keep a tight lid on the goldrushes and so delay political progress. The License fee was never just a fee, and the regulations were not made specifically for the gold industry. Rather, they were also political concepts that sought to address the many competing social, political and cultural interests of 1850's colonial society. This was clearly the intention of legislators when gold was first discovered in NSW as the NSW Colonial Secretary explained:

> … the circumstances in which the gold discovery had been made were such as to place the Government in a position of considerable embarrassment. The tiding of the discovery at first seemed to threaten a general bouleversement of society throughout the length and breadth of the land. In the regulations that had been made the Government were desirous to do justice to those who were anxious to engage in the pursuit of gold digging; and at the same time as far as possible to prevent interference with those industrial pursuits which have been and must be, so valuable to the community. The Government felt the necessity of protecting those pursuits as far as possible; and although it might not be able to prevent them from all interruption, he believed he had done all that could be done, and that there was much reason for congratulation that the great

---

[192] *Geelong Advertiser* Tuesday 4 November 1851, page 2, 'Debate in the Sydney legislative Council on the Gold Discovery'.

interests of the colony have suffered so little.[193]

As the *Empire* pointed out from the beginning, the license fee differed in principle from the method of imposing royalty rents in the mother country where people were not penalised for simply digging. In Britain, it was argued, the privilege of mining on Crown Lands was paid for by a fixed amount of the produce in lieu, which should have been the case in NSW where locating and extracting gold was particularly hazardous. Even more concerning, it was argued, was that it placed an undue amount of power in the hands of a commissioner. This was particularly relevant to the fourth clause on undischarged employees 'making the Commissioner, Inquisitor General into the circumstances of every man who comes before him to ask for a gold license, - a power with a high likelihood of abuse.' At a more fundamental level, the editor argued where gold was being extracted for the benefit of the Crown, the license fee violated the principle that governed British social institutions, 'that a man shall be at liberty to take his labour to the most profitable market and any violent interference with that natural liberty, becomes at once a most reprehensible tyranny'. [194]

In Victoria, however, there were few concerns about Government tyranny, at least in the beginning. Rather, gold discovery was considered a civic duty promoted by opportunistic Melbourne merchants and their political backers. For them, the prospect of instant and indiscriminate wealth outside of the pastoral economic and political systems would immediately open the door to prosperity and political power. Before 1851, however, there had been little real interest in gold or what could be accomplished by the relatively instant injection of vast amounts of money into the economy. A 24oz nugget on display in the window

---

[193] *Geelong Advertiser* Tuesday 4 November 1851, page 2, 'Debate in the Sydney legislative Council on the Gold Discovery'
[194] *The Empire*, Monday 26 May 1851, page 2, The Government and the Gold Seekers.

of a Collins Street jeweller from 1849, remained little more than a curiosity. Purchased from a shepherd boy who claimed it was from the Pyrenees, it was followed with another 22oz nugget which he sold to a Mr Duchene.[195]

From February 1851 there had also been numerous reports of gold in the same locality and it was urged, following the discovery in NSW, that a government-backed exploration of the district should be launched to investigate.[196] Immediately following this, a meeting was held in Melbourne led by His Worship, the Mayor, 'for the purpose of taking steps to offer a reward for the discovery of an available gold mine within the Province of Port Phillip.'[197] The stated purpose was to counteract the attraction of the NSW discovery and anticipated negative effects on the cost of labour, property and the economy in general that could be 'disastrous and entail ruin on many.' The meeting at the Mechanics Institute attracted about 400 which included most of the leading citizens, some of whom such as Westgarth, Greeves, and Fawkner, were later prominent supporters of the diggers in their roles as members of the Colonial Government.

The *Sydney Morning Herald* called it the Victoria Gold Movement, due to the high estimation of the mineral reserves, the anticipated economic boom that it would bring, as well as public interest and the encouragement of the new Victorian government.[198] Predicting what eventually transpired, it was their assessment that the rapid generation of wealth would ensure a political and economic advantage for Victoria and the Empire ensuring progress and prosperity by assimilating the gold-seeking

---

[195] *The Argus*, Tuesday 10 June 1851, page 4, letter to the Editor from 'Peru'
[196] *The Argus*, Tuesday 10 June 1851, page 4, letter to the editor from 'Peru'
[197] *The Melbourne Daily News*, Wednesday 11 June 1851, page 2, The Gold Meeting.
[198] *The Sydney Morning Herald*, Thursday, 11 September 1851, Advertising, page 3

population.[199] However, little thought was spared by commentators and legislators to the 'assimilation' process of all those gold-seeking immigrants. It was not foreseen that it would come with such a struggle and with such disastrous consequences. What the Sydney paper failed to account for was the intransigence of the government of the newly formed colony of Victoria and their pastoralist supporters.

For the Victorian establishment order, the predicted 'movement' was viewed as a disaster in the making and the end of their period of dominance. Others, however, with more radical political and economic leanings welcomed the gold 'experiment' as a means to break up outdated social and political structures and propel them into the modern age. This was the conclusion of an astute Scottish observer writing on his return to Glasgow - it would bring disorder 'for a time', but eventually things would stabilise and the new and expected society free of aristocratic domination and based primarily on commercial relations as predicted by Scottish philosophers Smith, Ferguson and their adherents, would triumphantly emerge.[200]

However, in the short term, a *laissez-faire* societal approach would not be adopted, and matters would not be allowed to take their own course. Instead, the 'gold movement' would be managed tightly by the new government and its unprepared and inexperienced members. Exemplified in the Goldfields Commission, it was a hasty measure put together with little legal or legislative scrutiny. So, their response, informed by the recent chaos of California, was like New South Wales, the adoption of the 'wise' policy of government control of the gold industry to control

---

[199] David Goodman, *Gold seeking: Victoria and California in the 1850s*, Allen & Unwin St Leonards NSW, 1994, pp27 - 37

[200] Ibid, p26, Christopher Berry, *the idea of commercial society in the Scottish Enlightenment*, Edinburgh University Press, Edinburgh, 2015, pp 1 – 32, 194 – 209, P Just, *Australia, or notes taken during a residence in the Colonies from the gold discovery in 1851 till 1857*, Dundee, Durham & Thomson, 1859

and guide the process of its development in a way that would not affect the stability of society.

However, public opinion in Victoria on the hastily formed Goldfields Commission and the license fee by the NSW legislature, as it did in New South Wales, quickly moved from supportive to concern over its detrimental effect on civil liberties and the future development of regional areas. To a large degree, this was influenced by the report by NSW MLC Martin tabled in November 1851 after six months of the operation of *their* gold legislation. Martin was scathing at what he saw as potential and actual abuses of power. With virtually no regional Victorian population, the establishment of any unwanted precedent that may affect the future social and political structure of the colonial regional areas was very worrisome. Particularly concerning was MLC Martins's assessment that 'there was no precedent in the British Constitution and (that it) may be applied in a way that was dangerous to the liberties of the people.'[201] The *Geelong Advertiser* therefore quickly reversed its earlier support for the Government's measures, calling for the gold legislation to be 'nipped in the bud as it was a gross violation' and would be an unacceptable escalation of centralization using arbitrary power to rob the Western District and 'cram the insatiate maw of ravenous government officials'.[202]

This proved to be an accurate assessment as, unlike New South Wales, Victoria had no regional civic infrastructure to speak of. This then made the Commission the only existing government to directly administer the tens of thousands of miners who flooded into the interior. It was a strange beast created with a formal charter that ostensibly was the management of all matters to do with gold and its extraction and sale. However, the multitudinous problems it created, which according to subsequent inquiries and miners'

---

[201] *Geelong Advertiser* Tuesday 4 November 1851, page 2, 'Debate in the Sydney legislative Council on the Gold Discovery'
[202] *Geelong Advertiser* Friday 29 August 1851, page 2, *Geelong Advertiser,* Tuesday 23 September 1851, Ballarat Diggings, page 2

complaints, lay with its *informal* powers which were undefined and largely ratified by clarification on the fly or with its Melbourne-based masters. Not surprisingly, it was this that generated the most amount of ire and opposition from many who were in no doubt about its role in society. The shared 'secret' among those who enjoyed the confidence of Lieutenant Governor La Trobe and other aligned members, was that the Commission represented a policy of 'conservative drag' to slow the expected demand for democracy that they feared gold and a huge influx of people would bring.[203]

Unfortunately, it was a strategy doomed to fail, as the enactment of the policy in NSW in the few months prior to Victoria's, had already firmly established the precedent for antagonistic relations. Thus, by the end of 1851 after six months of mining, it was not too surprising when issues began to emerge surrounding the oppressive and disrespectful way the gold laws were enacted. Miners quickly felt betrayed by the Government after the threatening tone of the regulations after initial suggestions that an affordable fee of £1 was trebled.[204] They were even more upset when assumptions of public courtesy enjoyed in town were not met in the countryside where diggers were met by armed police. In December of 1851, a meeting of over 2000 miners on the Turon goldfield gathered to petition the government for an inquiry. The complaints were:

> ... the injustice of the present system of licensing, and the exorbitance of the license tax, as the very justly designate it, levied upon the miners. There are other grievances urged, such as the vexatious mode of collecting the license fees; the insulting and, to a British spirit, galling display of an armed police force at the office of the Commissioner, and the prohibitory regulations regarding quartz-crushing and the draining of

---

[203] *The Argus* (Melbourne) Monday 1 September 1851, The Digging Licenses, page 2
[204] *The Argus* Friday 30 May 1851, page 2

waterholes.[205]

Protesting specifically against the new regulations advertised just weeks earlier, the miners were outraged at the 'utter absurdity' of the Legislative Council of NSW in believing that the mines could absorb large numbers of the population, and stimulate 'other industrial operations' while discouraging the same with oppressive taxation. With the advent of steam power and quartz crushing, the Government had decided to tax the machinery as well with one horsepower of steam to be deemed to be equivalent to seven men.[206]

It was viewed as a Protectionist reaction to predictions that the colony, with a great increase in commerce, would be ruined by Free Trade.[207] These measures had been adopted by legislators putting aside their differences and banding together to avert what many of them saw as catastrophic consequences for the colony if the gold industry was not tightly controlled. It was the topic of a circular that had been published and distributed amongst the NSW politicians to inform them when they met in the legislature.

It did not escape the attention of *The People's Advocate*, however, who had been quick to see the potential for fundamental social change in the discovery of gold. A response to the 'memorial' was promptly published exposing it as a measure for the protection of the rights of an 'unfortunate clique' of squatters and associated commercial enterprises such as tallow-makers that believed they were the custodians of the political and economic systems of the colony. With a view of the future, the Advocate thus comments:

> "The established branches of our productive industry" – meaning of course wool and tallow, the necessity of which will be in a great measure be superseded by the influx of a new

---

[205] The *Empire (Sydney)*, 27 November 1851, The Gold Miners' Petition, page 2
[206] *Geelong Advertiser*, Tuesday 9 December 1851, Additional Gold Regulations, page 2
[207] The *Empire (Sydney)*, 27 November 1851, The Gold Miners' Petition, page 2

commerce which will swamp the old system and render the squatter a mere secondary personage in our community. Persons of this now fated class are mindful of California; they remember but too well how that country was, as if by magic, transformed from a desert into a rising and prosperous state independent of pastoral pursuits, and they dread that the gold discoveries of Australia may lead to a similar result. We foresee the same result but not with the same apprehensions; we say that we look forward with no little hope to the time when a better spirit shall dawn in the land, … when the labourer shall be considered worthy of his hire and the councils of government shall not be ruled by the principles of favouritism or the intrigues of a faction.[208]

With similar protectionist concerns in Victoria, it was assumed the precedent set in NSW would be copied practically word for word. This was widely discussed in the press with the only regional newspaper, the Geelong Advertiser warning of economic and political tensions in December 1851 with the publishing of the latest NSW amendments to gold legislation.[209]

---

[208] *The People's Advocate and New South Wales Vindicator* Sydney, 11 June 1851, The Beggar's Petition, page 4
[209] *Geelong Advertiser* 9 December 1851, Government and the Gold, 9 December 1851, page 2

7. The Victorian Gold Rush

Implications of a Regional Population Boom

The early resistance of the pastoral establishment and the restrictive measures adopted by the government did little to deter public interest. It expanded exponentially as news of finds was announced during August and September of 1851. An early report describes 'parties of diggers' as the main types of travellers to the diggings. Several of them were wildly successful like the Cavanagh brothers who returned to town the week before the end of September. Their haul was quoted at sixty pounds of gold with the whole party averaging £100 per day. However, as reported, the Cavanagh's haul was easily eclipsed by the 'Galloways' on account of them finding a 'very rich hole.'[210] One such prospecting enterprise preparing to depart from Geelong in September 1851 drew a large crowd and was so described:

> In Moorabool Street today I saw two bullock drays being loaded for the diggings ... there were five or six cradles, two or three wheelbarrows, a couple of dozen dishes, and about the same number of beds and boxes on each: besides ropes, frying pans, ovens, stretchers, tarpaulins, quart and pint pots, buckets guns, sieves, picks, crowbars, spades, &c, &c &c[211]

Nevertheless, despite the fact that most of the forays into the gold districts in 1851 were by well-organized and cashed-up syndicates, there were growing signs that the attempts to restrict

---

[210] *Geelong Advertiser*, Monday 29 September 1851, News from the Diggings,' page 2
[211] *The Argus*, Friday 19 September 1851, Geelong, page 2

gold-seeking to such syndicates were not working. Reports of others more desperate and less prepared were becoming more frequent. A story of one prospector seen on the road from Geelong to Buninyong with nothing but an umbrella added to the growing levels of 'gold fever.' Another story described a digger pushing a loaded wheelbarrow 'appearing quite fresh and as indifferent to fatigue as the wheelbarrow itself.' Another case that drew a great deal of attention, was that of an ex-policeman who also pushed a loaded wheelbarrow and 'cradle' from Geelong to the Ballarat diggings.[212]

This is what the government feared and the reason for setting such a high rate for the license. Representing the pivot point of social change, the license was loaded with expectations for some sections of the community as well as the fears of cultural oblivion for others such as the squatters and their social and political adherents. The discussion and passing of the Victorian bill for the regulations of the goldfields in 1851 therefore immediately exposed divisions between 'the people' and the squatter-dominated government. Coming so close to the separation from New South Wales, the gold legislation invariably, therefore, became linked to the expectations of the new constitution.

With large swathes of the country in the hands of a few squatters, the growing numbers of people of small and modest means thus viewed the gold industry as an important way to prevent the introduction of the same exclusive political system that they had forsaken in Britain. Thus, as a matter of public debate beginning with the establishment of the new Victorian parliament, and an increasing number of immigrants, fair representation for an expanded population had been in the sights of reformers well before the gold rushes had begun.[213] But with gold discovery

---

[212] *Geelong Advertiser*, Friday, 19 September 1851, The Ballarat Diggins, page 2, *Geelong Advertiser*, Friday, 10 October 1851, The Ballarat Gold Field, page 2, *The Argus*, (Melbourne) Saturday 20 September 1851, Geelong, page 2
[213] Geoffrey Serle, *The golden age*, p 17, *Geelong Advertiser*, 25 March 1851, p 2

promising an even bigger increase in population in a shorter period, the campaign had taken on a greater sense of urgency.

Victoria 1851: Anticipating Social Change
In Geelong, a particularly strong movement for legal and political reform had developed by August 1851 represented by 'The People's Association.' Formed by leading citizens it encapsulated most of the later demands in the famous Ballarat miners charter of November 1854. Prominent members were T C Riddle who was one of the first to purchase land in Ballarat after the initial survey in January 1852, and Captain John Harrison, who became a well-known activist for the establishment of civic society and gold legislation reform on the Bendigo goldfields. With many ex-chartists among their members, they promoted the belief that there should be no privileged class in the community and the guarantee of equal rights for all. Strongly supported and promoted by the municipal councils of both Victorian cities, they aimed to also expose corruption, educate the public and ensure the most fitting people were elected to the Legislative and Municipal Councils.[214]

A few weeks later the movement had expanded to Melbourne with the creation of the Melbourne Reform Association. The aims were stated as:

- Adoption of a national system of education
- The introduction of vote by ballot
- The extension of the franchise
- A more just distribution of representation
- The proper revision of the electoral roll
- The economical expenditure of public money
- The obtaining of responsible government
- The entire control of colonial revenue

---

[214] *Geelong Advertiser* 28 August 1851 p 2 People's Association, Geoffrey Serle, *The golden age*, p 17

- The introduction of local improvements[215]

While the movement appeared to have faded as the gold rush gained momentum, its principles very soon were trumpeted on the goldfields in the various protests against the Goldfields Commission especially throughout 1853. At Ballarat, the Gold Diggers Association led by Drs Carr and Sylvester had compiled a similar list of demands based on the idea of local autonomy. This they presented to the Government during the 1853 inquiry. Leading the Geelong-based movement was the mayor of Geelong Dr Thompson, the Mayor of Melbourne, and other leading commercial figures, many of whom were members of the chambers of commerce.

Especially active on the emerging issue of gold and its implications, were many from the rapidly growing commercial sector and their supporters and any developments were closely followed. Thus, with the introduction of gold legislation, at the urging of 'the people,' a meeting on recent developments in Melbourne was called. Chaired by the Lord Mayor on Saturday 30 August 1851,[216] its stated purpose was to address His Excellency the Lieutenant Governor on the expediency of the late regulations as to the working of Gold and the mineral resources of the colony. While in agreement with the government in supervising the 'whole system of gold digging' and imposing a tax, it was the understanding of Alderman Johnstone from a private conversation with His Excellency, as was his favourite method of dispensing information, that the instructions to the Commissioners were that the fee was nominal and would not be enforced.[217]

---

[215] *Geelong Advertiser*, 26 September 1851 p 2 Melbourne
[216] *The Sydney Morning Herald*, Thursday, 11 September 1851, Advertising, page 3
[217] *The Argus* (Melbourne) Monday 1 September 1851, The Digging Licenses, page 2

Gold Legislation: 'a field for crude experiments'
From the outset according to Mr Hodgson, it was recognized that the amount of 30s was exorbitant with most earnings from gold not even on a par with the regular labouring wage. Dr Richmond Webb in agreement also explained,

> The reports recently received from all quarters were most unsatisfactory; he had seen scarcely anyone who had obtained gold in sufficient quantity to remunerate him for his labour, loss of time, and expense in procuring it; and until some portion of the country could be pointed out where digging might be pursued with profit, it was quite premature on the part of Government to impose any tax on what really could be termed nothing else but a prospecting tour. By the proclamation of His Excellency, any person working or digging in any locality, was liable to be collared by a constable and locked up.[218]

The effect of this proclamation, therefore, as Webb argued was to frighten people away. And this was already occurring as he explained, that whether true or not, many believed that the NSW goldfields near Sydney were more attractive and were already leaving Melbourne to try their luck. Concerns over the legality of its imposition also was raised as the status of crown land in the colony was brought into question and the fact that the fee in principle, as part of the general revenue of the colony should be determined by the people themselves.

To the miners and the public, however, the political ramifications were obvious. The *Geelong Advertiser* correspondent as a prelude to the later diggers' catch cry, called it

> "taxation without representation" – an imperial edict to raise an indefinite sum, by an absolute and unexplained levy, to be applied heaven knows how or where. What is a five per cent

---

[218] *The Argus* (Melbourne) Monday 1 September 1851, The Digging Licenses, page 2

taxed burgess compared to one of these men, paying £18 per annum? In this edict is a gross innovation: a principle is involved here, and the sooner it is nipped in the bud the better it will be for all classes.'[219]

The proclamation all agreed, was part of the policy of 'conservative drag' initiated in New South Wales. Already adopted in Victoria, by the nominees in the Legislative Council, its blind emulation was being resisted by the municipal councils. Alderman Johnstone thus argued

> It is ridiculous to talk of a 'conservative drag' when it was found that the present foolish step of the Government had the effect of draining our population and sending hundreds to Bathurst. The Sydney Government had not resorted to such a measure until it had been shown that gold digging was remunerative ... and now there was an apparent fear on the part of our own government that we should go ahead too fast and so they had put on the 'conservative drag' which only showed a necessity for a little of the "democratic impulse."[220]

However, more liberal-minded members of the government and the broader society recognized the opportunity that gold would bring and sought to embrace the mining population with open support. The Adelaide Times correspondent on seeing for himself on a tour from Geelong stated

> ... a digger who went down into a hole at daybreak a poor man, emerged at sunset with a competency – yes! This is true – every moment is a golden one and I am prepared to hear even more astounding intelligence than I record in this letter. I ask your attention, your reason, for there is much to ponder at the present crisis; for gold is revolutionising us, and now is the time for "master minds" to come forward and guide the change.[221]

---

[219] *Geelong Advertiser* Friday 29 August 1851, page 2
[220] *The Argus* (Melbourne) Monday 1 September 1851, The Digging Licenses, page 2
[221] *Adelaide Times*, Monday 13 October 1851, Ballarat Diggings, page 3

Unfortunately, there would be no 'master minds' coming to guide the process. Instead, it would be a government 'enforcer.' The arrival of the first Government administrator Commissioner Armstrong and his deputy Captain Dana with three mounted troopers on Saturday 19 September 1851, found a group of miners at Ballarat, numbering about six hundred. Among them was a hard-core element numbering about 60, who resolved 'to resist and avoid by all lawful means, the payment of the tax.'[222] Upon his arrival, another meeting was immediately called and the assembled diggers passed resolutions condemning the action of the government, electing two delegates to 'wait on the Commissioner.' A petition was also drawn up with a request that it would be presented to the Municipal Councils of Geelong and Melbourne calling for 'their interference on their behalf.' The meeting then ended with three groans for the Government.[223] Nevertheless, the Commissioner when he first arrived found, not a group of 'runaway scoundrels' that required domination, but as a representative of the press described it; 'a gathering of the most sober and industrious of our townsmen that were willing to conform to the laws and pay their fair share of taxation, provided they were treated with consideration.'[224]

Nevertheless, the initial 1851 protests found many sympathetic ears in the growing commercial and professional sectors in Melbourne and Geelong. The equally sympathetic Geelong Advertiser correspondent, who was at the very first meeting in protest at the arrival of the Commissioner at Ballarat, appealed to this section of the community in his initial report on the enactment of the license fee at Ballarat in September 1851:

---

[222] *The Tasmanian Colonist* (Hobart Town) Monday 15 September 1851, Bunninyong, Diggings, page 4
[223] *Geelong Advertiser*, Tuesday 23 September 1851, Ballarat Diggings, page 2
[224] *Geelong Advertiser*, Monday 29 September 1851, News from the Diggings, page 2

> I appeal to the whole constituency of Victoria, if taxation be not the province of the people of Victoria to fix, and if it be, shall we submit to the dictum of an individual or will he not be obliged to ask an act of indemnity from the first legislative Council for his unauthorised act; for be it remembered that the claim of ten thousand eight hundred pounds of taxation from six hundred men is no longer founded on a Royal Prerogative, but as a branch of the revenue by the terms of the license granted.[225]

Another *Geelong Advertiser* correspondent who arrived a few days later found that the ill feeling had not abated amongst those opposed to the license fee but had now spread amongst almost all. With no little venom of his own added, he expressed the outrage felt among many of the 600 or so that were present. Prophetically, it conveyed the core elements of the 1853 Red Ribbon movement and the Eureka uprising over three years later:

> Great God! It makes an honest man's blood to boil at the bare mention of it. It is the culminating point of tyranny and the author must be brought before the bar of public opinion. Liberty imperilled deposes on the altar of truth ... making the finest province of the British Crown, a field for crude experiments, to ascertain the greatest tension to which a people's endurance may be stretched. ... In the name of justice I appeal to the public on principle – I ask you men of Geelong, I ask you inhabitants of the Western District – I ask everyone who will exercise his reason, of what use is your boasted Bill of Independence? Of what use is your £10 suffrages and your representatives and your Legislative Council, if an imbecile Governor, moving on a universal joint and gyrating like a weathercock, can use an arbitrary power and trample on your boasted rights. ... How is it going to be expended after the Western District is robbed of that sum. I say robbed – for it is withdrawn from our general circulation to cram the insatiate maw of ravenous government officials, to be expended out of the province on the plea of police protection. But the Western District is but a provender of

---

[225] *The Geelong Advertiser* Tuesday 23 September 1851, Ballarat Diggings, page 2

a centralised government.[226]

At Ballarat during October of 1851, the issue of the license fee continued to simmer as many were becoming disillusioned with the inability to return a profit. *The Herald* correspondent's report, endorsed as reliable by the *Geelong Advertiser*, thus described 'ten out of every hundred reaping good harvests – ten more gaining a comfortable livelihood, another ten doing something, that is paying their expenses; and another seventy doing nothing.'[227]

These types of divisions highlight different loyalties among the miners as W S Gibson's account indicates. While opposition was general on principle, most successful diggers were more likely to comply with the new regulations highlighting divisions between the successful and not-so-fortunate, especially at Ballarat that grew deeper as time progressed. This led to an attempt to correct the many misconceptions that arose from a public meeting and further press publicity. The meeting was held at the Geelong Mechanics Institute on 4 October 1851, with a lecture delivered by Mr W S Gibson supported by Mr Clarke of the *Geelong Advertiser*. Amongst advice on adequate preparation and the harsh realities at Ballarat, Gibson describes the implementation of the license fee.

On the arrival of the Commissioner, Mr Armstrong, the meeting reported on earlier by the local correspondent was described by Gibson as 'turbulent' with very inflammatory language being used. It had been resolved that the license fee would be refused and resisted. However, with the meeting barely over, the Commissioner was rushed and within a short time, all the license stationery had been exhausted. For those who had refused, as Gibson explained, it was not enforced, confirming La Trobe's intention, but Armstrong made every effort to explain that claims would be protected once a license was obtained. After the initial disturbance, for the most part, it was therefore as Gibson

---

[226] *Geelong Advertiser*, Tuesday 23 September 1851, Ballarat Diggings, page 2
[227] *Geelong Advertiser*, Friday 10 October 1851, The Ballarat Mines, page 2

explained, viewed as good insurance and was usually more willingly taken out the more successful the find. For those not successful Armstrong was willing to extend credit along with protection until gold was obtained in sufficient quantities. The first Commissioner was considered by Gibson to be a public relations success often moving amongst the miners and directing the unsuccessful to more prosperous areas.[228]

With summer approaching, however, the need for water was becoming urgent and MLC William Westgarth was there on site to discuss it with the miners. As the first major local infrastructure proposal for regional Victoria, a solution in the form of a series of dams in the local watercourses was proposed at a large meeting of diggers on the flat opposite Golden Point. The expectation was that the cost would be met by subscriptions to allow the work to begin immediately with a government grant to be pursued later. The meeting was chaired by Mr Westgarth from the Legislative Council on the stump of a gum tree and opened by Geelong notary and businessman T C Riddle. It was recognized that that the £10,000 of gold they were daily producing was a 'new and most important export for the colony' and now after some initial disruption, 'the business of the country could be got through without any serious inconvenience.'

Westgarth's main concern was that 'good feeling would always be maintained between the Government and the people at the mines' and that they should avoid the evils that had befallen California. He accepted their complaints that the license fee at thirty shillings per month was exorbitant and hoped that it would be abolished along with the escort fee to Melbourne, considering that only 2200 had paid for licenses - less than a third of the 8000 who were liable at Ballarat. He considered ten shillings a more appropriate figure, 'reducing to five after harvest.'[229] This followed

---

[228] *Geelong Advertiser*, Friday, 10 October 1851, The Ballarat Gold Field, page 2
[229] *The Geelong Advertiser*, Monday 27 October 1851, Public Meeting at Ballarat Diggings, page 2

an earlier meeting on Saturday 4th where Lieutenant Governor La Trobe addressed the diggers on the need for a temporary withdrawal of the 'license to dig' on account of the need for the local harvest to be completed and safely stored – a proposition that was warmly received. At the same time, the proposal to dam the local watercourses was also discussed.[230]

Nevertheless, the 'good feeling' quickly dissipated with the arrival of Captain Dana and his contingent of police. With a completely different mindset to La Trobe, they took the law into their own hands. Declaring that 'he would be damned if he would offer protection to such a lot of fellows,' Dana's words were supported by a reputation for brutality in the execution of his and his officers' duties.[231] He also made it clear that no escort would be provided, stating that they were able to protect themselves. In response to such an arrogant dismissal, more than a few diggers, many of whom were of respectable backgrounds, believing their license fee was for both protection and administration, declared that they would not be returning to the goldfields to experience the 'inconvenience and malmanagement' that they had been subjected to.[232]

As time progressed the reputation of the government's men did not improve but worsened considerably. The recruitment drive for commission officeholders often resulted in the appointment of inexperienced staff placed by recommendation rather than experience. Likewise for the same reasons the expanded police force was considered by diggers to be corrupted by Vandemonians and criminals who showed no respect to law-abiding diggers. Thus, despite the overtures of consideration to the mining population by leading politicians, the practical application of the legislation on the ground conveyed a different message entirely. Thus, with the

---

[230] *The Cornwall Chronicle* Launceston, Wednesday 22 October 1851, page 671, *The Geelong Advertiser*, Friday 10 October 1851, The Ballarat Mines, page 2
[231] *Geelong Advertiser*, Wednesday 1 October 1851, Ballarat Diggings, page 2
[232] *Adelaide Times*, Saturday 18 October 1851, Ballarat Diggings.

actions of officials like Capt. Dana, many diggers and the larger body of colonial citizens from such an early stage, were coming to believe that the enactment of gold legislation was both unfair and violated the principles of freedom on which an orderly, civilized, and British society was based.

As the gold rushes developed the protests increased to a roar by both the people in Melbourne and Geelong as reports of the overbearing methods of the Goldfields Commission began to filter out into the public domain. Confirmed and repeated in government inquiries and reports in 1852, 1853 and 1854 it contributed in no small part to the loss of confidence in the government and support for the diggers' causes. It also confirmed earlier predictions that the license fee would be a source of social disorder as the Geelong Advertiser correspondent reported from Buninyong at the beginning of the gold rush:

> It is a monstrous imposition to levy on labour eighteen pounds per annum. It is the maximum of iniquity to wrench from a man a sum that is the equal to what he would be paid as a hutkeeper for a twelvemonth's service. It cannot be levied without disorder; or if levied it will crush the worker and create feelings antagonistic to the peace of society.[233]

Thus, from the very beginning, as a new colony, ideology around the state and individual liberty was quite mature among members of the public and found a focus through the imposition of the mining legislation and the resulting regulations. As it was eloquently put by Dr Owens in 1853, unlike the citizens of Melbourne, diggers on the goldfields had to suffer the indignity of being accosted by a policeman just for engaging in their normal daily work.

Much of this opposition was pre-formed based on experiences back in Britain with the aristocratic dominance of the social and

---

[233] *The Geelong Advertiser*, 25 August 1851, Buninyong, page 2

political system. The final chartist campaign was still in living memory having ended only three years earlier with prominent activists, like Henry Holyoake and the Nicholls brothers Henry and Charles, with them on the goldfields. Additionally, as the generation after the Great Reform Act of 1832, and the Municipal Reform Act of 1835, they expected much more from the colonial government, which from the end of 1851, was already discussing the rollout of planned townships and a similar local government project in the colonies. The formation of the Goldfields Commission as the sole administrative body on the goldfields, was for the well-informed diggers on the goldfields therefore, a retrograde step defying a decade of British social and political reform. Additionally, many had come from towns and cities where the adoption of the 1835 Municipal Corporations Act removed arbitrary control from out of the hands of the few and had begun managing towns and cities for the benefit of the public. This was an entirely new generation with a vastly different outlook on society from the old pastoral set that had been governing the colonies.

It is no surprise therefore that the well-laid plans of Fitzroy and La Trobe were met with resistance from the beginning of the gold rushes. The subsequent story, therefore, was one of increasing concession by the government to the diggers' demands. After the first initial cries of protest from a wide section of the community to the Government's measures, the volume and intensity increased year by year along with the population. A major escalation involving the diggers and the public in 1852 was met with a large roads and bridges project. Another in 1853 resulted in an inquiry and a reform bill which included a reduction of the license fee, and changes in the management of the goldfields. Dissatisfaction with the outcome, however, continued to provoke further unrest, as it did little to improve the lot of the average digger. Further agitation from the end of 1853 for the complete removal of the Commission, led to the announcement of a comprehensive inquiry in November 1854 that acknowledged most of the diggers' complaints with a commitment to comprehensive reform promised. The Eureka rebellion in December of that year confirmed the seriousness of the problem with the Goldfields Commission as a local governmental body leading to the comprehensive changes to the Goldfields in 1855. It came as no surprise to many because the government had been warned of an event like Eureka many times from the beginning by many people from various sources.

8. Victorian Regional Government 1851-1855

The Goldfields Commission, notwithstanding the criticisms directed at it, was the first form of local Government of inland Victoria. For over three years from September 1851 to June 1855, just like the old British chartered corporations, it operated under the oversight of the government, completely unresponsible to the people under its jurisdiction. It was a huge organisation governed from the Melbourne head office to which all Resident Commissioners reported. There were many stations and outstations all manned with Commissioners, Deputy Commissioners, clerks, police, couriers, and medical staff. It also encompassed and oversaw the legal arms of the Government in each locality such as the local Magistrates, and police who all, in an *ad hoc* sort of way, saw themselves as an essential part of a network of individual working communities.

For example, in the absence of a Resident Commissioner at Ballarat in December 1852, Acting Police Magistrate Eyre at Buninyong fulfilled this role as well as his own. He reported that he was informed by local diggers of a new discovery of gold and settled a criminal and medical matter where a man was shot, took a census of the district and reported on the need for staff at Creswick Creek which he deemed to be a permanent settlement. He appeared to be well informed on the amounts of gold discovered and was careful to distinguish between 'working miners' and others in the 6400-strong community such as the 600 women and 800 children whom he considered to be a great benefit to order and contentment.[234]

---

[234] VPRS001189/P0000, Unit 000090, *The Acting Police Magistrate Buninyong to Colonial Secretary 52/8836, 52/9029, 52/9453*

The camps also had structure and routine with 'knock-off time' notified by a cannon from the Government quarters, in the more established locations like Ballarat.[235] Living and working areas occupied separate locations and by 1854 in Ballarat, permanent government structures and private and commercial establishments were appearing in the township and along the main road to Buninyong and Geelong. Observation of the Sabbath was a weekly event for many diggers which were also attended by camp officials and public health was considered a priority with weekly reports filed.[236] Schools were beginning to make their appearance in 1854 as the total population approached 30,000.[237] Travelling shows, entertainment venues and a large variety of stores and service industries such as blacksmiths, and other mechanical services, gave the impression of a permanent city but its management was a far cry from the participatory civic arrangements of Melbourne.

Despite this, the commissioners generally showed a strong sense of responsibility for their charges, facilitating numerous cases of kindness and generosity that encouraged a sense of community. For example, at Ballarat after a tragic incident with a flooded mineshaft in November 1853, police were instructed to assist the diggers with the water dispersal.[238] In July 1854, Commissioner Robert Rede was elected head of a miners' committee and successfully lodged an application with the Chief Commissioner for £1000 as joint funding with the diggers for a hospital. Commissioner Robert Rede was an enthusiastic backer noting in

---

[235] Geoffrey Serle, *The golden age: a history of the Colony of Victoria, 1851-1861*, Melbourne, Melbourne University Press, p76

[236] *Ibid*, p79, Weston Bate, *lucky city*, p20,39, *Most Commissioners reports 1852-1854* VPRS1189/P0000 units 83-90

[237] Weston Bate, *Lucky city*, p49

[238] VPRS P0000/Unit 000089, 53/12676 *Resident Commissioner Ballarat to the Chief Commissioner, Weekly Report to 26 November 1853*

his correspondence that this was 'imperative for goldfields so extensive and populous as Ballarat.'²³⁹

A year earlier under Resident Commissioner Clow and at the behest of the Chief Commissioner of the Goldfields, fifteen-year-old miner John McMah (also of Ballarat), 'a friendless lad' with a deformed hand was awarded the £30 in fines imposed on those who stole his hard-won pay dirt while charitable allowances were made to local widows.²⁴⁰ At Ballarat in September 1853, at the height of the 'Red Ribbon' protests, the local miners' protest committee led by Dr Sylvester and Dr Carr, foiled an attempted robbery on the 'treasure tent' where gold was stored for transport, offering their services to the Resident Commissioner to act as special constables.²⁴¹ During the same period, the committee also instructed local miners to continue paying their license fees until instructed otherwise.²⁴² Early in 1854, Chief Commissioner Wright ordered that confiscated illegal liquor should be sold and the proceeds allocated to the provision of hospitals on the various goldfields.²⁴³

By 1854, the Commission was administering policing, health regulations, licensing, postal services, public buildings and roads performing many of the functions that a municipality would in

---

²³⁹ VPRS001189/P0000 Unit 000091, 54/170, *Resident Commissioner Ballarat to Chief Commissioner Melbourne, 11 July 1854*
²⁴⁰ VPRS001189/P0000 Unit 000086, D7636, *Chief Commissioner of the Goldfields to the Colonial Secretary, 3/8/1853*
²⁴¹ VPRS001189/P0000 Unit 000087, 53/250 D11093, *Resident Commissioner Ballarat, weekly report to 3/9/1853*
²⁴² VPRS001189/P0000, Unit 000087, C8771, *The Resident Commissioner Ballarat to the Chief Commissioner of the Goldfields, Weekly Report, 27/8/1853*
²⁴³ VPRS001189/P0000, Unit 000090, 54/444, *Chief Commissioner Wright to Colonial Secretary Feb 1854, Chief Commissioner Wright to Colonial Secretary 13/1/1854*, VPRS001189/P0000 Unit 000091, 54/170, *Resident Commissioner at Ballarat to the Chief Commissioner, 11/7/1854*, H54/8110, *Chief Commissioner to Colonial Secretary 26/7/1854*

normal circumstances.[244] At Ballarat, the Commission organized the mapping of the township boundaries and arranged for local roadworks.[245] Much of this came about with the recognition that by 1853, more permanent accommodation was needed. Thus, with its resources severely stretched, a massive building project along with the streamlining of the administration was undertaken. With legal matters like police subordination to the commission also settled, the organization was becoming more streamlined and looking to a long-term future based on virtually unlimited gold resources. However, it was occurring at the same time as those subject to its administration were becoming better informed and more organized thus exposing its vulnerabilities and the temporary nature of its original concept. Its focus remained where it began – on the gold resource, ignoring the basic principles of civic society and the social functioning and needs of human beings.

Local Government Policy 1851-1854
This placed the goldfields at odds with the social and political progress that was occurring elsewhere in the colony. Completely out of step with what was occurring at the same time in Melbourne, it existed as it was always intended, as a separate social system, as Withers described it, 'outside the mystic circle of government'. But change was always looming as travel, communication and trade increased between the goldfields and the cities, hastening the time when they would be fully integrated into the social and political

---

[244] VPRS 2500/P000/89/C53 13.112 *Chief Commissioner's Report to Colonial Secretary W/E 10/12/1853, C53/9933 A C Cruikshank application for Inspector of weights & measures & slaughterhouses 4 October 1853*, VPRS 2500/P000/90/*Resident Commissioner at Ballarat to Chief Commissioner in Melbourne applying for assistance for erection of public hospital 11/7/1854 54/170*, VPRS 1189/86/*To the Senior Assistant Commissioner Ballarat from Clerk of Works, 6 June 1853, details & cost of proposed works*, VPRS 1189/P000/91/54/150 & *circular 53/14.697 Chief Commissioner of Police Melbourne, 19 September 1853*
[245] VPRS 1189/P0000 Unit 000084, *Letter from Chief Commissioner Wright to Colonial Secretary, February 1854, Description of the boundaries of the Ballarat Township Reserve*

framework of the colony. This would always be a problem that would have to be solved sooner rather than later. Thus, with the creation of separate colonies, the political focus was on the creation of new constitutions and the unavoidable needs of a potentially huge permanent inland population of diggers. It would take a visionary with a view to the future and the establishment of a modern state with an all-encompassing civil society.

In Victoria, one such visionary was Secretary Foster of Victoria who proposed that representation for the upper house be based on regional representation or district councils.[246] However, as John Waugh points out, with few regional towns in New South Wales and virtually none in Victoria at the time, it failed to attract any support due to the absence of an established local government and civic network. Nevertheless, Foster's ideas in Victoria found fertile ground with Surveyor General Clarke who saw the merits of such a system, especially with the discovery of gold. His efforts resulted in moves to create a new bill to replace old legislation for the management of towns. It was accompanied by an almost frantic effort to create and survey towns in regional Victoria by colonial surveyor Urquart throughout 1852-1853.[247]

Lieutenant Governor La Trobe, however, was resolutely supportive of his solution for regional Victoria - the Goldfields Commission. He was convinced, as he later wrote, that its greatest benefit was in controlling a large, diverse, and 'excited' population and that it guaranteed a close connection between people and the Government. But he also believed that it would be a transitional measure until it could be 'abandoned with safety, when the financial and social advantages derived from it may be secured in

---

[246] See John Waugh, Framing the first constitution, 1853-1855, in *Monash University Law Review*, 1997, Vol. 23 (2), p., 342, *Report from the Select Committee of the Legislative Council on a New Constitution for the Colony; together with the Resolutions and Proceedings of the Committee and the Draft of a Bill, Votes and Proceedings*, Legislative Council (Vic) sess 1853-4, Vol 111, no Dl1, 15, 34.
[247] Weston Bate, *Lucky City*, p25

some other manner.'[248] Despite this, matters quickly took on a life of their own bringing the time of 'safety' much closer than La Trobe was expecting. The process for this 'abandonment,' therefore began during the same year of 1851, in December. Local diggers at Ballarat just a couple of months after the discovery of gold, requested the Government make land available for successful miners to purchase and settle down. In response, W S Urquart, the District Surveyor appointed in December 1845, was sent almost immediately by La Trobe and commenced the survey of the Ballarat township completing it by 17 January 1852.

Once surveys were completed in 1852 in settled areas, the Goldfield townships with their private allotments, became subject to the existing Town and Country Police Act which vested power in local magistrates to administer licensing, permits, crimes, sanitation, commerce and public records.[249] Large expenses for roadworks, public buildings, and other local needs were met by application to the Department of Works and the Colonial Treasury due to the absence of any local road board or rate-collecting body.[250] These powers, however, were effectively suspended in favour of the Goldfields Commission which acted as a mediatory body for the township until it was disbanded in June 1855.[251]

The next major step was initiating the Select Committee on the Administration of Local Funds. It was commissioned in December of 1853 and reported to the Legislative Council in February.

---

[248] *Argus*, Saturday 27 August 1853, page 4 Council Papers, copy of despatch from His Excellency the Lieutenant Governor of Victoria to His Excellency Sir Charles Fitzroy 1 August 1853 Colonial papers Latrobe to Fitzroy
[249] Bernard Barrett, *The civic frontier*, p17
[250] Sir George Frederick Verdon, p10, Bernard Barrett, *The civic frontier*, pp84-90, J B Hirst, *The strange birth of colonial democracy*, Sydney, pp244-246
[251] VPRS 2500/P0000/Unit 91/ Circular 53/H6971 19 September 1853, *Chief Commissioner Melbourne to officers in charge of police on the goldfields respecting their position in relation to the Resident Commissioners*, Bernard Barrett, *The civic frontier, p159*

Victorian Regional Government 1851-1857

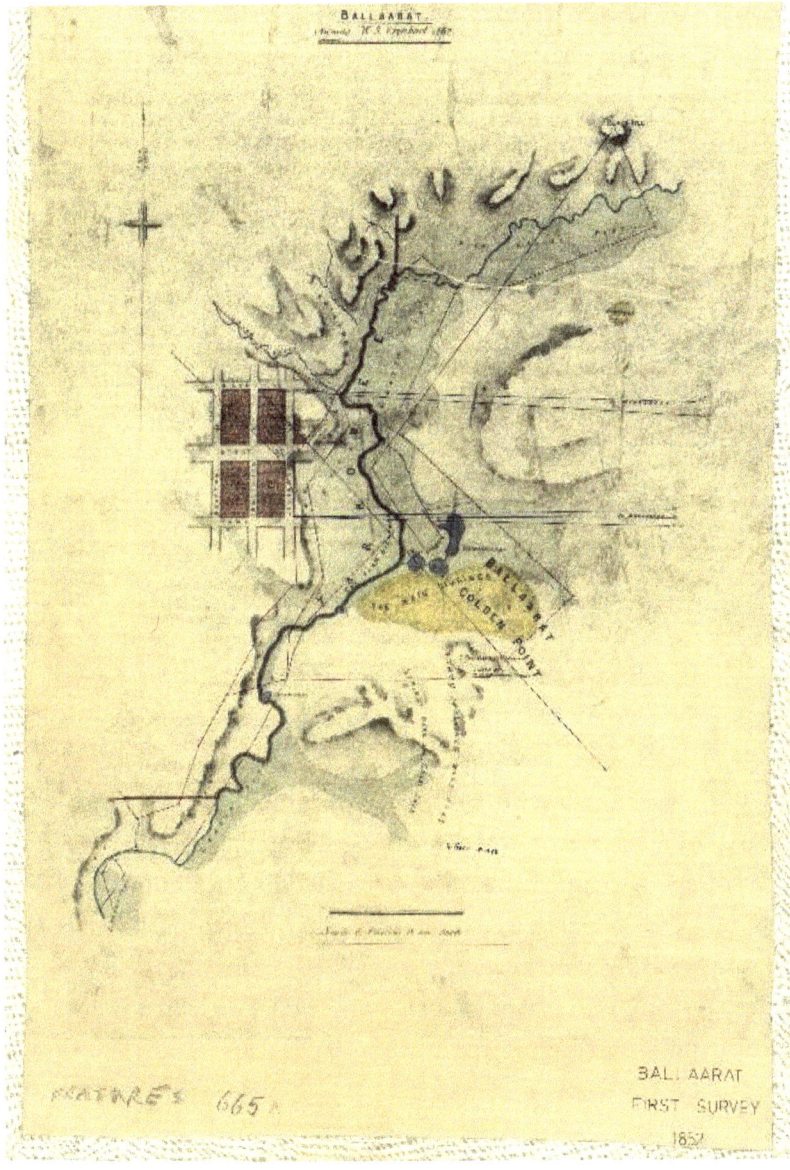

Ballarat First Survey 1852 VPRS 8168 P0005 FEAT 665A. The escarpment runs North to South and the 'Flat' is the river flats of the Yarrowee. Potential gold reefs are detailed as red lines. Streets from right to left are Lydiard, Armstrong, Doveton and from top to Bottom are Mair, Sturt, Dana.

1854.[252] While its original brief was to examine and assess the growing size of the city of Melbourne and its budget, Colonial Secretary Foster also decided, given the growing townships on the goldfields and other locations, to include a proposal for the application of municipal government colony-wide. This would then provide the means for local communities to levy rates, create bylaws and manage their own defined areas. According to Foster, this would alleviate problems caused by the growing size and cost of infrastructure as well as the bureaucracy to manage it, which he argued, was 'creating a dangerous level of centralization that was prejudicial to almost every individual in the colony.'[253]

Throughout 1854 the committee began drafting the Act led primarily by the expertise of Andrew Clarke a former army engineer and now the new Surveyor General. Clarke provided a list of localities which included the goldfield districts of Castlemaine, Ballarat, Buninyong, and Heathcote. They would be democratic with a franchise that included any adult male who owned or occupied property for six months and would be empowered to make bylaws, levy rates and tolls and be responsible for local utilities and infrastructure.[254] The Government then put the final pieces of its colony-wide local government system together presenting it to the Legislative Council in October 1854. Royal Assent came on 29 December 1854 just a few weeks after the Eureka uprising. The new legislation was a quiet but revolutionary Act that came into effect virtually unnoticed, drowned out by the disturbances surrounding the events at Ballarat and the Eureka Stockade.

---

[252] *Report from the Select Committee of the Legislative Council on a New Constitution for the Colony; together with the Resolutions and Proceedings of the Committee and the Draft of a Bill, Votes and Proceedings,* Legislative Council (Vic) sess 1853-4, Vol 111, No Dl1, 15, 34
[253] Bernard Barrett, *The civic frontier*, pp116-124
[254] Bernard Barrett, *The civic frontier* p124

The Municipal Institutions Act was a view towards a diverse future both socially and economically. It was designed to encourage economic development and the growth of modern infrastructure throughout the colony, not just in Melbourne and Geelong. As several politicians argued, it was, like their Canadian counterparts, promoting the 'true development' of the colony of Victoria.[255] The idea of a true, decentralized, and liberal approach to the development of the colony acknowledged that the exclusive methods of the pastoral era and the Tories back in England were behind them. The introduction of the bill, therefore, was not to be underestimated nor taken lightly as it was believed, according to the Surveyor General, that its passing would 'alter the state of society and of local government in the country.'[256] The liberal members believed that the Victorian Act likewise would have a revolutionary effect on the populations in regional Victoria, which had laboured since 1851 under the Goldfields Commission, without rights civic recognition and representation. For them, the Commission was another 'Tory' institution standing in the way of progress. For the government however, many of whom were often labelled as Tories, their majority represented the old order before the discovery of gold, and for most of them, it was the means to preserving it. For them, their majority in the legislative council was an instrument to prevent social change, not to embrace it.

The more progressive members of the Legislative Council, however, were well aware of the potential of the proposed bill arguing during 1854 with the anticipation that it would remedy the discontent on the goldfields. Andrew Clarke echoing the Colonial Secretary almost nine months earlier, declared at its second presentation to the Legislative Council in October 1854 that this was a departure from the past that would "destroy the spirit of centralization – a spirit which had made distant localities

---

[255] *The Argus* (Melbourne) Thursday October 19, 1854, The legislative Council, page 4
[256] *ibid*

discontented and rendered nugatory many efforts of the government." Pointing to the prosperous state of Canada, Clarke praised the wisdom of Lords Metcalf and Sydenham in granting Canadians municipal councils reminding the Council of the preamble of the Canadian Act where it stated that "the true development of the country would thereby be promoted."[257]

Strong support for the bill came from the 'diggers' friend' in Council J P Fawkner, who believed that the facilities enjoyed in Melbourne should be available for the regional areas, while Mr Campbell argued that the bill signalled a "new era in the history of a country when a system of self-government was thus provided." Moreover, the consensus of the Legislative Council was that the introduction of municipal government on the goldfields was essential to their transformation and 'progressive success' and was a timely concession that would bring system and cohesion to the formative arrangements of the community.[258]

The bill was also viewed by the *Age* as a remedy to the goldfields' animosity towards the government.[259] The primary grievance was the lack of recognition in return for the large amounts paid to the treasury. This was supported by the Statistical Report for Victoria 1852 which showed that the license fee formed the greatest category of general revenue and was successfully utilized in successive petitions filed by the Bendigo and Mt Alexander miners in 1852 and 1853 for roadworks, escorts and lowering the license fee.[260]

---

[257] *Argus*, (Melbourne) 19 October,1854, The Legislative Council, p4
[258] ibid
[259] *Age* (Melbourne) Friday, November 3, 1854, page 4, Local Government.
[260] VPARL 1853 – 54 No31 *Statistics for the Colony of Victoria*, page 39, *Argus* (Melbourne) Thursday 22 July 1852, page 4 Bendigo, *Cornwall Chronicle* (Launceston) Wednesday 28 July 1852, page 472, 'Mems from the Mount' VPRS 1095 P0000/5 1852/2760 *Petition To La Trobe and members of the Executive Council, from the Gold Diggers and others residing at the Bendigo Goldfield.* 2 July 1852

9. Ending Local Government by Commission

By 1853, in the settlements where the miners lived, many were witnessing the construction of Commission residences for the staff, barracks and other buildings paid for by their hard-earned and often fruitless license fees.[261] This had the effect of creating a class divide between the tent-dwelling miners and increasing the volume of the universal slogan that had been voiced from the very beginning of the goldrushes: 'taxation without representation is tyranny' or in many other cases 'robbery.' It was the main catchcry, and the slogan carried all the way to Eureka the following year.[262]

The budget that it commanded was huge employing clerks at all locations, a commissioner at a declared gold field, many assistant commissioners and a large head office staff in Melbourne. The head office itself in Melbourne for the 1853/4 financial year commanded a budget of almost £12000 while, as the below example of Mt Alexander illustrates, outposts such as Ballarat, Castlemaine and Sandhurst also commanded huge budgets. This included provisions for escorts, assorted buildings, clerks, storekeepers and provisions, and other general labourers. In the Ballarat district alone preparations were being made to allocate large amounts towards the building of new Government offices.

---

[261] VPRS1189/P0000/87 *Letters from the Chief Commissioner of the Goldfields, Inwards Registered Correspondence* I, 53/10.742, Fred B .... Staff Officer, *Letters from the Chief Commissioner of the Goldfields VPRS1189/P0000/91*Inward Registered Corr I 54/82

[262] *Argus*, (Melbourne) Friday 26 August 1853, page 5, Important meeting of the diggers of the ovens. VPRS 1095 P0000/5 1852/2760 *Petition To La Trobe and members of the Executive Council, from the Gold Diggers and others residing at the Bendigo Goldfield*, *Argus*, (Melbourne) Tuesday 15 February 1853, 'Scraps from the Ovens', Page 4, Friday 11 Feb 1853, Friday, 18 Feb 1853, 8 Feb 1853, *Argus* (Melbourne) Friday, 5 August 1853, 'Grievances of the Gold Diggers', page 4

> *Estimate of the probable amount that will be required for establishing an Escort for conveyance of Gold from Mount Alexander to Melbourne during the year 1853. as per Statements annexed.*
>
> | № | | | £ | | |
> |---|---|---|---|---|---|
> | 1 | Buildings | | 10,000 | 0 | 0 |
> | 2 | Equipment | | 7,050 | 0 | 0 |
> | 3 | Forage & Farriery | | 31,200 | 0 | 0 |
> | 4 | Supplies | | 1,390 | 0 | 0 |
> | 5 | Salaries | | 6,350 | 0 | 0 |
> | 6 | Contingencies | | 500 | 0 | 0 |
> | | Total Estimate | £ | 57,490 | 0 | 0 |
>
> *W. H. Wright*
> *Chief Commissioner*

which included a large brick and stone military barracks (shown below) that would be housing the 'pensioners' battalion. It was stressed that this was a matter of urgency as it was considered unsatisfactory for them to be housed in tent accommodation. The new buildings, as the report stated, would provide comfort and shelter 'from the inclemency of winter and the heat of summer.' Once repatriated, it would then be re-purposed as government offices. At a time when many diggers across the goldfields were struggling to pay the license, seeing the revenue collected from them going towards the comfort and protection of their oppressive overlords was a step too far. It reinforced in the most visible way

Ending Local Government by Commission

that the Goldfields Commission was there to stay and expected to for the long term. It became a 'bookend' issue, particularly on the northern goldfields. The infrastructure project was a major complaint by delegates to the inquiry later that year. In addition to the diminishing returns for gold-seeking, it had finally pushed them to action against the goldfields administration, continuing for the better part of 1853.

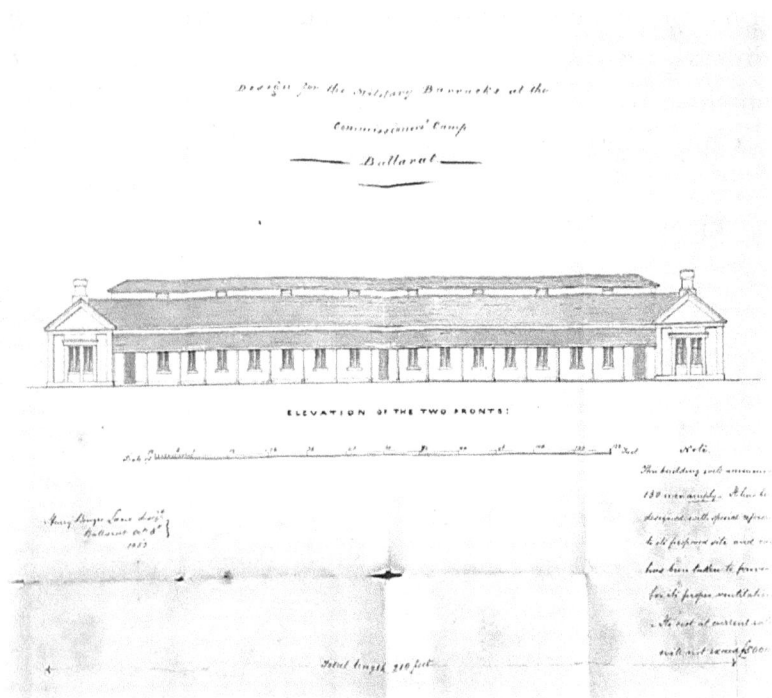

263

The miners' campaign was given a boost from diggers in New South Wales when from July to September 1853, 'Captain' Brown panicked the diggers on the Bendigo, Mount Alexander and Ovens fields with the news of a looming population increase. Large posters on trees, poles and anywhere they could be attached announced that 400,000 immigrants under Governor General Fitzroy's 1851 scheme were on their way from the home countries in the next few months. This raised the prospect of greatly diminished returns and potential impoverishment for everyone. As a result, a successful passive resistance campaign for a fee

---

[263] Monthly Goldfields Officers return Sept 1853, *Letters from the Chief Commissioner of the Goldfields VPRS1189/P0000/91* Inward Registered Correspondence I 54/82

reduction was waged from July to September 1853 where miners at most locations offered themselves for arrest.[264]

In September 1853, reports of unarmed police being overpowered by a mob at Sandhurst and of licenses that could not be collected at Waranga, heightened concerns of the Chief Commissioner as to the viability of the present structure of the goldfields and its policy[265] As the protest gathered momentum, Chief Commissioner Wright, in a report to the Colonial Secretary, argued that 'no amount of police could reverse the passive resistance to the license' while the staff and costs to process the thousands of fines or prosecutions were beyond the capacity of the organization. The application of 'coercive measures' he believed would 'throw serious obstacles in the way of establishing any regulations that could be enforced.'[266]

1853: Ballarat Miners and Local Government
Meanwhile, in Ballarat, the Ballarat Gold Diggers Association had been formed in support of their colleagues' campaign in Bendigo, Castlemaine, and the Ovens. Led by Dr Alfred Carr, W Sylvester, and Dr Kemp, regular meetings were held up until the Select Committee inquiry into the goldfields in October of that year. As a result of these meetings, a list of items was voted on and presented as a petition to the Government in much the same tone as the famous Miners Charter the following year just before Eureka. This petition contained six points:

    1. A reduction of the license fee.

---

[264] *Argus* (Melbourne) 9 July 1853 Bendigo, page 3, *Sydney Morning Herald*, Tuesday 23 December 1851, page 2 'Legislative Council 22 December 1851'

[265] VPRS 2500/P000/87/53/932 Copy, *Resident Commissioner Panton Castlemaine, 5 July 1853, to Chief Commissioner of the Goldfields, 8/3/9/1853*, VPRS 2500/P0000/87/D11093, *Asst Commissioner Waranga, Weekly Report 3 September 1853*

[266] VPRS 2500/P0000/87/53/341 EC *Reports by Chief Commissioner Wright to Colonial Secretary*, 28 August 1853, page 3

2. Enfranchisement of the several districts of the goldfields
3. Local government
4. That a sum of money from the proceeds of the license fee, and fees of escort, be laid out in the formation and repair of the roads to the goldfields
5. That there should be regularly licensed tents established on the goldfields, for the sale of fermented and spirituous liquors, (under stringent regulations) for the benefit of the diggers
6. That there should be offered for sale to the digger (on the ground) small sections of land abutting the goldfields for the purpose of cultivation and for permanent establishments.[267]

Leaders of the Association, Alfred Carr and W Sylvester, as delegates to the inquiry, both argued that funds extracted from the miners should be spent where they were collected. Dr Carr also declared to the inquiry: "the first thing we want is local self-government." The chairman then asked Sylvester: "you wish in fact to establish a municipality?" Sylvester answered in the affirmative, adding: "if we had Local Government on the diggings … I believe that the 30s license fee would be collected as easily as a penny."[268] The core issue of the protests, according to the *Geelong Advertiser* correspondent, was the fact that the miners, as Westgarth later pointed out, were not considered citizens of the Colony of Victoria and yet as a class they were heavily taxed and were contributing to society just like those in Melbourne and Geelong. Therefore, the

---

[267] *Argus* (Melbourne), Tuesday 6 September 1853, page 4, William Kelly, *Life in Victoria*, London, Chapman and Hall, 1859, p251 - 254

[268] *Report of the Select Committee of the Goldfields together with the Minutes of Evidence and the Appendix*, 1 November 1853, Parliament.Vic.gov.au/papers/govpub/VPARL1854-55NoA76p[1], item 1610, p74, item 1623, item 1343, p60

Select Committee by proposing no remedy, had failed 'to attain a fair allowance of political and social justice on the goldfields.'[269]

1854 and the Commission of Inquiry
The overriding factor behind the protests was the large amounts of people who had become permanent residents. Most residents were loath to forfeit their claims when the weather was unfavourable, as had been the case in earlier years. In addition, as predicted the year before, individual returns had greatly reduced. Many who could not afford to leave, remained to pick up income from employment in other working enterprises or from the government on the roads or other building and maintenance work. According to the Chief Commissioner, this accounted for 'one-third of the whole adult population.'[270] These demographic changes were recognized in the 1854-55 Royal Commission. Seasonality, longer-term projects such as deep sinking (which was more characteristic of Ballarat), and the puddling enterprises in Bendigo and steam technology, were thus contributing to a return to normal social relations. A permanent population with employers and employee relationships was beginning to emerge.[271]

Commissioner Wright's concerns about the uncertain success of 'coercive force,' were finally realized in December 1854. At Ballarat, the population had trebled from 8,200 in October 1853 to almost 25,000 in December 1854.[272] The aggressive method of license collection from October 1854 thus created the spark that

---

[269] *Geelong Advertiser and Intelligencer* 11 October 1853, page 6, The social aspect of the Diggings.
[270] VPRS001189/P0000 Unit 000086, C53/7859, *Chief Commissioner of the Goldfields to the Colonial Secretary reporting on the state of feeling on the Goldfields with reference to the petition to the Lieutenant Governor for a reduction of the license fee*, page 13
[271] VPARL1854-55NoA76p *Report from the Commission to inquire into the condition of the goldfields: to His Excellency Sir Charles Hotham, KCB, Lieutenant Governor of the Colony of Victoria*, point No 156
[272] Geoffrey Serle, *The golden age*, Appendix 4, Mining Population, p388, this includes 4500 women and children shown on census return from Ballarat 1854, not included in Serle's figures

ignited the Eureka uprising. The large group of unsuccessful Irish miners on the Eureka lead, who had been exercising violence against fellow miners and threatening 'physical force' for more than twelve months, were driven to the point of desperation.[273] This triggered the famous license burning, the uprising and hastened the Government inquiry announced at the end of November 1854.

The inquiry found that the causes for the unrest were three-fold:
1. The license fee and its method of collection
2. The land grievance and the impossibility of investing their capital in a section of ground
3. The want of political rights – large numbers without gradations of public rank, political representation, or any system of self-elected local authority in short contributing largely to the wealth and greatness of the colony without enjoying any voice whatever in its public administration.[274]

This finding matches reasonably with the 'Ballarat Reform League Charter' or declaration and list of demands handed to the Colonial Secretary in November at the trials of the Eureka Hotel riot and Bentley murders. It also maintained the localisation tone of the petition of the year before by the Ballarat Gold Diggers Association calling for 'a thorough agitation of the goldfields and the towns' and the immediate disbanding of the Goldfields Commission.[275] Local government, which had been the major

---

[273] *Geelong Advertiser and Intelligencer* 27 August 1853, Supplement page 1, 'Meetings at Ballarat', (Irish physical force faction warned against taking action) VPRS001189/P0000 Unit 000084, 54/59, 54/2796 *Resident Commissioner Ballarat to Chief Commissioner, reporting on a serious disturbance (1000 people, Irish arrests) 14/3/1853*, Weston Bate *Lucky City* p51, 55, p276 notes (Tipperary mob & Eureka as Irish territory)

[274] VPARL1854-55NoA76p *Report from the Commission to inquire into the condition of the goldfields: to His Excellency Sir Charles Hotham, KCB, Lieutenant Governor of the Colony of Victoria*, p10

[275] VPRS 2873/ P0012, Unit 27, *Ballarat Reform League Charter* November 27, 1854

theme of the earlier petition, had already been guaranteed in the new Act passed in October of that year. But it passed with little fanfare, eclipsed by the crescendo of miners' agitations over the gold license, ending with the Eureka Stockade a few months later. Nevertheless, it was a confluence of related events and social pressures that became a wake-up call to the fledgling Government, on the urgent social and political needs of the regional populations that existed without any civic status. As James Oddie reminded the citizens of Ballarat many years later, the miners rose up against tyranny and the rule by commissioners winning municipal government, democratic concessions and local autonomy.[276] In the first instance, this resulted in the disbanding of the Goldfields Commission and the election of local representatives to the newly formed Miners Courts early in 1855. However, this did not address the urgent needs of the township which, from its inception in 1852, had been neglected due to the large expenses required to maintain the Goldfields Commission. It had also expanded significantly and was becoming the focal point of more agitation but this time amongst the diggers themselves.

---

[276] *The Ballarat Star*, Tuesday 19 Dec 1905, The Jubilee of the City Council, page 1

PART 3

Creating Civil Administration at Ballarat 1855-1857

10. Local Consolidation after Eureka

To preserve the liberties and institutions of their fatherland

By 1855 as the above map illustrates, the town had had physically doubled in size. The original central grid of six streets had been extended southward and divided into lots with their imminent sale anticipated. With this expansion naturally came a growing expectation for the corresponding extension of the services and facilities of the state – a need reinforced strongly at the ballot box in the election for the expanded Legislative Assembly in 1856. With the Goldfields Commission now largely irrelevant as a local civic body after the Eureka disaster and the huge public outcry against the government over its actions surrounding it, the people at Ballarat began looking to integrate themselves into the rest of society. For them, it was the establishment of what they had been denied for the past four years – civic society and public institutions. They envisioned the proper operation of a police force dedicated to the protection of the population and the enforcement of civil laws, not the protection of the Goldfields Commission, its people and its assets and policies. For the diggers, as they argued on numerous occasions, this was an inversion of what the state was about and a violation of constitutional rights.

The role of the state in the lives of communities and the individual was a long-held and debated principle of British society as articulated by the father of Liberalism John Locke and his predecessor Thomas Hobbes. It had matured considerably with the now well-established concept of property both public and private which had taken hold in British political thought. Locke's

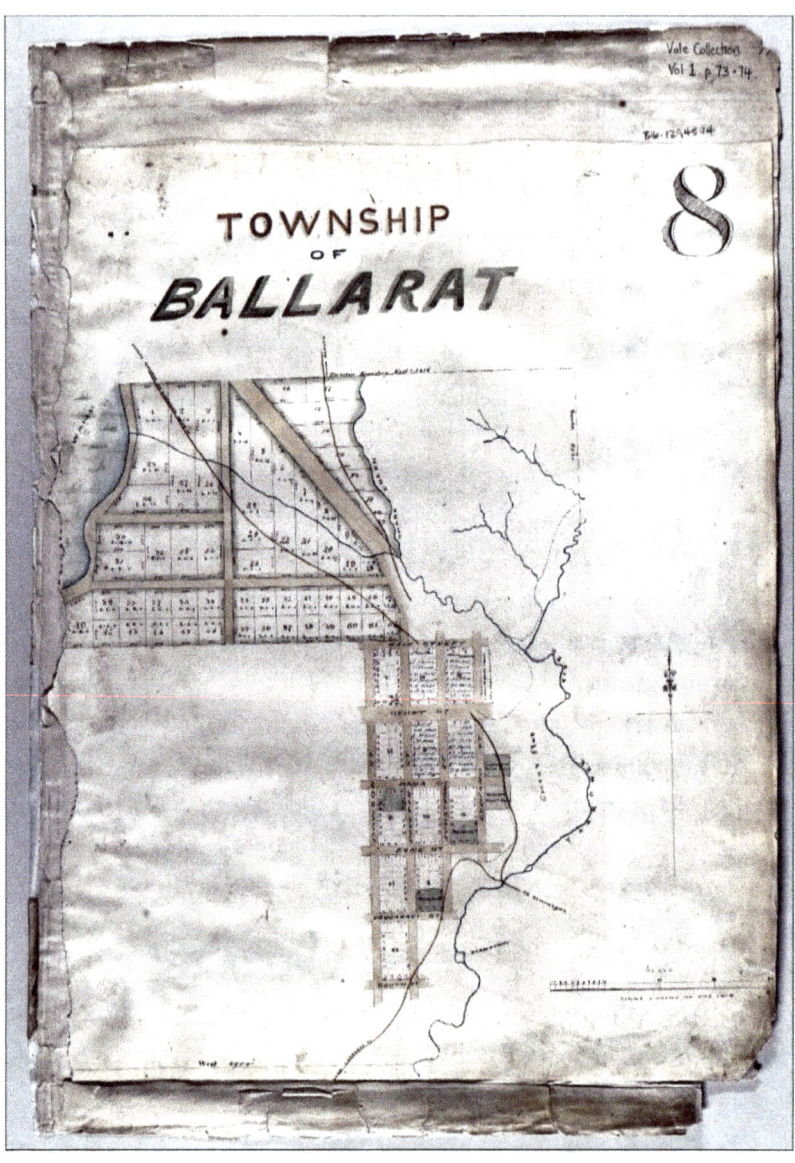

Copy of a parchment map of the Township, possibly late 1854, certainly dated between 1853 and 1855 without Drummond, Errard, Lyons and Raglan streets, very likely the one referred to by the Age 28/6/1855 *Township of Ballarat [cartographic Material]*. Vale Collection1851. http://handle.slv.vic.gov.au/10381/192258

ideas were based on the concept that 'political authority is bestowed by individuals on government for the purpose of pursuing the ends of the governed'.[277] This powerful tradition derived a great deal of credibility from the victory of the parliament over Charles 1st, spawning groups like the levellers and their derivatives who began to agitate for electoral, legal and local government reforms. Particularly relevant for local government was the repeal of socially divisive legislation like the test acts in the early 1800s which opened the door to many prominent citizens previously excluded from holding public office on religious grounds.[278]

There were strong indications of pride in this heritage in the Ballarat community which emerged during a long and vigorous toasting session in the victory celebrations for J B Humffray in October 1856. Dr Allison thus reminded all present to

> Let them remember the free and happy land of Britain … where constitutional liberty had long been enjoyed; there the laws were mild. The standard of liberty and religion had long been erected in Britain (Cheers). In Britain all were free and he thanked heaven they were not under such a rule as that of the king of Naples. Their duty was to preserve the liberties and institutions of their fatherland and transmit them unimpaired to future generations. [279]

Thus, of primary concern for Britons, from a Hobbesean perspective, was the expectation that the institution of government should be conceived as an instrument for the defence of the life, liberty and estate of its citizens or that the reason for its existence

---

[277] David Held, 'The development of the modern state, in Stuart Hall and Bram Gieben eds., *Formations of modernity*, Polity Press, Cambridge UK, 1992, pp 110-112

[278] Brian Manning, *The English people and the English revolution*, Penguin Books Harmondsworth UK, first published by Heineman Educational Books 1976, pp 322-340, E. P. Hennock, *Fit and proper persons*, p. 309-310

[279] *The Star* (Ballarat) Saturday November 1, 1856, Complimentary Dinner to J B Humffray Esq, M P, page 2

is the protection of individuals rights as laid down by God's will and enshrined in law.[280] This belief was at the heart of the moves to establish the municipality. It informed a sense of outrage around two basic issues. The first was being let down by the government which had failed in its duty to protect the rights and the property of its citizens. The second was collecting revenue from which no direct benefit was derived. This was completely out of step with the rest of the colony as Sir George Verdon pointed out in 1857. [281] In Melbourne and Geelong, residents were enjoying the benefits of political representation as well as municipal government. Rates and taxes were not collected with armed escorts and all to varying degrees enjoyed or suffered the effects of progress and civilization. Adding insult to injury with many miners a major 'point of grievance' under the Goldfields Commission was seeing their taxes being squandered on unnecessary government buildings and overbearing staff rather than expenditure on legitimate local needs such as roads, courthouses, gaols, and other necessary public facilities.[282]

During the shallow alluvial phase settling down permanently was not considered by many miners due to the expectation that new and richer gold discoveries were yet to be found elsewhere – a point made very clear to the Government in the 1853 Investigation into Conditions on the Goldfields.[283] This was Secretary Foster's main justification for not providing adequate services as he explained in a series of letters to the *Age* in 1855. [284]Understandably, in the early stages, it was impossible to keep up

---

[280]David Held, 'The development of the modern state', 1992, p110

[281] Sir George Verdon, *The present and future of municipal government in Victoria*, Melbourne, 1858

[282] Ibid, pp 52-53, *Report of the Select Committee of the Goldfields together with the Minutes of Evidence and the Appendix*, 1 November 1853, points, 458, 714, 1610, 1611, 1613, 1623, 1343, 2007-2011, 118-123

[283] *Report of the Select Committee of the Goldfields together with the Minutes of Evidence and theAppendix*,1November1853,Parliament.Vic.gov.au/papers/govpub/VPARL1 854-55NoA76p[1]

[284] *Geelong Advertiser and Intelligencer* Tuesday June 5, 1855, Three Letters, 3

Local Consolidation After Eureka 155

with a rapid and constantly moving population, but by 1853 it was becoming clear that some centres, like Ballarat and Bendigo, were becoming permanent and needed more resources directed to them and less to other less permanent mining camps.

Commissioner Hardy, the NSW Goldfields Commissioner until 1854, called for fundamental reform that was based on local funding and services and voiced opinions that led to his eventual removal.[285] Hardy was not alone in this opinion which was vindicated and expanded on by R.H. Horne, the late Commissioner of Waranga who was even more specific calling for 'responsible government' both local and colonial.[286] This is what inspired the Ballarat Reform League Charter which stated:

> That it is the inalienable right of every citizen to have a voice in making the laws he is called upon to obey – that taxation without representation is tyranny ... Immediate objects of the Reform League An immediate change in the management of the Goldfields, by disbanding the Commissioners.[287]

Although primarily about the colonial government with the political changes 'contemplated,' in the new colonial constitution yet to be made into law, the more immediate concerns were local – with the Goldfields Commission and its behaviour and to ensure that they had a say in how their taxes were spent. This is an important and overlooked part of the Eureka miners' demands as it did not stop there. It was part of a campaign that continued after the Stockade and into 1855. As also noted, the charter included a call for 'a thorough and organised agitation of the goldfields and the towns.' While this is a matter of interpretation, the actions of

---

[285] Hardy, J R, *Squatters and Gold Diggers, their claims and rights*, Piddington, Sydney George Street 1855
[286] *The Age* (Melbourne) Monday May 28, 1855
[287] *Ballarat Reform League Charter*, Inwards Correspondence, VPRS 4066/P0000 Unit 1, November 1854 No 69

Victorian Reform League & Local Leadership

An article in the *Age* on 15 Jan 1855 claimed that the 'spirit of reform was dead' suggesting that after forcing changes to the Goldfields Commission, the Ballarat Reform League had achieved its aims. In reply, the newly formed Victorian Reform League declared that 'it was far from dead' indicating a change in focus to social issues stating, 'men are now beginning to perceive the close connection between their political freedom and social prosperity.' They, and it can be safely assumed that this included its leader J B Humffray, who added shortly after, we will not be frittering our time away on useless schemes but will be establishing local self-government through the application for municipal institutions.[288] It was the first shot fired by the local diggers to establish local control of the Ballarat goldfields after three years of tyranny under the Goldfields Commission and to implement their vision for a fair and prosperous future.

1855 began with a high level of uncertainty with the expected reorganisation of the current Commission administration and a tentative application of martial law. There were also large rallies in Melbourne, Geelong and Ballarat supporting the miners. With the expected official demise of the Gold-Fields Commission, it was unclear who was in charge at a local level and a crisis in governance quickly developed as crime got out of control and reactions by mobs and officials alike to local issues, created a sense of a community without leaders and on edge.

The events in Ballarat also reverberated loudly in Melbourne. The clash at Eureka reinforced a widely held perception by the

---

[288] *The Age* (Melbourne) Tuesday, January 23, 1855, 'Bendigo and Ballarat', page 4, Victoria, *Colonial Times* (Hobart) 21 March 1855, page 2 as published in the *Ballarat Times*

people of Victoria that the government's lack of timeliness in updating policies and laws was behind much of the social unrest. This was the point made by the *Age* early in January 1855:

> Social and political developments in this colony are so rapid, and the events of recent occurrence have been of so extraordinary a character, that a vigorous and independent policy might well be justified by circumstances. We can no more afford to wait for despatches to be transmitted to Downing Street and directions based upon them to reach us by post, than Lord Raglan could have afforded when he saw the enemy posted on the heights of Alamu to send to London for an order of Battle. The government here must be conducted on the spot.[289]

Immediately following Eureka, the insecurity of the Colonial Administration became evident as a rally was organised by the Mayor of Melbourne, at the instigation of the authorities (as claimed by the *Age*) in support of the 'laws and institutions of the colony'. Specifically targeted towards the recent events at Ballarat the rally spectacularly backfired, and turned instead, by the large crowd present, into an overwhelming condemnation of the Government.[290] A second meeting followed the next day that was reported to have attracted over ten thousand. Chaired by respected businessman and one of Melbourne's largest employers, Henry Langlands, the purpose was to emphasize that 'great constitutional principles were endangered.' Resolutions with 'enthusiastic unanimity' were made calling for the removal of the soldiers and a transitional body of seven citizens (the number necessary to form the Municipal Council) with the confidence of the community to be put in place for the transition for the restoration of peace at Ballarat.[291]

This submission was denied by Governor Hotham who chose instead to await the results of the Commission of Inquiry, pledging

---

[289] *The Age,* Melbourne, Saturday January 6, 1855, 'Summary',4
[290] *Ibid,* page 5
[291] Ibid,4

'to construct a new system of management in accordance to its report[292]. Nevertheless, the *Age* continued its attack on the Colonial Administration with its prophetic declaration of the solution to the current disaffection on the Gold-Fields:

> There are radical defects in the present system which must be remedied by radical reforms. The Ballarat affair renders it impossible that this should be deferred any longer. The fate of the license fee is sealed, and some source of revenue less obnoxious must be devised. For the rest, it is probable that an honest and thorough application of the principle of Representation to 'the digger' in connexion with central and *local government*, will do more than anything else to restore contentment, a cheerful obedience to laws, and that stern confidence in the integrity of power, which in free states is the only guarantee of public order. [293]

In the hiatus period at Ballarat, while Governor Hotham deliberated and prevaricated, the various groups such as the soldiers and police tended to look after their own affairs as the expected transition to the new Goldfields management was in process. The management of the township was more directly responsible to the Central Roads Board and the District Police Magistrate. However, with the local Police Magistrate D'Ewes discredited after the Bentley affair, people were in limbo as a replacement was being arranged. With responsibility for legal issues such as by-laws and criminal justice vested in a travelling Stipendiary Magistrate based outside of the locality, there was a growing perception that nobody was acting on behalf of the local population on critical issues.

Despite this, there were moves afoot to establish some form of civic leadership in the community and the source of this new movement was in the township, rather than amongst the diggers. The first local stirrings were reported by the correspondent for the

---

[292] Ibid
[293] Ibid

Colonial Times (Hobart) on 13 January 1855 who reported on 'a meeting of considerable importance' on the 4 January at Bath's Hotel. [294] The meeting, as the correspondent reported, was chaired by auctioneer, Henry Harris, later to lead the Chamber of Commerce, with the objective of garnering support for the establishment of a local branch of the Free and Accepted Masons. Its purpose was reported to be 'for the furtherance of loyal, constitutional and fraternal principles, which have been much required on these diggings.' The meeting was well attended with a 'respectable' and collegiate element that included 'the principal Camp Officials, merchants, storekeepers, and residents of the township. Nevertheless, however important this coming together of camp and township leaders and residents may have been, it did little to arrest the rising tension caused by the maladministration of the Goldfields Commission. This would need swift and decisive action and there was only one organisation with sufficient goodwill, especially amongst the mining population.

The Ballarat Reform League enjoyed respect and a high profile maintaining the wide support in the Ballarat District that it had generated in the lead-up to the Eureka Stockade. Its emphasis on consultative and considered action was a big factor in a developing sense of local self-government within the community. After the handing of the six-point charter to the Government, the future direction of the now Victorian Reform League was publicised in the *Ballarat Times*. *The Colonial Times* of Hobart thus reports:

> The objects of the Victorian Reform League are reviewed in the Ballaarat Times, and the opinion is expressed that such action as it contemplates is unnecessary till the arrival of the New Constitution. In the meantime, certain directions are indicated, in which the energies of the committee may be beneficially employed. Instead of frittering away their energies in vain attempts at public usefulness, the committee can use their best endeavours, as we understand they mean to do, to secure the

---

[294] *Colonial Times*, (Hobart) Saturday 13 January 1855, Ballarat, 2

> release of the remaining state prisoners; … Then too, they might see to the application of the Municipal Institutions Act of the Surveyor General to our district, by so doing we would gain a local self-governing power of unquestionable advantage, and at the same time be training ourselves for a more extensive interference in the management of the colony. [295]

Thus, after the dust had settled after Eureka, its role did not diminish but rather widened to take on local civic priorities as it waited for the delivery of the contemplated political aims of the Miners' Charter in the New Constitution. Thus, its actions were also timely and greatly needed as a general perception of lawlessness and lack of safety was pervading the community. Relations between the locals, the police and the military continued to be hostile. The military presence, even before Eureka, was viewed as unnecessary and in a very poor light as a Geelong correspondent noted in September 1854:

> The utility of any soldiers on the goldfields is more than questionable unless we except those (sappers and miners, I believe) who are at present engaged in taking a survey from which to make a model of Ballarat for the forthcoming Paris exhibition.[296]

Their reputation was made worse by their heavy drinking and only the publicans were sorry to see most of them re-assigned in the new year[297]. Ill feelings towards the soldiers intensified and skirmishes between the locals and 'joes' occasionally exploded into unrestrained violence. One episode on Friday night of 5 January 1855 at Hanmer's theatre, saw two drunken troopers harassed by the jeering crowd at the close of the performance. One of the troopers in response fired his pistol into the crowd, wounding a

---

[295] *Colonial Times* (Hobart) Wednesday 21 March 1855, Victoria, 2
[296] *Geelong Advertiser and Intelligencer* (Vic), Monday, 18 Sept 1854, 'Ballarat', 4
[297] ibid

man in the chest. His mate retaliated with a 'loaded whip' fatally injuring the uniformed assailant.[298]

The Law & Order Crisis

This was not unexpected as the *Colonial Times* correspondent reported that the diggings were under a very close watch by police, who patrolled each night dishing out 'just deserts' to the rowdy mob elements.[299] However, the close monitoring of the diggings soon fell away as the likelihood of a mass uprising began to appear less likely. By April, it was the miners and townsfolk complaining of a need for protection as crime began to increase to an alarming level and it was this issue that sparked an even greater impetus for Municipal Government. That criminals were becoming very audacious in the face of poor law enforcement is exemplified by the 'audacious scoundrel' who tried unsuccessfully to make off with the cash box in a well-patronised Charlie Napier Hotel on the Saturday night session on 7 April.[300]

Adding to the general feeling of unease, the large contingent of redcoats continued to throw their weight about. *The Age* reported that 'since the Eureka massacre, there had sprung up a very bad feeling towards the soldiers.'[301] An altercation on 31 Jan received a great deal of attention when a party of over fifty redcoats attempted to gate-crash a party of Cornishmen in the township and were ejected after a 'lively skirmish'.[302] A few weeks later they were reported as refusing the roadworkers access to government land for roadmaking materials at gunpoint causing lengthy delays as an appeal was made to the Resident Warden and eventually to the Colonial Secretary to overrule them.[303] As the year progressed

---

[298] *Colonial Times*, (Hobart), Saturday 6 January 1855, Ballarat, 2
[299] *Colonial Times* (Hobart) Saturday 13 January 1855, Ballarat, 2
[300] *The Age* (Melbourne) Tuesday April 10th, 1855, Ballarat, 5
[301] *The Age* Melbourne, Thursday 1st February 1855, Ballarat, 5
[302] ibid
[303] *The Geelong Advertiser and Intelligencer*, Monday 19th March 1855, Ballarat, 2

there were reports of 'pranks' such as demanding to be included in local 'shouts' at drinking establishments and harassing people on the roads.[304]

Overblown reactions to petty crimes also were an indication of a community on edge. An attempted pickpocketing incident at the end of January 1855 attracted a large crowd of two to three hundred diggers who captured the miscreants and escorted them to the police camp. The police reaction was out of proportion as Sub-Inspector Kirk made a charge at the crowd with all available mounted and foot police to disperse them.[305] As the year progressed the malaise of governance deepened and the numbers and severity of the crimes increased to the extent that people had had enough of the poor responses of the police and the gold-fields oversight.

There were well-founded rumours of collusion and collaboration of the soldiers with criminal elements that persisted for most of the year.[306] This more than anything forced the townsfolk and diggers to band together to find solutions to the serious threats to civic harmony. The *Geelong Advertiser* correspondent noted this increased attention to civic concerns in his summary of Ballarat local events on 12 April:

> Political grievances are about to give way to the consideration of social evils and from the temper which is already manifest on all sides, there is a fear that death may again become too familiar to our ears and eyes.

Conditions in the Creswick area early in the new year of 1855 were described by the Age correspondent as 'unsettled and revolutionary' due in most part to the 'inefficiency of the police force.' He noted that:

---

[304] *The Age* (Melbourne, Vic: 1854 - 1954), Tuesday 17 April 1855, page 5, see appendix 2
[305] *The Age* Melbourne, Thursday 1February 1855, Ballarat, 5
[306] *The Geelong Advertiser and Intelligencer*, Ballarat, Wednesday 15 August, 1855,3

> The laws affecting the management of the Goldfields are no doubt both unjust and inoperative; but the evil alluded to requires immediate attention, else lynch law must soon assume the place of the imbecile executive.[307]

These were serious concerns by many responsible locals who feared the social breakdown that could come with outraged locals taking the law into their own hands. But the catalyst for permanent change came in the weeks between the end of March and the middle of April.

A group of horsemen had become incredibly bold in their activities pillaging the local population openly during the daylight hours. Camped in the bush at Slatey Creek, about two kilometres south of Creswick under the guise of conducting a legitimate business, they had become the most notorious element in a wave of crime that was experienced from Ballarat almost to Melbourne and across to Geelong. As the *Age* correspondent reported:

> The organised villainy was content at first with simple stick up and rifling the person of their victim of any valuables. We now have gone through all the stages from that to deliberate murder. ... Not only are individuals selected, tents gutted in open day, articles of small value as well as those of importance carried off. Hotels are stuck up, and if a strong hand is not brought to bear on the present state of things, not only to prevent its spread, ... we will but too soon hear of the conveyances, the banks, aye, and even the government escorts being laid under tribute to these 'plunderers' and armed ruffians. [308]

While some considered banding together for 'mutual protection' to put down the evil scourge, most were not in favour of vigilantism and the lynch, preferring to trust the leaders who had

---

[307] *The Age* Melbourne Thursday 1 February 1855, Creswick's Creek, 5
[308] ibid

guided them through the last six months to seek a more legal and constitutional solution.

Nevertheless, 'Self Protection' societies, were attracting a lot of interest, the most well-known calling themselves 'the Crow Club[309]' formed after the inquiry chaired by the local Victorian Reform League, local residents and commercial establishments. Unlike other such organizations originating in the central goldfields around Bendigo,[310] it existed purely for 'protection' denying any religious and political affiliations.[311] The *Age* reporting on this development screamed 'Lynch Law at Ballarat' making wild accusations that the population now was at war with a band of Vandemonians, two hundred strong, manned in some part by rogue police.[312] However, the reality which was much less sensational, was serious enough to galvanise local leaders to stand up for the community and garner support for action. The shooting death of the perpetrator of an attempted robbery at the George Hotel did evoke a response that there should be more such shootings to assist the police in their endeavours.[313]

The bushrangers were eventually captured along with a treasure trove of loot that filled several large drays, in a daring night-time raid that caught the gang asleep and unarmed in their bush hide-out at Slatey Creek.[314] The heroics of Sub-Inspector Nicholson and his band of six officers restored some faith in the local constabulary, but the three months of terror inflicted by this gang on top of everything else did too much to arouse the outrage of the local community which would not be silenced. And as Eureka had demonstrated, once stirred up, the mining community and in

---

[309] Because they met at the "Crow' tea rooms next to the Exhibition Mart on the Melbourne Road

[310] *Bendigo Advertiser*, Wednesday 26 September 1855, Original Correspondence: The Working Miners' Protection Society, page 3

[311] *Mount Alexander Mail* Friday 4 May 1855 "Storekeepers' Association, 3

[312] *The Age* 11 April 1855 Lynch Law at Ballarat, 5

[313] *The Geelong Advertiser and Intelligencer*, Thursday 15 February 1855, 2

[314] *The Geelong Advertiser and Intelligencer*, Friday, 20 April 1855, Ballarat, 2

this case, the storekeepers themselves were directly impacted by the bushrangers plundering their stock and trade and personal possessions. The search for a permanent solution thus gave rise to the beginnings of the Municipal Corporation. This action, following the tried-and-true methods employed in the mining dispute, led to the election of committees to establish facts and seek redress through parliamentary petition.

As a sub-committee of the newly formed Victorian Reform League, the Ballarat members, by their consultative approach, in early April 1855, appointed a commission to enquire into these and other events sitting for three days from seven PM at the Star Hotel with the intention of compiling a report.[315] The report stated that it was a

> memorial of the miners and storekeepers of Ballarat … proving that the police are totally inefficient in affording protection … and that your Excellency will take immediate steps for providing a sufficient force of police … and thereby save your memorialists the expense and inconvenience of organising themselves for mutual protection. … signed R Muir Chairman.'

Nevertheless, as a response to public concern, it was moved by Mr Binney of the firm Binney & Gillot and seconded by Mr Allen, a miner, that a committee also be formed for the purpose of the 'protection of life and property' made up of Mr Robert Muir, Rolf, Oddie, Wilson, Abrahams, Mr H R Nicholls, Lester, Norman, C F Nicholls and W C Weekes with the power to add to their number as they saw fit.[316] It would appear, however, that this was not the only initiative taken with the Geelong Advertiser reporting on the ferocity of the 'silly' freelance activities of a 'Mr Goodman' and his squatting and mercantile supporters in keeping the mining interests 'down.' Such activity was condemned as running counter to the

---

[315] *The Age* Melbourne, Vic, Wed 4th April 1855, Ballarat, 5, see full article appendix III page 196-198
[316] *The Age*, Melbourne, Vic, Tuesday, April 17, 1855, 5

aims of the reform movement which needed to be 'settled equitably for the peace and prosperity of the colony'.[317] As the *Age* reported, Mr Weekes (who later served on the Miners' Court) in reading the report stated that the matter was of the highest importance and that he wished always to act constitutionally. [318]The report was then approved for printing and duly signed by H R Nicholls, H T Holyoake, and C F Nicholls.[319]

Cr Robert Muir: from the collection of The Ballarat Historical Society, section of B/W photo of *Ballarat's first Council 1856, Cr Dr J. Stewart, Cr J Oddie, Cr A B Rankin, Cr R Muir, Cr W Tulloch, Cr J S Carver.* Catalogue No 106.81

The Hon John Basson Humffray, pastel on brown paper by Thomas Flintoff, 10 August 1859. State Library of Victoria catalogue No H325

Thus, in this vein, in response to the law-and-order crisis, a meeting was called on Saturday 16th April, to hand the matter over to the local community for action. The meeting was chaired by Mr Robert Muir of the drapery firm, Muir Bros a man whose energy and ambition for Ballarat West would be highly influential in its rapid development over the next few years. Mr J B. Humffray then took

---

[317] *The Geelong Advertiser and Intelligencer Thursday* 10 May 1855, Ballarat, page 2
[318] *The Age*, Melbourne, Vic, Tuesday, April 17, 1855, 5
[319] Ibid, for a full copy of the article see Appendix 1II

Local Consolidation After Eureka

the chair and following the pre-amble of the Miners' Charter asserted, as reported by the *Age* correspondent:

> ... there was a well-known sound political maxim, that for a people to be well governed they must govern themselves, would it not be better for them to take the law into their own hands. He did not mean in the seditious sense about which so much learned nonsense had been uttered of late. But that the people should insist on the due administration of justice; and that in as much as the people of Ballarat paid their proportion of taxation, they ought to have their proportion of protection to life and property. Ballarat must be declared a municipality, and the people will secure two important political rights, namely, the raising of local taxation and expending of the same for the benefit of those who pay it, and thus prevent its being squandered by a system of official centralization.[320]

Ballarat vs the Miners

In elaborating on the meeting, the *Mount Alexander Mail* reported that the petition drafted by the Victoria Reform League and read by J B Humffray also requested that 'steps should be taken for declaring the township a municipality in order that the police might be placed under the management of those who understood local requirements."[321] However, as it transpired, the colonial government, although severely chastened by the public over their handling of the Eureka affair, was only prepared to propose a partial remedy in accepting the petition, being unmovable on the issue of granting local control over the Ballarat police force.

Thus, after submitting the petition to the Governor, the response came in the form of a suggestion from the Colonial Secretary on May 25 endorsing the measures already adopted:

> His Excellency will direct that such police as can be spared from other districts shall be sent to Ballarat, but he desires me to say that in the present condition of the country no amount of police

---

[320] *The Age*, Melbourne, Tuesday April 17, 1855, page 5
[321] *Mount Alexander Mail*, Friday 4th May 1855, 3

> force which could, consistently with the financial interests of the colony, be maintained, would, in his judgement be sufficient for the protection of the present widely scattered goldfields of Victoria. The Governor is satisfied that a general desire exists at Ballarat to maintain the law and uphold order, and he confidently trusts that the holders of property on the Ballarat gold-field will enrol themselves as special constables and unite with the police in quelling disturbance; and what is of more consequence, show that they are lovers of order, and firm in their determination to aid the local authorities.[322]

It was clear that police matters would remain with the central government as it was for all municipalities in the Australian colonies with local government not necessarily local self-government as proposed by Joshua Toulmin-Smith and his chartist colleagues back in England.

Nevertheless, although this was the spark that began the movement towards municipal government, law and order was just the first hurdle to cross. There was an even bigger obstacle in the path of the township and its residents and that was its position concerning the gold deposits underneath its streets. It was the one defining issue on which everything hinged.

In early 1855 Ballarat was a typical mining town serving the commercial needs of the mining population However, by early 1856, Ballarat West could legitimately claim to be the regional centre of commerce. It was the only place in the district where private town land could be purchased for residential purposes. It also could legitimately claim to be Ballarat itself by the official survey of the township in 1852 and where almost all the government and financial service offices were located. However, maintaining that status in 1855 was more a result of faith than anything else because for a while nothing was one hundred per cent certain as confidences waxed and waned following the fluctuating fortunes of the mining activity. Nevertheless, by the

---

[322] *The Age* (Melbourne) Monday June 4th, Ballarat News, 5

end of July 1855 fears for public safety at least, had eased due in no small part to the success of the crime prevention measures employed by the local committee. This also resulted in the disbanding of the Ballarat Volunteer Protection Society or the 'Crow Club' as it was commonly named.[323]

Although the 1852 survey by W S Urquart showed Sturt Street as the main 'boulevard', it was Lydiard Street in 1855-1857 that was the main centre of business. It included the district transport hub of Cobb & Co and the booking office of Carrington & Rollins on the Sturt Street south corner on land owned by Thomas Bath. This large transit centre came with a livery of twenty-seven stables and a large storage and staging facility. All traffic from Geelong and Melbourne came through this centre – the first stopping place for those seeking their fortunes on the goldfield. It was a large allotment that covered almost half an acre and arguably was Ballarat West's most prime real estate asset. Next door was Bath's Hotel, the premier establishment in the district and the weighbridge, which until 1856 was the only one until the council facility was set up at the market square on the corner of Mair and Doveton Streets. The gold buyers were also located in this central precinct along with the three major Banks – the Bank of NSW, the Bank of Victoria and the Colonial Bank as well as all the branch offices for the Colonial Government including the post office and Surveyor's Office. It was the post office and its location that was to be one of the major delineations between east and west Ballarat in 1857 as the different municipalities asserted themselves in the district.[324]

---

[323] *Geelong Advertiser and Intelligencer*, (Victoria) August 9, 1855, The Ballarat Volunteer Protection Society, page 2, *Mount Alexander Mail*, Friday 4 May 1855, 'Self-Protection,' page 3

[324] *The Star* (Ballarat) Wednesday 29 July 1857, 'Post Office Removal'

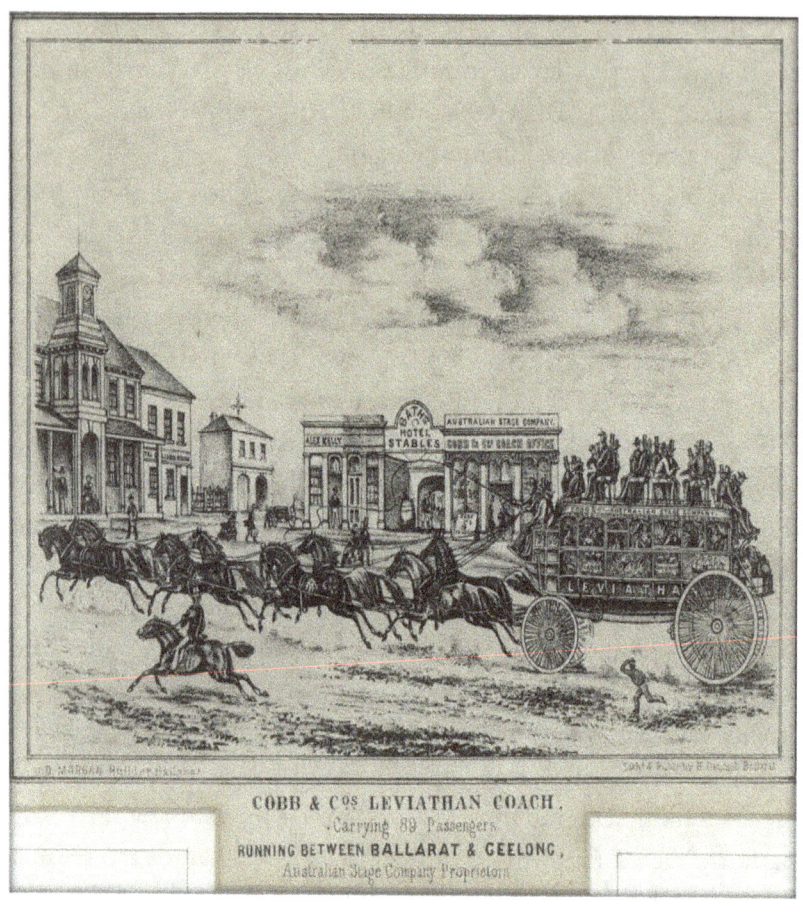

Cobb & Co Leviathan Coach arriving at Bath's Corner ca 1860. The booking office was on the corner of Sturt and Lydiard and Bath's Hotel was next door with a 'right of way' approved in 1856 by the council, separating the two buildings. Note the front entrance to the hotel on Bath's Lane. Deutsch, H. Cobb & Cos. *Leviathan Coach Carrying 89 Passengers, Running between Ballarat & Geelong* [Vic.] H. Deutsch., 1862, accessed online http://search.slv.vic.gov.au/primo-explore/fulldisplay?vid=MAIN&docid=SLV_VOYAGER1817940&context=L

After serving as chairman of the new Council, James Oddie believed that West was where it should stay to service a growing population and agricultural industry to the north and west of Ballarat as well as the financial establishments and land agents –

most of which were in Ballarat West.[325] Besides, as Wymond of Lydiard Street drapery firm Wymond & Vasey asserted, long-term township landowners like himself 'knew what they were about.'[326]

However, as events transpired, that confidence was severely tested as it wasn't the post office that provided the biggest challenge to the township in 1855. Mining was threatening its very existence. During 1854 and 1855, this uncertainty was increased by opportunist traders along the flat on the Main Road from Buninyong, leasing government land to cater to the needs of the nearby miners. This was not surprising as it had become customary for suppliers to be as close as possible to where the work was taking place. Therefore, from early 1855 the flat along the Yarrowee through to the bridge below Bakery Hill was experiencing a building boom supplying all sorts of goods, primarily drink. As the planning and survey documents for the newly created Ballarat East municipality confirm, intense competition for positions had resulted in an alarming number of exceedingly small lots so described by a news correspondent as 'moving forward in battalions on each side of the new road leading to the bridge.'

While in the township on freehold land, there was also growing evidence of a more permanent appearance with 'several buildings of stone, brick, wood and iron springing up.'[327] The activity along the flat, however, had raised the ire of those in the town who increasingly saw this as a threat to their long-term security, the value of their assets and more importantly, their profit margins. By the middle of 1854, the mining activity and the buildings that accompanied had crossed the river and were approaching the township boundary at Lydiard Street on the escarpment just above present-day Albert Street.[328]

---

[325] *ibid*
[326] *ibid*
[327] Ballarat, *The Age* Melbourne, Vic, Wednesday 4 April 1855, page 5
[328] See page 46 for 1855 map of township.

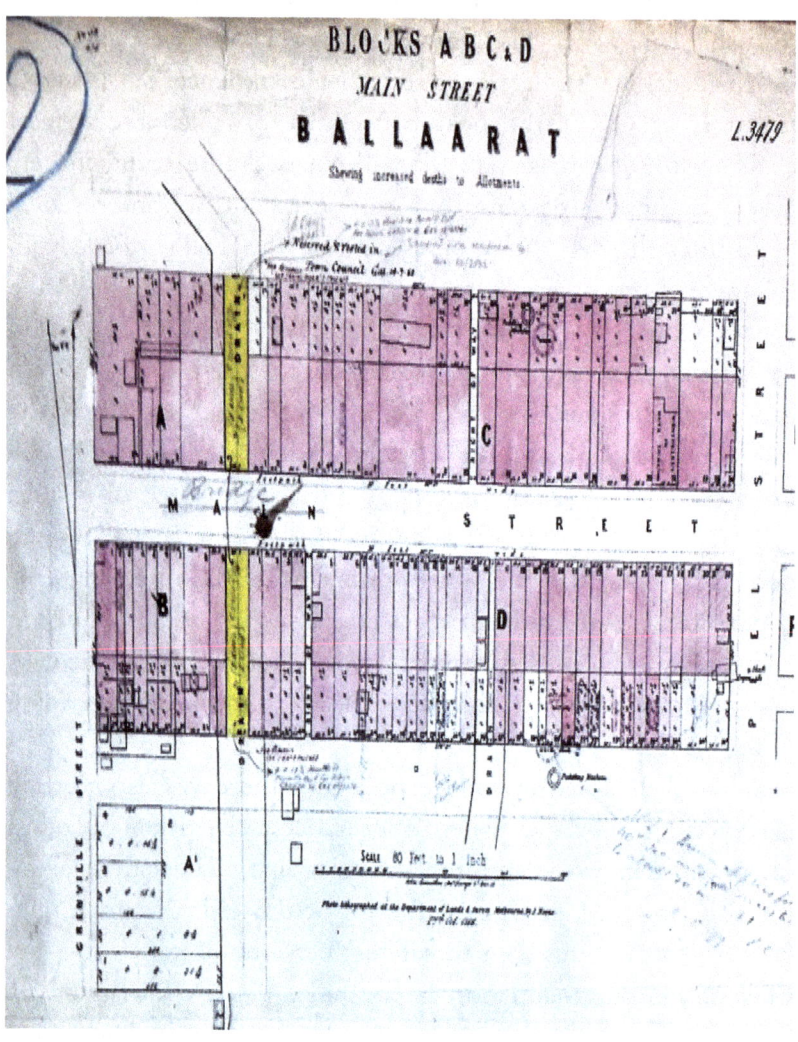

1857 Plan detailing surveyed lots for Main Street (now Bridge Street) Ballarat East and Bakery Hill. Public Records Office VPRS 2500 P0000/1 Ballarat Municipal Council Letters Inward January – December 1856-1857 *Bridge over the Yarrowee in yellow marks the boundary set in 1856 – lots on the west side fell into Ballarat West.*

Local Consolidation After Eureka

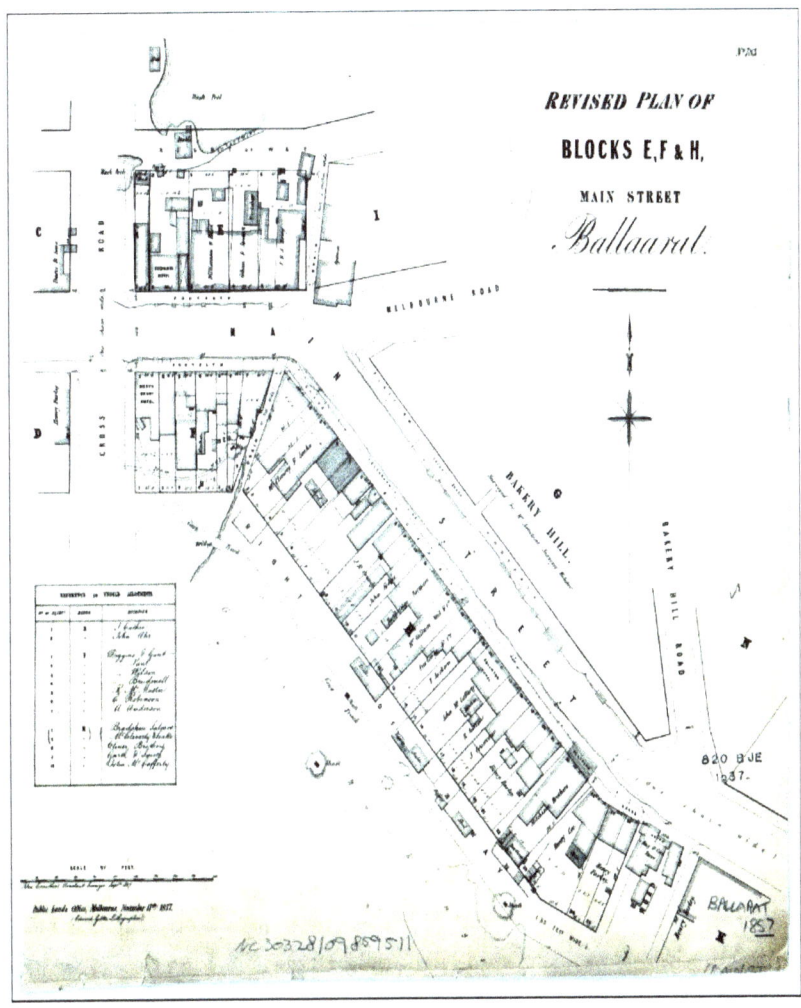

1857 Plan detailing surveyed lots for Main Road to Peel Street Ballarat East and Bakery Hill. Public Records Office VPRS 2500 P0000/1 Ballarat Municipal Council Letters Inward January – December 1856-1857

It was the careful construction of a drinking establishment provocatively erected on the boundary line that was the final straw, dubbed by the *Geelong Advertiser* correspondent, that had the potential to be 'of greater interest than the occupation of the Danubian Provinces by the Russians.'[329] The freeholders in the town were reported to be 'very wroth that tents and stores were allowed so near to their property on which they had expended so much money.'[330] This situation reached an impasse in September 1854 as the Gravel Pits lead finally reached the township boundary where building activity stopped as deputations from miners and town storekeepers were lodged with the Governor for protective measures. The question on the lips of the population was 'how is the Government going to act if the Gravel Pits heads into the township?'[331]

The Governor ruled first in favour of the township and then as he had prevaricated for over six months, overturned his decision in favour of the miners on the flat early in 1855[332]. This was due in no small part to the enterprising actions of entrepreneurs who, in the meantime had established a wide variety of commercial premises, even speculating substantial sums with options placed on possible shopfront positions. *The Age* correspondent described it as 'a great centre of business, frontages began to command high prices, and though on crown lands, the stores along the road were transformed into permanent premises.'[333]

By June of 1855, there was a growing belief that the township would soon be overtaken as some commentators began calling it a 'parchment township.'[334] As the leads progressed at a quicker pace with steam technology[335] in that direction some were expecting that the Government should provide the means to repurchase the

---

[329] *Geelong Advertiser and Intelligencer*, Wednesday, 20 September 1854, Ballarat, page 4
[330] *Ibid*
[331] *ibid*
[332] *The Age* 21 Feb 1855, Ballarat, page 3
[333] *The Age*, 21 Feb 1855, page 3 *Ballarat*
[334] *The Age* (Melbourne) Thursday 29 June 1855 Ballarat, page 5
[335] *The Age* (Melbourne) Wednesday 28th June 1855 Ballarat, page 5

Local Consolidation After Eureka 175

township land from the sale of the occupied lots on the flat.[336] More weight was added to this position later in the year as the London Chartered Bank of Australia established a branch on the flat, providing a great deal of relief to the local diggers who had been compelled to make an uphill 'trudge to the township to do their banking business.'[337] In addition, the residents and traders along Main Road were now viewing the locality as a permanent arrangement. One enterprising trader Mr F Reid, in competition with the establishments in the township, had fitted out his premises with gas renaming it 'the Gas Saloon' illuminated by gas manufactured on the premises.[338]

October 1855 however was a turning point as diminishing returns from the Gravel Pits and Golden Point leads sparked a search for the lead in several directions. While the westward ventures continued to threaten the township premises on Lydiard Street another series of operations had plans of digging up the government camp to the northeast. If allowed unrestricted access, the practice of shepherding would have overwhelmed the whole central township grid with shafts on the claims already marked out. Consequently, the Resident Warden of the Gold Department declared a pause on mining while he lodged an appeal to the Governor for direction.[339] The Geological survey map below shows the extent of the alluvial shafts (rows of dots) following the Golden Point Lead (left) and Gravel Pits lead (centre) and Red Hill (right), relevant to this period stopping at the escarpment. The concerns were valid and greatly worrying as to the future of the local gold industry.

---

[336] *The Age*, 21st Feb 1855, page 3 *Ballarat*
[337] *The Age*, Friday 10th August 1855, Mining intelligence Ballarat, page 5
[338] *The Age*, Saturday, August 11, 1855, Ballarat, page 5
[339] *The Age* (Melbourne) Saturday 13 October 13, 1855, Ballarat, page 6, *The Argus* (Melbourne) Saturday October 13, 1855, Domestic Intelligence, 5

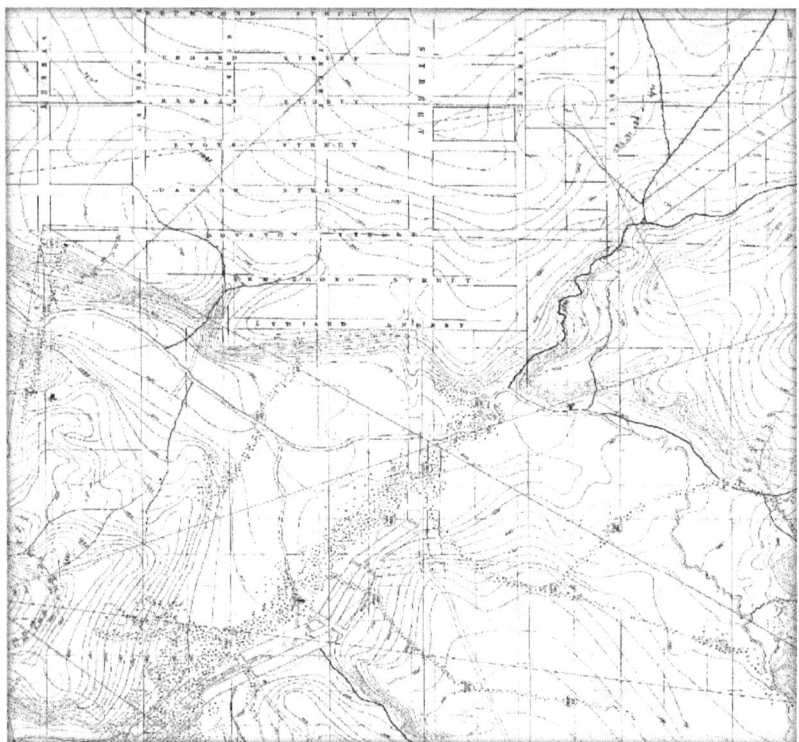

Rows of dots indicating shafts sunk along leads leading to the Township. This survey map is dated 1906, however without the mines along the escarpment or any shown inside the town as does the 1857 survey of Ballarat South, we can assume that it refers to the period 1855 – 1856, VPRS 8168

Considering the width of the Gravel Pits lead and the possibility of them all joining under the township, it raised the prospect of even bigger returns by employing heavy engineering and other capital-intensive methods. However, this brought into question the viability of the township itself. Thomas Bath, therefore, the largest local proprietor as the owner of the Bath's Hotel complex that included a weighbridge, stables and other buildings on the Sturt Street and Lydiard Street corner, had to put the concerns to rest while also hoping to cash in on the speculation. Employing a syndicate of hopeful diggers, substance was provided to the much-touted potential of riches, by a shaft being sunk out the front of

Local Consolidation After Eureka

his hotel in Lydiard Street, the unofficial main street at the time.[340] As Bath and his associates continued to descend without success during 1855, Wymond & Vasey, drapers on the Mair Street side of Lydiard Street, also decided to try, announcing that the lead would be found at 240 feet.[341] While ultimately unsuccessful, it inspired several other ventures to look for the extension of the rich lead. This then resulted in the fortuitous find of a branch of the Gravel Pits lead running in parallel with the Yarrowee, the results of which became the economic foundation for the municipality and its massive extension from 1856. Thus, with the attention diverted southward towards White Flat[342] and under the basalt of Ballarat South township was spared from further serious disruption from mining.

Nevertheless, Bath's 'fishing expedition' remained a thorn in the side of the township and with the new municipality in the year following. By June of 1856, he remained in the grip of gold fever, having sunk to almost three hundred feet. A party of Cornish miners that had joined him with an engine and had declined offers of £500 each for their shares which appeared to be based more on speculation than on any real discovery.[343] Nevertheless, this had given encouragement to other enterprising groups convinced by similar contrarian theories about the south branch of the Gravel Pits lead. Falling just inside the township's southern boundary along the Yarrowee it would test the authority of the new council in the following year.[344]

While the issue of mining in the township continued to fester, the coming of the telegraph was greatly anticipated in Ballarat

---

[340] *The Age* Saturday, 13th Oct 1855
[341] *The Age* (Melbourne) Friday 9 November 1855, Ballarat, 6
[342] *Portland Guardian and Normanby General Advisor*, Thursday 25 October 1855, Ballarat Goldfields, 3
[343] *Geelong Advertiser and Intelligencer* Wednesday, 4 June 1856, Ballarat, 2
[344] Ibid, Ballarat, Friday 6 June 1856, 2 *Portland Guardian and Normanby General Advertiser*, Monday 16 June 1856, Mining on the Ballarat Township, 3, Ibid, Wednesday 11 June 1856, Ballarat, 2

West. Apart from solidifying faith in the township's future into something more concrete, it was also

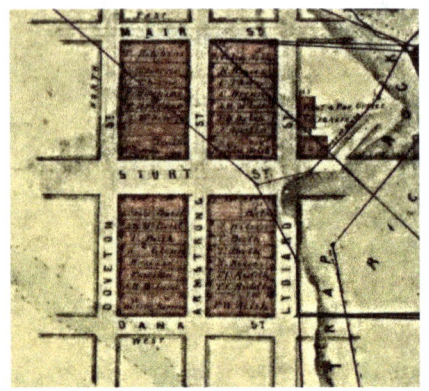

Enlargement of Township -shown on Ballarat First Survey 1852, with 1856 proposed sites of Telegraph, Patents Office and new Post Office on Lydiard Street. Note also red lines drawn by the Court of Mines noting possible future mining activity. VPRS 8168 P0005 FEAT 665A

viewed as the solution to the flow of information, social cohesion and as a deterrent to crime with particular benefit to the commercial interests in the township where an exchange would be located. The correspondent for the *Geelong Advertiser* tabled a letter from W H Butcher of the Proposed Joint-Stock Company, listing the benefits of instantaneous communication for ordering, pricing, news as well as putting down unfounded rumours of gold discoveries, greatly reducing the numbers of itinerants wandering the countryside.

He also emphasised the crime-prevention merits of the telegraph especially regarding endemic horse theft as brands could be 'instantly transmitted to all the places at which horses are usually sold.'[345]

While such endorsements were providing a greater sense of security for Ballarat West, the interests of the miners and traders east of the river continued to cause complications and delays for the process of municipal incorporation that had gained impetus after the law-and-order crisis in April. This was due to competing petitions raised that represented the township only and another that included the Main Road traders on the eastern side of the Yarrowee River. Unfortunately, as it stood, both petitions were

---

[345] *Geelong Advertiser and Intelligencer*, Electric Telegraph to Ballarat, Thursday 2 August 1855, 2

returned with one of them twenty signatures short as the *Age* reports:

> Oh, routine, routine! When will you learn that the letter of the law killeth but the spirit giveth life? No doubt, the serious obstruction to our wishes will soon be removed; but while we are straining at gnats at official difficulties, we are swallowing camels in the shape of serious accidents to life and limb, hindrances to business and general discomfort among a population of twenty thousand people, and all because the petition wanted twenty names. [346]

Following this, a meeting was called on Monday 13 August 1855 [347] where it was decided that the petition put up by Mr H R Nicholls[348], which included most of the Main Road proprietors, would be replaced by combining them both into one petition that was based on the provisions in the Surveyor-General's Municipalities Act.[349]

This confusion resulted in the final petition being gazetted twice as the Government sought clarification. The second petition gazetted on October 2, 1855, thus is a resubmission of the combined petition gazetted on September 4, 1855. This indicates the disputed process with the accepted version being an amalgamation of Township landowners and Main Road proprietors and residents who would be part of a future extension, as suggested by the Governor.[350] Significantly this final version omits most of the officers and councillors of the Municipality with

---

[346] *The Age,* Melbourne, Tuesday 14 August, Ballarat, 5

[347] *The Argus,* Melbourne, Ballarat, Monday, 20 August 1855, 7

[348] Due, no doubt to his flood mitigation project at White's Flat on the Yarrowee

[349] *The Argus*, Melbourne, Monday 20 August 1855, 7

[350] *The Age* (Melbourne) Saturday 25 August 1855, Ballarat, for a list of petitioners see Ballarat (Vic.). Council. *City Council of Ballarat: the Mayor's special report, 25th anniversary, 1881* Ballarat 1881, appendix VII, page 202-205, See also Appendix VI & V, page 199-200, State Library of Victoria\ *Victoria Government Gazette* No. 86 Tuesday September 4 1855, page 2242, No. 97, Tuesday October 2 1855, page 2472, neither of which includes the list of petitioners.

Thomas Comb, the future Town Clerk, and Councillors Robert Muir, William Tulloch, and James Stewart the only participants.

This was a problem that reflected the differences in land tenure. On one hand, there were those who had purchased and occupied lots surveyed in the township and on the other were those such as the Main Road traders who were occupiers of Crown Land and would not be subject to the authority of the proposed municipality. This difference was at the heart of the East-West division. As the Act stated, the petition was to be presented by 300 householders within an area of nine square miles and extended to incorporate an area with an average of thirty-six householders to the square mile. The Ballarat East lots, however in 1855 and at the commencement of the municipality in 1856, were leasehold, Crown land and commercial rather than residential and occupiers would not be required to pay rates or abide by council bye-laws. The township on the other hand immediately met all the requirements of the Act, which proved to be a powerful reinforcement of the validity of the Western position. Thus, once the petition was finalised, the Ballarat West Township faction immediately tossed aside all overtures of accommodation with Main Road. A further meeting to address the issue of commercial establishments occupying crown land in the township was immediately called.[351]

With Mr Robert Muir in the chair, a committee was formed to monitor the situation and to petition the Governor to enforce their pre-eminent rights as freeholders. The committee stated that it viewed 'the erection of business premises on unsold lands within the town boundary, as a violation of the rights of landed proprietors, and it pledged itself to unite for the removal of all such places within the town boundary.'[352] This, no doubt, was due firstly to the loss of rental income endured by squatting, but also by the promise of Acting Governor Haines to consider moving the

---

[351] *The Argus*, Melbourne, Ballarat, Monday, 20 August 1855, 7
[352] ibid

Local Consolidation After Eureka 181

township boundary 'towards the flat' to incorporate the commercial premises along Main Road.[353] The intention was to force the issue of making lessees become owners, remove their competitive advantage and significantly boost future rate revenue.[354] This promise was only partially kept with the eastern municipal boundary extended only as far as the Yarrowee River[355]. The option to extend beyond the river nevertheless was seriously considered early in 1856 by the new council with an approach to the Government considered to extend the eastern boundary by two miles to incorporate proposed eastern property sales.[356]

However, this plan was discarded after incorporation in 1856 in favour of extending southward towards Sebastopol and the new cooperative mining projects.[357] The hard-line was maintained due partly to the problems of cost and inconvenience in creating a road three chains wide despite approval given by the Central Roads Board to extend 'the Main Road' into the southern end of Sturt Street[358]. More importantly in its existing state the Main Road district was not considered compatible with Ballarat West due to 'its insalubrity as an extension to the township.'[359] This would also have been driven by the expectation of major developments mooted during 1856 such as the telegraph exchange, railway terminus on Soldiers' Hill[360] and a new post office making them

---

[353] *Geelong Advertiser and Intelligencer*, Wednesday August 22, Ballarat, page 2 and Thursday August 30, 1855, Ballarat page 3, State Library of Victoria*Victoria Government Gazette*, Tuesday, December 18, 1855, page 3275
[354] *Geelong Advertiser an Intelligencer*, Wednesday August 22, Ballarat, page 2
[355] State Library of Victoria*Victoria Government Gazette*, Tuesday, December 18, 1855, page 3275, see Appendix VI, page 201 for proscribed boundaries.
[356] VPRS 13007 P0001 Council Minutes March 4, 1856
[357] Ballarat South Extension found in Public Records Office VPRS 2500 P0000/1 Ballarat Municipal Council Letters Inward January – December 1856-1857, Council Minutes Wednesday July 23, 1856, as published in *The Star* (Ballarat) Thursday July 24, 1856, page 2, see also appendix IX page 208
[358] VPRS 13007 P0001 *Council Minutes*, February 29, 1856
[359] *ibid*, April 2, 1856.
[360] *The Star* (Ballarat) Thursday September 18, 1856, The Railway Route, page 2

the commercial hub in the near future[361]. The relative security of the high ground on the escarpment was always considered their greatest asset, especially on the north side of Sturt Street which was less likely to be affected by mining.

With such a multiplicity of competing interests during 1855, it was no surprise to anyone in August 1855 when the Argus reported that local progress had stalled under the present arrangement. It was recognised by all concerned wrote the correspondent 'that it was high time that some change in public affairs took place … the want of some official whose duty should be to watch progress and point out the requirements of the township is most seriously felt'.[362] There was not long to wait, with the emergence of leaders like Robert Muir, of the Melbourne drapery firm Muir Bros, James Oddie of Auctioneers J & T Oddie, Dr. James Stewart, solicitor, Mr Rankin, seeking nomination for foundational positions on the new council early in 1856.

---

[361] *The Age* (Melbourne) Saturday May 24, 1856, Postal, Rail and Telegraph Communication, page 2
[362] *The Argus*, Melbourne, Ballarat, Monday, 20th August 1855, 7

Local Consolidation After Eureka 183

Black and white photo of Ballarat's first Council 1856, Cr Dr J. Stewart, Cr J Oddie, Cr A B Rankin, Cr R Muir, Cr W Tulloch, Cr J S Carver. From the collection of The Ballarat Historical Society, Catalogue No 106.81. *This is a collage made much later as all were young men in 1856*

The Municipal Council of Ballarat have in their hands a power that is of the utmost importance to the wellbeing of this community, and which is deserving of the utmost consideration. – The Age 22/1/1856

11.1856 Ballarat West: Fit and Proper Persons

The First Election

After his elevation to the Legislative Council in 1855, J B. Humffray took on the matter of the Municipality as a priority. On the agenda for the Legislative Council on December 11 of 1855, J B Humffray gave notice, as he had on many occasions, that on the thirteenth he would be requesting information on the three most pressing issues for Ballarat, the progress on plans to erect a court house and County Court, to grant municipal institutions to Ballarat and the progress on the telegraph from Geelong to Ballarat.[363] They were all of equally vital importance in the integration of Ballarat into the fabric of colonial society conceptually and physically. The petition for municipality, however, ended up being the first to be achieved, granted on 15 December 1855 and formally announced in the press on 24 December 1855.[364]

There was little time wasted in taking advantage of the attainment of the new status for Ballarat. In less than two weeks after the announcement in the press and despite all the festivities of the Christmas and New Year period, a meeting was called for Saturday 5 January 1856 to propose the composition of the new

---

[363] *The Geelong Advertiser and Intelligencer*, Wednesday December 12, 1855, Wednesday Morning, December 12, 2

[364] William Bramwell Withers, *History of Ballarat*, Ballarat Star Ballarat, 1887 p 243, *The Geelong Advertiser and Intelligencer*, The Municipal Extensions Act, Monday December 24, 1855, 3

council.³⁶⁵ Noticeably missing from the description of the meeting was any representation from Ballarat East or the mining interests, as the press reported that there was a 'large attendance comprising the most influential portion of our trading and legal community.'

The names mentioned as possible candidates were 'Messrs Lynn, Douglass, Oddie, French, Rainy, Seekamp, Muir, Wigley, Dunne, and Welsh', all long-term and well-established owners of lots in the township. This contrasts with similar moves in Sandhurst occurring at the same time that were not taken at all seriously. Names put forward for their proposed municipality included Lord Nelson, Lord John Russell, Charles Dickens and General Simpson.³⁶⁶ All accepted nomination except for Wigley and Douglass (of Ranken & Douglass gold brokers) with Douglass, after some dispute over the status of the returning officer, agreeing to stand in as temporary chairman until a formal election took place. The meeting was described as very animated and indicative of the degree of interest and commitment shown by those present, auguring well for the future.³⁶⁷ Once this was settled, the first order of business was the formation of a committee for the establishment of a fire brigade. An agreement was made to meet a week later to take nominations for the declaration of a poll the following day with both to be held in the 'large room' of the Golden Fleece Hotel on Lydiard Street North.³⁶⁸

This important meeting followed immediately after a sale of town lots over the previous two days where fifty lots were put up for sale. Many 'old miners and mechanics were described as eager purchasers intending to build comfortable cottages and settle down, using Ballarat as a base to take advantage of any new finds.

---

³⁶⁵ *The Geelong Advertiser and Intelligencer*, Monday, 7 January 1856, Ballarat, 3
³⁶⁶ *Bendigo Advertiser*, "Progression: our rights and our resources", Tuesday January 8, 1856, 2
ibid Thursday 10 January,1856, 2 *ibid*, Saturday January 12, 1856, 2
³⁶⁷ *The Geelong Advertiser and Intelligencer*, Monday, 7 January 1856, Ballarat, 3
³⁶⁸ *Geelong Advertiser and Intelligencer*, Ballarat, Monday 7 January 1856, page 3, & Wednesday 16 January 1856, page 2, Ballarat.

Golden Fleece Hotel in Lydiard Street where the first meeting took place to discuss the formation of the council in 1855. From the collection of the Ballarat Historical Society, Ballarat Victoria, catalogue No 248.81

It was also noted by the *Geelong Advertiser*, that several Geelong residents had made purchases. By far, however, the overwhelming majority of lots sold, were existing owners and occupiers, who were increasing their holdings.[369] This was a solid endorsement of the view becoming more prevalent among those on the township, that permanent settlement should take precedence over mining, the preservation of the Surveyor General's original and amended plans, existing streets, and reinforcing the need for official municipal management and organisation as an essential foundation for economic and civic progress.

---

[369] *Geelong Advertiser and Intelligencer*, Ballarat, Monday 7 January 1856, 3, see also rate book for 1856 where J Jackson, R. McNiece, T. Randall, J Chisholm, D. F. Main, W Stewart, T Oddie, E A Wynne, Tulloch & McLaren, all appear as owners of multiple lots.

Ballarat West: Fit & Proper Persons 187

It all passed by with little notice or fanfare. In contrast, the laying of the foundation stone of the Ballarat Hospital on Christmas Day 1855, was colourfully attended by the Masons and the Oddfellows,[370] while the Miners' Court elections attracted large numbers to a series of rowdy outdoor meetings.[371] Held on 14 January 1856 in the large room at the Golden Fleece Hotel, the nominations, though open to all landowners and householders of the district, were described by correspondents from the *Age* and the *Geelong Advertiser* as 'not very numerously attended' and 'of little interest.'[372] The general lack of interest continued into the next day as the poll was declared open. The *Times and Southern Cross* article of 17 January reproduced in the *Age* observed prophetically:

> Many people are inclined to treat the whole affair as ordinary and commonplace, and not worthy of more than a passing thought, but they are labouring under a mistake as events will soon prove. The Municipal Council of Ballarat have in their hands a power that is of the utmost importance to the wellbeing of this community, and which is deserving of the utmost consideration. Anyone carefully reading the act for the establishment of Municipal Councils as published in yesterday's Times, will see the importance of their trust and the extensive power they possess. [373]

The scepticism of the press, however, was unfounded. Although not as numerous, entertaining or as boisterous as the Miners Court

---

[370] *The Age*, Melbourne, Vic, Ballarat, Monday 31 December 1855, 7

[371] *The Age*, Melbourne Vic, Ballarat, Friday 18 January 1856, 3 & *Geelong Advertiser and Intelligencer*, Wednesday 16 January 1856, Ballarat, 2

[372] *The Age*, Melbourne, Ballarat, Friday 18 January 1856, 3, The *Geelong Advertiser and Intelligencer*, Wednesday 16 January, 1856, Ballarat, 2: This description differs from that of Nathan Spielvogel in the *Spielvogel Papers, Vol. 1, Version 3* First published 1974, edited by J A Chisholm MBE, p1 & 73 where he states that the meeting was taken over by a Ballarat East crowd leading to its abandonment. According to Spielvogel, the meeting was rescheduled for the 14 January at Bath's Hotel where police refused entry to Ballarat East residents and the councillors and officers were elected.

[373] *The Age*, Melbourne, Ballarat, Tuesday 22 January 1856, 3

elections, a fair crowd arrived on Tuesday 15 January for the vote. The proceedings were conducted free of controversy with the turnout and behaviour of the crowd indicative of the overwhelming support for the new administration in the community. Eleven hundred and fifty-one votes were cast from which the first seven were selected. The successful candidates were:

James Oddie	132	(Land Agent and Auctioneer)
Robert Muir	126	(General Merchant/Draper)
Dr. J Stewart	115	(Medical Practitioner)
W. Tulloch	107	(Merchant – wines, Spirits, horses & general)
A.B. Rankin	97	(Gold Buyer)
J.S. Carver	81	(Government Land Agent and Auctioneer)
P. Bolger	81	(Hotelier – Clarendon Hotel)

An interesting result was the lack of endorsement for Henry Seekamp, editor of the *Ballarat Times* who had led opposition to the miners' license fee. Receiving only 17 votes, it was presumed by some correspondents that it was due to his ongoing disagreement with fellow proprietors at the *Star*.[374] Once concluded, they all adjourned to the George Hotel where the 'health of the Chairman, the successful and unsuccessful candidates was pledged in some of Howe & Herring's best champagne.[375]

During the following week, a town clerk was appointed with Mr Thomas Comb the successful candidate and advertisements were placed for valuators in preparation for rating the new municipality. This was a much needed and anticipated development that began with no reported protest or opposition as the residents were eager to see some well-deserved and needed improvements. As some commented, it would make Ballarat a 'neighbourhood somewhat more civilized in so far as the means of communication are

---

[374] *The Geelong Advertiser and Intelligencer*, Ballarat, Friday 18 January 1856
[375] *The Geelong Advertiser and Intelligencer*, Ballarat, Friday 18 January 1856, *The Age*, Melbourne, Ballarat, Saturday, 19th January 1856, 3.

Ballarat West: Fit & Proper Persons

concerned.'[376] By 1 March the surveyor Samuel Baird, a man with considerable experience in the west of Scotland, was appointed along with the inspector Alexander Dimant. [377] The Chairman James Oddie, was sworn in as a Justice of the Peace.[378]

The political significance of this foundational period, however, is ignored in Bate's account of Ballarat, overlooking the efforts of residents and proprietors, J B Humffray and the Victorian Reform League. Instead, Weston Bate interprets the creation of a municipality in Ballarat West rather vaguely as due to the pressure from 'fantastic development.'[379] However, with a lot of proposed development along Main Road mooted for the east during 1855, Bate's history of Ballarat, not surprisingly appears to have a greater focus on the Ballarat East municipality founded a year later. While this may be due to a lack of available hard local sources on Ballarat West and an abundance for Ballarat East at the time of his writing, it provides a limited view of that crucial period. It also glosses over the mindset of many who recognized the value of a municipal corporation to the local community and the struggle to wrest control over their affairs from the Goldfields Commission. Since Weston Bate's iconic history, however, the National Library of Australia has made many and varied sources available through its digitization program particularly the articles of visiting correspondents from locations all over Australia, thus providing a greater insight into the events.

For example, in covering the election the *Times and Southern Cross* correspondent conveyed his impression of the proceedings under the banner of 'Advance Ballarat.' He presented a picture of a

---

[376] *Geelong Advertiser & Intelligencer*, Ballarat, Tuesday 29th January 1855, 2
[377] Alexander Dimant's contribution to establishing and maintaining sanitary and regulatory guidelines was both lengthy and highly valued, given special mention at the First Grand Gathering of The Ballarat Pioneers in August 1872, he is mentioned with J. Oddie, T Bath, H Foster, Warden Daly and other notables, *Ballarat Star*, Tuesday, 27th August 1872, The Ballarat Pioneers, 2
[378] *Geelong Advertiser & Intelligencer*, Ballarat, Tuesday 4th March 1856, 4
[379] Weston Bate, *Lucky city: the first generation at Ballarat 1851-1901*, p165-166

progressive and independently minded group reminiscent of the widely acclaimed independent British member for Aylesbury,[380] fighter of privilege and man for the people:

> It was not a turbulent, factious party, rabble sort of election, but one conducted with all that solemnity and decorum that it deserved. ... Since Mr Layard's happy speech, the watchword of progress has been 'the right men in the right place,' and never, we believe, has the principle been carried out so fully as at the election yesterday, and the principle has been still further carried out today by the judicious choice of the chairman from among the members of the council. ... to advance the prosperity of the community ... if we all pull together ... we may yet see Ballarat the first city in Australia.[381]

Similarly, in Nathan Spielvogel's accounts during his tenure on the radio in the 1970s, the election was portrayed as mired in controversy and had to be rescheduled due to a public disturbance. However, as records now available to us show, the visiting correspondents report that it was quite the opposite.

Inaugural Chairman James Oddie
The *Age* in the same vein, also expressed hope that Chairman James Oddie and his colleagues, like Layard, the British independent member for Aylesbury,[382] a fighter against privilege, champion of fairness and an advocate of progress in government would also attract the same sort of esteem. James Oddie particularly fitted the mould. Portrayed by Anne Beggs-Sunter he was a highly respected local businessman (auctioneer) deeply committed to political causes and an active supporter of fairness in business.[383]

---

[380] Mr Layard at Aylesbury March 27, *Empire*, Monday 15 June 1857, page 2
[381] republished in *The Age* Melbourne, Tuesday, 22 January 22, 1856, 3
[382] *The Age* (Melbourne) Monday August 6, 1855, Attacks on Mr Layard, page 6
[383] Beggs-Sunter, Anne, *James Oddie, (1824-1911) his life and the Wesleyan contribution to Ballarat*, MA Thesis, Deakin University, 1989

Chairman James Oddie From the Collection of Federation University Australia Historical Collection (Geoffrey Blainey Research Centre) Federation University Australia E.J. Barker Library (top floor) Mount Helen Victoria *Copy of a painting of James Oddie* held by the Art Gallery of Ballarat. Object registration 18825

Later in the year, Mr Oddie took a personal interest in the occupation of unsold land below Lydiard Street to the Yarrowee by a few local notables. In one case in particular, Mr Rainy the Lawyer had mounted appeal after appeal against Oddie's removal orders on land he occupied that was reserved for the Mechanics' Institute.[384] A cunning and difficult operator he had aroused the ire of Oddie by his blatant lack of civic sensibilities.[385] In commenting on Oddie's actions, Warden Sherrard of the Gold Department declared: 'he (Oddie) would rather be clement to a blacksmith, or the keeper of a fruit stall, than to a wealthy man who would not lay out the money to purchase a freehold.'[386]

His political affiliations were likewise just as clear, chairing the Ballarat Early Closing Association and the local eight hours movement.[387] In their well-attended meeting on 9 October 1856,

---

[384] Council Minutes Wednesday 10th September 1856, as published in the *Ballarat Star* the next day, page 2

[385] Lawyer Rainy had declared that he was only going to stay in the colony for three years boasting that in the short time he had been there, he had already made £2000 – see Council minutes as published in the Star 18th Sept 1856, page 2, However, his overconfident plans took a blow when he purchased most of the residential lots released at Clarendon on the Geelong Road – a gamble that never paid off as expected.

[386] Comments made by Warden Sherrard as relayed to the Council by Mr Oddie, see Council minutes Wednesday, 17th September 1856, as published in the *Star*, Thursday, 18th September 1856, Municipal Council, 2.

[387] *The Age*, Melbourne, Friday, 2nd May 1856, The eight hours question at Ballarat, 3

Mr Oddie commenced by commenting on the justice of shorter hours but emphasised he was also committed to doing something about it.[388] Oddie was also personally committed to the political career of Irish ex-patriot Charles Gavan Duffy, chairing the local meeting to help raise the £2000 needed for his property qualification. In the company of other well-known Eureka activists Black, Seekamp, and Nicholls a committee was formed of which he was a member, to actively canvass the district for donations.[389] His commercial acumen was of the highest calibre, serving as a director of the local branch of The Bank of Victoria[390] along with fellow councillor Dr James Stewart both of whom in addition were also named along with other dignitaries such as Warden Sherrard and J B Humffray as trustees of the newly announced savings bank established in anticipation of a boom in freehold occupation south of Sturt Street. [391]

James Oddie, in response to the miners' right legislation in 1857 had formulated a plan to erect homes for the district miners on the township in Ballarat South to take advantage of the cooperative mining ventures opening up on the deep leads extending south to Magpie. Unfortunately, his intentions were temporarily thwarted during 1857 by misinformation and the local Gold Department that prevented the municipality from exercising any jurisdiction over the unsold lots in Ballarat South.[392] Despite this early setback, the first Council under his leadership, was later given credit for implementing this popular scheme together with Duncan Gillies

---

[388] *The Ballarat Star*, Saturday 11th October 1856, Ballarat Early Closing Association, 2
[389] *The Age*, Melbourne, Saturday, 29th March 1856, Ballarat, 3
[390] *The Star* (Ballarat) Thursday 25th September 1856, page 4 (advertisement)
[391] Ibid
[392] *The Star* (Ballarat), Thursday November 12, 1857, page 2, 'Meeting at Council Chambers'

and Mr Fraser of the local Miner's Court, opening up large sections of the district to affordable home construction.[393]

Robert Muir
Although not as politically active as James Oddie, Robert Muir was arguably the most active in the foundation of the new municipality. Sharing the same values as his colleagues, he was a persuasive public speaker who chaired many meetings for a variety of causes. Joining with local activists such as James Oddie, Thomas Bath and C F Nicholls on 9 May 1855 they presented a united community supporting efforts by the Victorian Reform League in negating the influence of the squatting interest in the framing of the bill for political enfranchisement on the goldfields.[394] Robert Muir's contribution to the establishment phase of the municipality is more remarkable. He is not remembered in Bate's history of Ballarat as among its eminent founders but what he achieved in the three years he is known to us is substantial. With an excellent pedigree in commerce and politics, he was one of five well-travelled brothers who emigrated to Australia seeking mercantile success. The eldest brother was William Patterson Muir, a respected Melbourne merchant, who could be more accurately described as his mentor and possibly advisor, considering his many trips to Melbourne.

A citizen of the world would be an accurate description of the older brother having served some years on the legislature of British dominions in the Caribbean as well as achieving business success in Scotland. He was a member of the Melbourne Chamber of Commerce enjoying a personal affiliation with O'Shanassy and had been approached on several occasions to stand for office in the old and new parliament as for Ballarat.[395] Robert Muir along with his

---

[393] *The Star* (Ballarat) Friday 1 April 1904, page 2, A Pioneer Citizen, see also Anne Beggs-Sunter, *James Oddie, (1824-1911) his life and the Wesleyan contribution to Ballarat*, MA Thesis, Deakin University, 1989, page 63
[394] *The Geelong Advertiser and Intelligencer*, Thursday 10 May 1855, 2
[395] *The Star* (Ballarat) Thursday 24 July 1856, Melbourne, 2

Ballarat West: Fit & Proper Persons 194

older brother are named as members of the board of directors of the Colonial Bank of Australasia[396] as well as being the proprietors of several trading establishments – two in Ballarat East, one in the Township on Lydiard and Dana streets and a successful store in Melbourne as well as a successful farm on the outskirts of Ballarat of 171 acres.[397]

Apart from his role with J B Humffray in initiating the law-and-order measures and the call to petition for the municipality, as a councillor Robert Muir was also heavily involved in the founding of many local initiatives. He was elected as the founding chairman of the Chamber of Commerce, a position he declined due to inexperience.[398] He was also chairman of the Agricultural Society[399] as well as holding the highly influential position of Foundation President of the Ballarat branch of the District Roads Board[400] and serving on the committee for the Ballarat Industrial Institute.[401] Not afraid of controversy or making enemies, he was also the main advocate of a hard-line approach to removing the traders on Main Road, a cause that he had been on the other side of during 1853-4.[402]

Unfortunately, his promising career was cut short by a series of legal actions against him throughout 1857 and 1858.[403] The story of Robert Muir as a local political and commercial leader ended towards the end of 1857 as he resigned from all his official

---

[396] *The Star* (Ballarat) Saturday 8 November 1856, Colonial Bank of Australasia, 2

[397] *The Star*, (Ballarat) Friday 26 February 1858, Insolvent Court, 3. See also the Star (Ballarat) Friday 14 August 1857, Supreme Court, 2 for a summary and verdict.

[398] *The Star*, (Ballarat) Saturday 6 September, Chamber of Commerce, 2

[399] *The Star*, (Ballarat) Tuesday, 19 August, Advertising, 3

[400] *The Star* (Ballarat) 25 October 1856, District Roads Board, 2

[401] *The Star* (Ballarat) November 1, 1856, Ballarat Industrial Institute, 1

[402] *The Argus*, Melbourne, Monday 20 August 1855, 7

[403] *The Star* (Ballarat) 13 August 1857, Supreme Court, 2, The Age, (Melbourne) Saturday 15 August 1857, Matrimony and Mammon, To the Editor of the Age, 6, *The Star* (Ballarat) Friday August 14, 1857, 2

positions.[404] A significant factor in this turn of events was a widely publicised scandal that involved a successful lawsuit against him for breach of promise for not marrying his fiancée. The awarded damages of £2000 significantly affected the Muir family business relationships with creditors simultaneously calling in their securities shortly after amid an international financial crisis.[405]

Another person of note was Alexander Dimant the town inspector. Of Jewish extraction,[406] his service was given acclamation at the pioneers' memorial dinner in 1872 along with other notables like James Oddie. He was also honoured for his support for the supply of educational materials to the library and Mechanics Institute.[407] His role was designated as Inspector of Nuisances, but he also served in many other capacities with sworn authority as a special constable. This gave him wide powers of arrest and the ability to enter premises as well as the ability to prosecute. Sanitary matters were his primary concern, but he also saw it as his duty to ensure all bylaws were adhered to. He was well known for prosecuting trading violations, weights and measures, burning off, building code violations and animal husbandry violations.[408] Mr Dimant's enthusiasm for the new regime was never in doubt. While this may have been due in some degree to his right to a part of fines collected[409] and the building he was

---

[404] See Robert Muir biography, Graeme s Cartledge: *A nineteenth century Scot in Colonial Australia: the adventures, misadventures & enterprises of an entrepreneur & pioneer in the Eastern Australian Colonies*, Local Research Publishers, Ballarat 2023

[405] *The Age*, (Melbourne) Saturday August 15, 1858, Insolvent Court, Monday 12 July 1858. (Before F Wilkinson, Esq. Chief Commissioner) in Re Muir Brothers, 2

and Pictures, (W B Withers), 4[406] *The Ballarat Star*, Saturday, 6 October 1888, Ballarat Chronicles

[407] *The Ballarat Star*, Tuesday 27 August 1872, The Ballarat Pioneers, 3

[408] See for example, Dimant vs McCullough for illegal Sunday trading, and Dimant v Carmichael for roaming pigs on the township streets, *the Star*, Ballarat, Summons Cases, Saturday, 25 October 1856

[409] This right was confirmed by a letter from the Attorney General, see Council minutes for Wednesday 10th September 1856, as published in the *Star*, Ballarat, Municipal Council, Thursday 11 September 1856, 2

provided with by the council in his capacity as council messenger,[410] he nevertheless was both feared and respected by all as he showed no partiality in the execution of his duties. A good example of this was his long-running dispute with Councillor Carver over his water closet which Mr Dimant deemed unsanitary and not compliant with legislation.[411]

While municipal matters were of primary importance, the men selected were also men of ambition for the success of the Ballarat district and viewed the municipal council as an important step in facilitating a modern and progressive agenda. They were also 'safe' choices with no Eureka activists, all firmly committed to progress and British Liberalism. With newly attained powers of jurisdiction over planning and development and maintenance of local infrastructure, there was no time wasted in moving forward on several fronts. In relatively quick succession important initiatives were started in the district strongly supported by the newly sworn councillors. One of the most influential was the Chamber of Commerce with an inaugural meeting called on Tuesday 5 August 1856.[412]

Creating Local Institutions

Once again, as with the beginnings of the movement towards the municipal council, the meeting was led by Robert Muir and J B Humffray. Nominated for the chair, Councillor Robert Muir

---

[410] VPRS 13007 P0001 Council Minutes, 2/4/1856 and 8/4/1856
[411] See Council minutes for Wednesday 3 December as published in the *Star* Saturday 6 December Municipal Council, 1, councillor Carver raised this as a matter of discussion but Mr Dimant had the full backing of the Chairman and the council, he was told by them 'that if he did not follow the direction of the Town Inspector, that officer could summon him to the Police Court, where the matter would be investigated.' The Councillor was summonsed in Dec that year. See Council Minutes 21 December. This appears to conveniently coincide with a campaign to have Carver removed from the council over his passionate backing of the market square location in Mair Street.
[412] *The Star*, Ballarat, Ballarat Chamber of Commerce, 7 August 1856, 3.

opened the proceedings and gave an illuminating address as reported by the *Star* Correspondent:

> As an inland town in the Australian colonies, they were assured that it was second to none, and he believed that here-after it would be second to none to no inland town in all of Her Majesty's dominions. ... The amount put on the estimates for improvements to Ballarat was absurd. This was a matter which a Chamber of Commerce could deal with. They required inland communication by railroad before Ballarat could be great, commercially or otherwise.

With Geelong, viewed by Dr Allison as the 'seaport of Ballarat,' it was deemed necessary to promote this as a priority.

J B Humffray then moved for the resolution and then commented that the Chamber of Commerce was a necessary adjunct to the Municipal Council as their jurisdiction was not complete over the district. A large number lived outside of the township boundary and remained at the mercy of the Central Roads Board that operated to suit themselves and unsold lands within the township were the property of the crown under administration by the Gold Department. A Chamber of Commerce thus could be an intermediary body that could lobby between the public and the government on necessary public works. He also reinforced the importance of attaining access to the electric telegraph to be 'quickly and thoroughly informed of the state of Melbourne markets' to avoid injury to local commerce by price variations and gluts.[413] Mr Rodier, of the yet to be formed Ballarat East Council, reminded them also, that it was necessary to have a body such as this to properly represent the interests of the local community in Melbourne. He reminded them that a great deal of hardship had been inflicted by Government Acts over the past two

---

[413] *ibid*

years largely unintentional but nevertheless caused by the lack of proper representation[414].

The next major initiative was the proposed Ballarat Industrial Institute at a meeting convened on Tuesday 28 October 1856. It aimed to keep abreast of innovations in 'the arts and sciences in connection with the mining, manufacturing, and general interests of the district' through periodical meetings and exhibitions. At the first meeting in the Star Concert Room, a resolution was passed to make an application to the government for a grant of five acres and £3000 to erect the building. The local members for North Grant and North Grenville were appointed as *ex-officio* members. Among the office bearers named were Councillors R. Muir, treasurer and J. Oddie on the committee of twelve.[415] It was an enterprise with ambitions that far eclipsed those of the Chamber of Commerce.

The first resolution proposed was by Mr Baker, the promoter of the Bakerian System, which established the Ballarat South mining district on an equitable basis and introduced a new phase of technology and heavy machinery to the local industry. Establishing the Institute was, he said, proposed with

> a feeling of pleasure and a feeling of regret. The feeling of pleasure arose from the conviction that the movement, if carried out, and he felt convinced that it would be, would be beneficial not only to the district of Ballarat, but to other districts, to the whole colony, and perhaps to the whole world. [416]

But, like the Chamber of Commerce it was viewed as a project that was representative of the unique liberal values that characterised the colonial culture. This came on the back of a growing technological emphasis, as solutions to mining and the supply and containment of water issues were being addressed locally.

---

[414] *ibid*
[415] *The Star*, Ballarat, Ballarat Industrial Institute, Thursday 23 October 1856, 2
[416] *The Star*, Ballarat, Ballarat Industrial Institute, Saturday, 1 November 1856, 1

[417]Though the institute failed to flourish it remains an indication of the local technological and innovatory emphasis that was behind the creation of the famous Ballarat School of Mines. Thus, once established, the influence of the new municipal body was pervasive in almost all aspects of local governance and commercial activity, not just land and services. It stands as a prime example of the uniquely colonial implementation of the project of modernity and liberal values and the eager desire to lay these down as founding principles.

Creating a Modern Society: Liberals and Old-fogeyism
Thus, in the Australian colonies, deprived of its 'natural enemy' as Stuart Macintyre puts it, liberalism unhindered by the structural inequality of Britain, 'acquired a new energy.' [418] It certainly impressed Alexis de Tocqueville when he first saw the progress of immigrants to the American new world 'cutting their institutions like their roads amidst the forests where they have just settled.'[419]

Likewise, in the Australian colonies, as Gascoigne explains, the project of modernity could be more easily implemented as

> the Enlightenment's ideal of a state which could deal with the individual citizen without the interference of privileged orders such as the church, the aristocracy or guilds, was largely realised in the character of the Australian state. ... Through the outcome of many influences and traditions, the character of the Australian state and politics indicates the extent to which the political ethos of the Enlightenment could flourish in a

---

[417] See H R Nicholls letter to the *Ballarat Star* 6 Sept 1856, page 2, where he describes the work of the White Flat Drainage and Mining Company, in damming the Yarrowee and constructing races to divert flood waters using steam technology. See also Casselli's letter to the *Ballarat Star*, on 4 Sept 1856 on the benefits of ceramic over iron pipes in the proposed water supply system and the fact that all the talent and raw materials were located locally for their manufacture.
[418] Stuart Macintyre, *A Colonial Liberalism*, p12
[419] *ibid*

landscape where the hold of its traditional adversaries, the Established Church and the aristocracy was weak. [420]

While Gascoigne writes in hindsight, in the present of the mid-1850s, there was a widely held understanding that these progressive values should be laid down as founding principles.

The *Age* thus reported in October, in the lead-up to the first election for the Legislative Assembly in 1856:

> that with so many of the real friends of progress watching over our interests no time should be lost in rendering to the colony, that protection and encouragement ... ought to be granted to the scientific and ingenious ... This is particularly desirable in a new country like this where improvements are so much wanted, but where the same field is not available as in England for their development and little encouragement ever extended towards their authors ... when no valuable idea will be lost to the country merely because its author happens to be a poor man.[421]

The Argus in a similar manner was calling for 'rational government' declaring that 'the day has gone by for tolerating arbitrary laws, arbitrary legislators, or arbitrary judges. They are required to conform to reason and justice.' [422] The drafting of the new constitution in 1853 and 1854 with its liberal character was positively received by the press offering hope that it was an opportunity for a new beginning and to avoid the social problems back home. *The Argus* praised the government for its congruence with the 'spirit of the age' and its liberal outlook. *The Argus* thus

---

[420] John Gascoigne (with the assistance of Patricia Curthoys), *The enlightenment and the origins of European Australia*, Cambridge University Press, Melbourne, 2002, p69
[421] *The Age* (Melbourne) Friday October 24, 1856, The Requirements of Progress page 4.
[422] *The Argus*, (Melbourne) Friday September 15, 1854, A Rational Government, page 4

reported on the Committee on the new Constitution in January 1854, almost twelve months before the events at Eureka

> Mr Secretary Foster adopts an extremely liberal and philosophical tone. ... The Committee he says 'unanimously concurred in thinking that the social condition of this colony renders a close assimilation to certain British institutions impossible, and that an attempt to imitate them is likely not only to fail but to introduce the evils without the advantages experienced from them in England. ... Being convinced that nothing could be more impolitic than to legislate against the spirit of the age – viewing the universal tendency throughout the world towards the spread of popular institutions. [423]

The impossibility of reproducing the social conditions of Britain was no more obvious than on the goldfields. This was based on a widely held aversion to the 'old fogey-politics' of class and privilege or as it was also labelled on the goldfields – 'Toryism' along with all the negative connotations that it generated. This was an essential part of the politics of J B Humffray declaring his position on liberalism and free trade, as he stated in his candidature speech at Ballarat for the Legislative Assembly in 1856:

> It is true in my earlier days I have at home taken a share in politics and played the part of a humble village Hampden in denouncing unjust taxation; but protection was too strong for my puny arm ... I think the members of the goldfields have removed the cobwebs from the eyes of old fogeyism. [424]

This was also clearly expressed by large rallies during 1857 when the popular O'Shanassy government was deposed. With the successful motion of no confidence led by squatter representative Thomas Howard Fellows in April 1857, the report in the *Age* of the rally in response at Ballarat reveals some of this deep-seated feeling as conveyed by Mr Dunne and the other speakers:

---

[423] *The Argus (Melbourne)* Wed 4 Jan 1854, The New Constitution, page 4
[424] *The Age (Melbourne)* Friday April 18, 1856, 'Ballarat' page 3

> We have come out 16,000 miles to avoid this Toryism and old fogeyism and are we to meet with it again? [425]

And in describing Michie, Haines, Fellows and their associates he continues: 'It is because they are out-and-out Tories of the oldest Tory school.'

Mr Cope (lawyer) as the next speaker spoke for most when he commented:

> ... after all, even the best of us have no religion at all, so we need not fight about it. So long as the heart is in the right place I do not care whether a man be Jew gentile, or crocodile - (laughter) - it does not matter which. If a man only votes right, ... he'll be a man after my own heart and that's the way with most of us.

In the *Ballarat Times*, Fellows was branded with the mark of Toryism along with the people he represented – 'the squatter lords' and deemed 'the champion of squatter intolerance and monopoly.' [426] C F Nicholls also spoke for all when he declared in December 1856 at a large rally for the formation of the People's League:

> We would tell the Governor ... that we did not come 16000 miles to live under the same mal-arrangements as at home. Our duty was to leave the country better than we found it, whether we left it to go home again or to lay down in the cold graves of Australia. [427]

---

[425] *The Age* (Melbourne) Thursday April 30, 1857, The Ballarat Demonstration, page 6
[426] *The Age*, Tuesday, April 21st, 1857, The Opinions of the Country, page 5.
[427] *The Star*, Tuesday, December 9, 1856, page 1, The Governor's Speech.

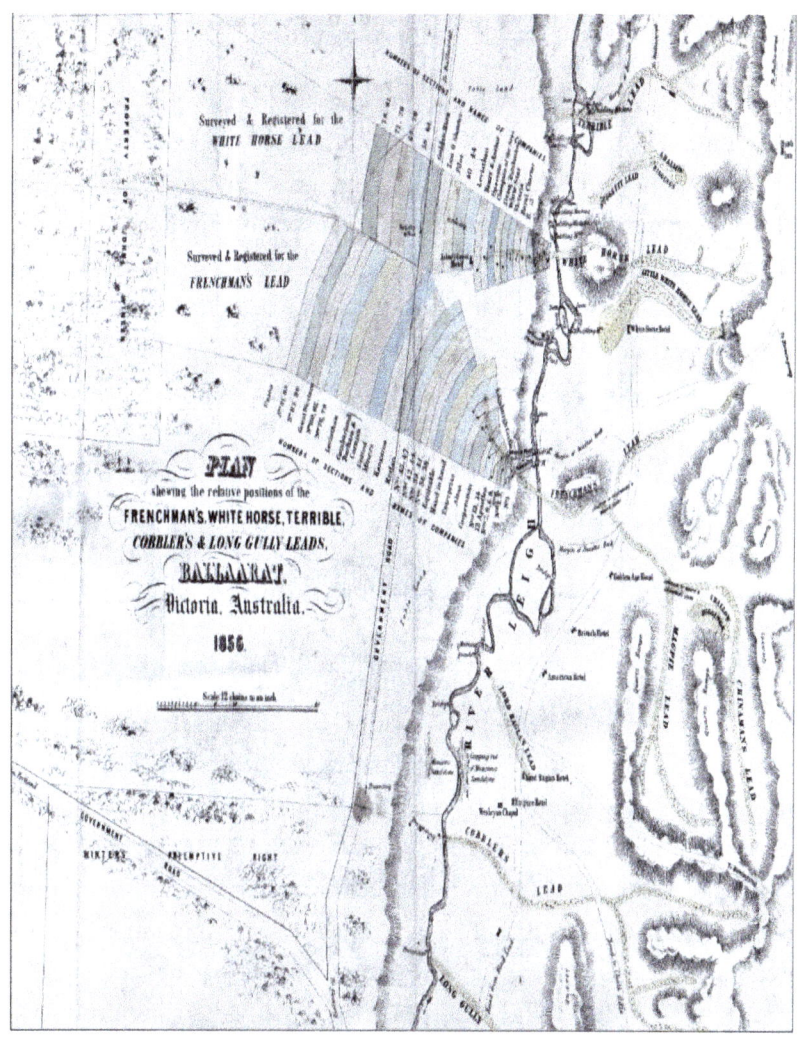

1856 *Survey map with details of companies, claims and relative positions on the Whitehorse, and Frenchman's Leads to the South of Ballarat located in present-day Sebastopol and Magpie.* Lithographed at the Surveyor General's Office, January. 29th 1857, by J. Jones. SLV, Vale Collection. Melbourne: Surveyor General's Office, 1857

The modern and progressive philosophy behind the development of Ballarat, however, could be best encapsulated by the hugely ambitious project to develop the deep leads of Ballarat South. Largely responsible for the massive extension of Ballarat West, it was the engine room that stimulated the local economy. Its management body was named 'The Amalgamated Committees of Management Appointed by the Miners of Frenchman's and Whitehorse Leads for the Effectual Working of the New Regulations.'[428] This ambitious undertaking launched local mining and its methods into the modern era, drawing together the latest ideas of financing, technology and commercial acumen. Conceived by the local Miners' Court and as a direct outcome of 'the Eureka Stockade Movement',[429] it was, despite initial resistance from the defenders of 'individual' mining[430], widely accepted. This was mostly due to the enthusiastic promotion by Mr James Baker after whom the scheme was known: 'the Frontage or Bakerian System.'[431]

It ushered in a new age of mining as the old methods of 'potluck' and 'shepherding' that arose under the administration of the Goldfields Commission no longer worked. Mining the leads under the basalt plain required greater technical skill and knowledge of blasting, drilling and other mechanized methods. It required a new approach that incorporated technology and cooperation, something that the old claim and licensing system was incapable of dealing with. However, for those proponents of the new system such as James Baker and other leaders of the Miners' Court, it also represented the values driving the new society that they were in the process of creating. This is exemplified by Baker at the meeting to

---

[428] *The Star*, Ballarat, Wednesday January 9, 1856, page 3, 'Ballarat: Public meeting at Magpie, *The Star*, Ballarat, Friday May 30, 1856, page 3, Correspondence: The Bakerian System; *The Star*, Ballarat Thursday September 4, 1856, page 2, 'Frenchman's and Whitehorse Leads' see map previous page
[429] See appendix ii
[430] *The Star* Ballarat, Friday April 26, 1856, page 5, 'Serious Riots at Ballarat'
[431] See appendix I, page 189

launch The Industrial Institute in November 1856. The purpose he stated was

> to be more than just a mere show for the day, but something more substantial so that the resources of the district might be developed. It would also be for the 'purpose of exhibiting productions of art and science tending to promote the mining, manufacturing, agricultural and general interests of the district. … It would he hoped 'be a point where they could all meet and forget to differ. In this country … labor and industry were the passports to wealth and honour. A Coningsby no longer considered it to be a disgrace to associated with a Millbank, and the aristocrat thought it the greatest honour to be allied to the manufacturer's daughter. [432]

Mr Cope the lawyer seconded the proposal giving a very entertaining and humorous speech on machinery and social change and the benefits of new skills and occupations that it would bring. It was thus a recognition that class was not an issue in the new society they were actively creating but status would be based on hard work and the ability to acquire professional skills in technology, science and the arts.

This promising future for Ballarat envisioned by Baker was embraced by most with even the most radical and revolutionary amongst them getting personally involved. H R Nicholls particularly appeared to have set aside his socialist and physical force leanings, embracing the new opportunities with enthusiasm. While acting somewhat as a spoiler for Ballarat East, he was nevertheless caught up in the mood with his enterprise at White Flat in 1856 described as 'perhaps the greatest mining operations ever performed in this colony.'[433] Designed to solve the water problems involved in local deep sinking enterprises, the Yarrowee

---

[432] *The Star*, (Ballarat) Saturday 1 November 1856, Ballarat Industrial Institute, page 1
[433] *The Star* (Ballarat) Saturday, September 6, 1856, 'White Flat Mining and Drainage Company'

was tamed with a series of dams and channels constructed with the labour of 75 men for six weeks along with two steam engine pumps that worked around the clock. [434]

The freedom of opportunity that enabled Chartists and socialists such as H R Nicholls to become entrepreneurs on such an impressive scale was made possible not only by an 'anti-Toryism' stance but also by a strong position against monopolies. This more than anything else characterised Toryism to the miners of the 1850s. Back in Britain, it was the monopoly of the political system, the harsh half-century under the oppressive tariffs of the Corn Laws and the lack of access to landownership and political power. Any hint of it reappearing on the goldfields therefore was steadfastly resisted. In the Ballarat District, such outrage was directed specifically at two substantial landowners and squatters, Jock Winter, and W J 'Big' Clarke who sought to exploit local miners by schemes to entice them to prospect on their land, paid for by a share of any discoveries.[435]

As mining began to become increasingly mechanised during 1856 cries of monopoly in conjunction with the evils of capital began to be heard elsewhere. A meeting in Ballarat on 2 August 1856 opposing this development was condemned in the Ballarat *Star* while the *Mount Alexander Mail* editorial as reprinted in the Ballarat *Star*, compared the opposition of the 'individual miner' to machinery to winding back the clock and making all lands common and the chaos and detriment it would bring to modern agriculture.[436] The editorial, however, praised the use of machinery as a weapon against monopoly bringing benefits to the many and denying the unfairness of rewards to the lucky few 'individual miners' which characterised the surface mining period which was drawing to a close.[437]

---

[434] Ibid.
[435] *The Star* (Ballarat) Thursday 30 October 1856, page 2, Mining
[436] *The Star*, Ballarat, August 12, 1856, page 4, Capital in Mining
[437] *The Star*, August 7, 1856, page 4, Machinery in Mining

The solution to such turmoil was the focus on progress and the liberal application of legislation to establish a society where liberalism could flourish. This was most appropriately expressed by John Fitzgerald Leslie Foster (son of a Tory) regarding the elections for the new Victorian parliament in 1857:

> Here ... we had nothing to preserve, and nothing to destroy. We landed on a naked shore to form, to found, to create.[438]

And put just as succinctly by Attorney General George Higginbotham as reported in the *Argus* 5 January 1858:

> A man for the times must lead the way – must know how to build the great edifice – must be in reality, not in name, a liberal.[439]

There was no doubt that this concept was behind the growing size and commercial diversity of the Ballarat Township. This was also the political ethos behind the main movers and shakers for the Ballarat district in 1855 and 1856 – J B Humffray the elected representative for North Grant and Robert Muir for the Ballarat West Municipality. J B Humffray, despite being elected the member of North Grant in September of 1856, was able to successfully negotiate the varying shades of grey to promote the locality of Ballarat in general. This often involved representing the interests of constituents in Peter Lalor's seat of North Grenville, many of whose constituents resided in the new municipality of Ballarat West. Portrayed by Carboni as a consummate politician with wide appeal, Humffray wasted no time after the Eureka incident making solid connections early, well before his election to

---

[438] Stuart MacIntyre, *A colonial liberalism: the lost world of three Victorian visionaries*, 12
[439] *ibid*

the Legislative Assembly.[440] He made wide connections, with the progressive miners south of Ballarat and both their Main Road and township supporters and the township commercial establishment. He was also invested personally in partnership with his brother as co-owner of a bookshop on Main Road[441] as well as owning property in Doveton Street on the township and his house on Main Road.[442]

Main Road merchant, W B Rodier declared he 'rejoiced in the return of Mr Humffray as he felt concerned that he would do all in his power to advance the commercial prosperity of Ballarat.'[443] Humffray with his platform of local and regional development as Quaife concluded from his study of the 1856 election, reflects the dramatic shift that had occurred from the early 1850's where 'a nomad population hungry for political reform … was replaced by a settled populace hungry for jobs, roads and bridges.'[444]

---

[440] Carboni Raffaello, *The Eureka Stockade; the consequence of some pirates wanting on the quarter-deck a rebellion*, Carboni Raffaello, Melbourne, 1855, p32
[441] Anne Beggs-Sunter, *"Eureka: Birth of a nation?"* P33
[442] Ballarat Rate Assessment Book 1856, VPRS 7260/P0002/1 *Ballarat Rate Assessment Books 1856 – 1857*
[443] *The Star* (Ballarat) Saturday, November 1, 1856
[444] G R Quaife, The Diggers: 'Democratic Sentiment and Political Apathy' in: *The Australian Journal of Politics and History*, Vol, 13, Issue 2 August 1967, pp221-230

12. Establishing Local Authority

A Town Hall & Local Opposition

Effective administrative functions began immediately with the first meeting on 28 January 1856 where it was clear from the outset that this was a practical and committed Council. One of the first binding regulations addressed attendance at Council Meetings. It was agreed and placed on the record that any member of the council absent fifteen minutes after the appointed hour would be fined a sum of no more than five shillings and if absent the whole time without reasonable excuse, ten shillings, with the fines to be contributed to a local charity.[445] The first to fall foul of this rule was Councillor Stewart who was fined ten shillings for non-attendance on 5 February 1856.[446] Of equal importance was the place of meeting with local Hotels (Golden Fleece and Bath's) being very inappropriate as a permanent arrangement.

An urgent application for a grant of land for the building of a town hall was therefore made as a matter of urgency. Shortly after, unfortunately, official notice was received from Melbourne by solicitor Wigley, that the grant of land requested for council chambers had already been made and allocated to Mr Taylor the District Surveyor for his own premises. However, as a gesture of goodwill and not desirous to hold up progress on the new premises, Taylor promptly requested that the land, (where the council buildings exist today) be allocated to the council. It thus indicates the enormous amount of local support for the new municipal council and the respect enjoyed by the chosen members. This section of land was originally granted to Taylor the district

---

[445] VPRS 13007 P0001 *Council Minutes 31 Jan 1856*
[446] *ibid 5 February 1856*

surveyor for his office and residence. However, in recognition of the importance of the position, Mr Taylor very generously agreed to ask the Surveyor General to allocate the lot to the new council.[447] Thus, in a truly remarkable effort that took just over three months, the Council Chambers had been commissioned and erected on the site at a total cost of £662 which included all the fixtures and fittings.[448]

However, while enjoying such a positive endorsement from the Surveyor, relations with the Roads Board were not as cordial, deteriorating as the year progressed. Reminiscent of similar contested transitions in Britain between the Tory old guard and the elected municipal officers in the newly formed municipalities, the local officers of the District Roads Board were not willing to give up their powers and jurisdiction over rates and responsibilities to the newcomers. With extensive powers over district roads, construction, rates, levies and tolls it had enjoyed a close and well-established connection with the Colonial Public Works Department, the Gold Department, and the local squatters. Municipal authority had to be asserted as all the old channels of communication remained in place. Despite the creation of the new local government in the district, there was little to no attempt by the old guard to defer or engage with any new authority. By the end of July 1856 irritations with the disrespectful actions of the Central Roads Board, particularly their Engineer Mr Rowand, who was based in Geelong, had reached boiling point.

A very sarcastic letter was received from Mr Rowand over temporary drainage undertaken by the Council in Sturt Street, suggesting that seeing as they were doing improvements, they could do all of Sturt Street themselves. At the same time, the

---

[447] Ibid, Public Records Office VPRS 2500 P0000/1 *Ballarat Municipal Council Letters Inward January – December 1856-1857*, see original letter appendix VIII page 206

[448] Mary Sandow, *The Town Hall Ballaarat 100 years, Ballaarat City Council*, 1970, page 6

Establishing Local Authority

Central Roads Board under Mr Rowand were also operating a quarry at the Western end of Eyre Street within the Council boundary without municipal sanction. The operator, a Mr Breganza, had refused to comply with a request from the Council to desist as his reply was that he only answered to Mr Rowand. The Council thus moved at the next scheduled meeting, that as the District Roads Board were treating the new council 'like a parcel of children who had nothing to do with the township' they would have to appeal to the Government to have it stopped.[449] By October, however, a more permanent solution was found as an Act of Parliament declared that the districts could elect their own District Roads Board.

The District Roads Board

A meeting was held for this purpose on Friday 24 October 1856 at the Court House on the Camp, and nine members were elected from a well-attended group of interested hopefuls with 707 votes cast. It was a process that was driven and directed by the municipal council who showed a great deal of determination to control the new body, encouraging all the council members to stand for election. The election itself also took place under the oversight of Council Chairman Oddie and Councillor Stewart, with Robert Muir voted into the chairmanship. W C Smith who became a councillor in 1857, was also elected.[450] This effectively ended the reign of the Central Roads Board and Mr Rowand over local affairs and provided a close working relationship with the Council with at least two council members leading its operation. This 'coup' was achieved with the assistance of their local ally in the colonial government, J B Humffray with his ability to draft new bills enabling a creative solution despite the limitations of the Municipal

---

[449] Municipal Council Minutes for Wednesday 30 July 1856, published in the *Star* Thursday 31 July 1856, 2
[450] *The Star* (Ballarat) Saturday 25 October 1856, District Roads Board, 2

Corporations Act. There can be no doubt about his guiding hand in the fortunes of Ballarat and none more than the enactment of what came to be known as the 'Miners Programme.'[451] The program, as reported by the *Age* was essentially the development of the regions based on three issues: the Land Question – to induce miners to spend their riches on land and permanent settlement; mining on private property, and Local Government and decentralization of public works. It represented the under-reported aims of the Eureka moral force majority – integration with the rest of the colony and local independence through the spending of local taxes on local development.

This programme was much more than enfranchisement and representation; it was essentially the economic, political and social development of the goldfield regions which certainly was not limited to the miners themselves but was in accordance with the aims of the Government as the tone of the 1855 Commission of Inquiry indicated. The *Age* states:

> The fullest powers of self-government must be granted to the miners. All tendency to unnecessary centralization in the Government must be closely guarded against. Every great central locality must be accorded its fair share of the public expenditure for local objects. Every possible encouragement to social improvement must be held out to miners. In schools, literary institutions, hospitals and so forth … in a word, miners must be regarded as an integral and most valuable section of the general community and not as a horde of social aliens. [452]

However, the program was primarily based on the expansion of private land ownership and the ability to levy rates and this was where the major challenge to the authority of the new municipality was based. Just because the municipality boundaries were clearly

---

[451] So-called by *the Age*, Melbourne, Thursday 2 October 1856, The Miners' Programme, 4.
[452] *Ibid*

defined, it not did necessarily follow that their authority did also. Exercising authority was hard work, involving a great deal of correspondence and liaising with other government agencies. In the district, it was also clear that jurisdiction was not well understood by officials of the relevant agencies resulting in long delays, prevarication and sometimes confusion as to who could make decisions over land and its uses.

Nevertheless, despite being twice reminded by the Attorney General that the municipal council had no jurisdiction over unsold lands,[453] the new council continued to use the power of bluff to exert authority. In the case of Rainy the lawyer who refused to remove a building on land leased from the crown within the township boundary, it proved unsuccessful. Their impotence was also further reinforced by the dispute with the public works department in the removal order for two ramshackle buildings that were obstructing the Bank of Australia and encroaching into the roadway on Sturt and Lydiard Streets. In this case, the Council were advised that they would have to wait the pleasure of the Public Works Department as replacements were organised in a new location.[454]

Land & Council Jurisdiction

At a meeting in April 1856, correspondence was also aired from the Attorney General and Solicitor General advising the Council that they had no jurisdiction over those involved in leasing arrangements with the Colonial Government. This was in response to attempts to eliminate mining in the township, Ballarat West's campaign against the Main Road traders in Ballarat East and any other such establishments within the municipal boundaries.[455] Not to be deterred, however, an appeal was made to the Resident

---

[453] VPRS 13007 P0001 *Council Minutes, Wednesday 30 April 1856*
[454] *Ibid.*
[455] VPRS 13007 P0001 *Council Minutes, Wed 30 April 1856*

Warden to exercise his powers to get such activity to cease.[456] The Councillors were encouraged by the response from the Acting Resident Warden James Daly, requesting a list of enterprises which was ordered to be furnished as quickly as possible.[457] However, this process became further complicated as the local Miners' Court entered the debate claiming that any dispute over land allocations under the Miner's Right Legislation was their responsibility. This gave a green light to many local miners who began occupying lots on the new extensions in Ballarat South and on Soldiers Hill from the second half of 1856. The new township extension into Ballarat South dated 5 March 1857 illustrates the enormity of the task that confronted the council. Although surveyed, a significant portion of the land was either impassable with deep gullies or subject to mining activity. In addition, tents and other structures were scattered across marked lots and streets with little regard for the planning of the area. By the end of 1857, most of these lots would be occupied by those waiting in anticipation of the new bill on the occupation of crown lands.[458]

Therefore, one of the first tasks of the Council was to perform an audit of available land to get a clear picture on what was available to them and how they may gain jurisdiction over parts that were subject to other agencies such as the Central Roads Board or the Gold Department or the Miners' Court. This was conducted over the course of 1856 and a list was compiled to provide clarity going forward while also providing a basis for Chairman Oddie's plan for creating affordable homes for the miners.[459]

---

[456] *ibid*

[457] ibid, May 7, 1856

[458] *Ballarat Rate Assessment Books* VPRS 7260/P0002/2 1857 -1858 Although still crown land, most lots were occupied and valued and expected rates listed in preparation of lots being sold in the near future - Appendix 4

[459] See valuator's report 15 March 1856, appendix I page 306, also W B Withers, *History of Ballarat*, 1887, p245 listing 267 tenements and 297 vacant lots valued at £40,061

Establishing Local Authority 215

As time progressed into 1857 confusion prevailed allowing opportunists to take advantage of a lax oversight with some speculators claiming and fencing lots on the township. This generated a great deal of ill will and created a problem that nobody wanted to deal with. However, matters were brought to a head when Robert McNiece, one of the original landowners, fenced off a large lot near the post office purely as a stunt to highlight the absurdity.[460] The intention of the Act as it stood, was to provide for homes for diggers on the gold-fields. This was the basis of a scheme in planning by the Chairman of the Municipality James Oddie and the Council whereby homes would be constructed and mortgaged.[461] The expected amendment to the Goldfields Act was to protect genuine miners and make it more difficult for speculators by allowing the holder of a miner's right or a business license as a tenant on crown lands, a right to 20 perches or be compensated in case of removal.[462] The famous case of the Queen vs Hill in 1857 in Castlemaine however, highlighted serious problems with a *laissez-faire* oversight and the spirit of the act calling for intervention on behalf of bona-fide miners.[463] The concern was that speculators who were not bona-fide diggers were occupying town lots and building structures on them to enhance their value and receive like compensation if made to vacate due to sale.

One notorious case of a builder who built houses on crown land and sold or let them in expectation of realising a much higher price with the passing of the amendment aroused a great deal of outrage. It was an issue taken up by the Ballarat *Star* who came down on the side of the diggers. The *Star* editor while acknowledging that 'we are ultra-liberal' in our ideas of the freedom and facilities that

---

[460] *The Star* (Ballarat) Thursday 12 November 1857, The Meeting at the Council Chambers, 2
[461] *ibid*
[462] *The Star (Ballarat)* 'Meeting on Soldier's Hill', Thursday 22 October 1857, 2
[463] *The Star (Balarat)*, The Gold-Fields Squatters, Saturday, 14 November 1857, 2

should be accorded to private enterprise,' called for a more protectionist facility for the miners in Ballarat. [464]

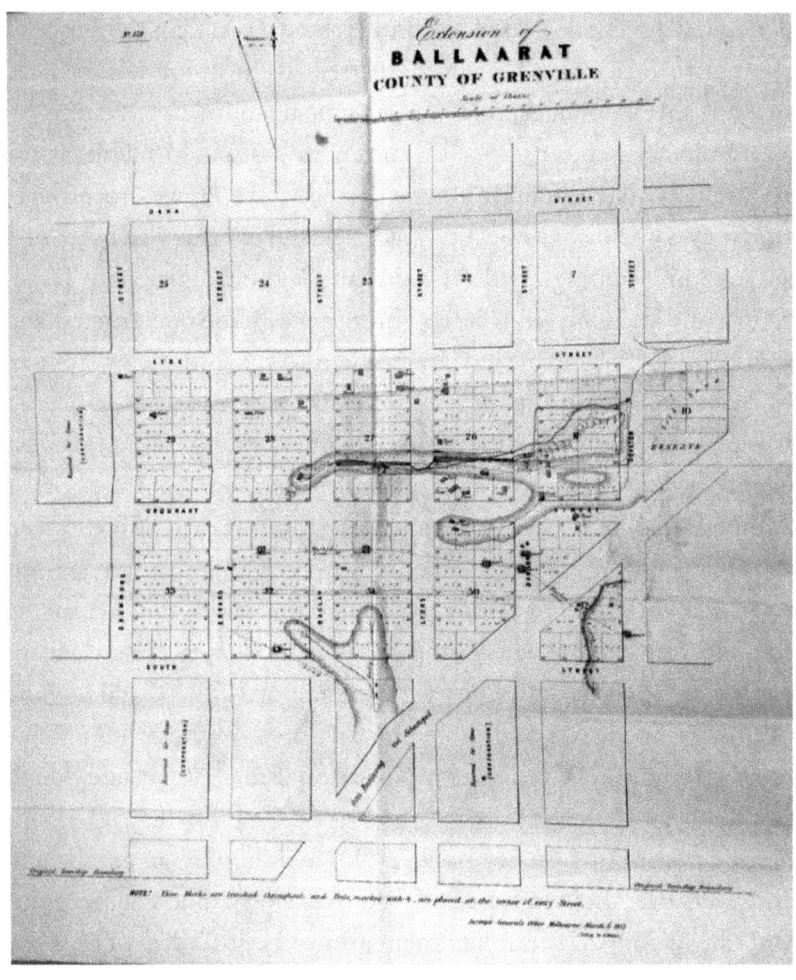

---------■---------- Mining Lead with shaft   ▌ Tent or other unofficial structure such as a bark slab hut

Proposed Ballarat South Extension 1857 with surveyed lots detailing terrain, mining activity and occupation Ballarat South Extension, Public Records Office VPRS 2500 P0000/1 Ballarat Municipal Council Letters Inward January – December 1856-1857

---

[464] ibid

Establishing Local Authority 217

An 1860's black and white photograph, showing 1860s Ballarat South from the Ballarat Benevolent Asylum. Evident in the photos are houses, gardens, shingle roofs, fences, St Patrick's Cathedral, Black Hill, Ballarat West Fire Brigade tower, mine dumps, mullock heap, and large chimneys. From the collection of Federation University Australia Historical Collection (Geoffrey Blainey Research Centre) Federation University Australia E J Barker Library Mount Helen Victoria, object registration 04657

However, this did not deter those with real power to exercise it. Although now quite benign compared to the rapacious administration of Robert Rede, the Gold Department (formed in 1856 to replace the Goldfields Commission) still had plenty of power to wield which they did arbitrarily when an opportunity presented itself. A notice put out by Warden Sherrard dated 1 October 1857 ordered all the occupants of crown land at Soldier's

Hill to remove themselves forthwith – no reason was given except that the land was unsold. [465]

1859 Plan of Soldiers Hill Ballarat with eastern boundary with Ballarat East on Havelock Street, Historic Plan Collection CN94: VPRS 8168 P0005

---

[465] *The Star (Ballarat)* 'Meeting on Soldier's Hill' Thursday 22 October 1857, 2

This was an affront to the occupiers as settled community had been established. In October 1857 149 unsold and occupied lots included 87 permanent homes: (63 cottages, 24 houses of which 4 were brick) 16 stores, 4 butcher shops, 2 bakeries, a slaughter yard, refreshment tents, a hotel, a smithy, a boarding house, and a school comprised of 3 tents. There were also several occupied tents (29). Following closely on the discovery by Weeks and Frazer of the Local Court of an attempt to 'smuggle' the Soldier's Hill lots[466] into a sale at a recent auction, this latest action according to the outraged locals, had all the hallmarks of a conspiracy to hurt poor diggers who wanted to settle down.[467]

A protest meeting of the residents at Knight's North Star Hotel was crowded and led by J B Humffray, Mr Weeks of the local court and Mr George Cuthbert. The meeting resolved unanimously that a memorial would be presented to both Houses of Parliament complaining of the Warden's action in contravention of the Goldfields Management Act. This was in response to the Warden's evasive and non-committal responses when questioned on the matter giving considerable weight to the belief that this latest act was part of a 'land-jobbing scheme' with which he was either involved or had given sanction. On the same day, a meeting of the municipal council also declared that the actions of the Warden were 'highly injudicious' and would prove to be 'very injurious to the future settlement and prosperity of this municipality.'[468]

Just as important were matters of administration of the municipality. This was of critical importance as all the new councillors were without any previous experience in any kind of public administration. One could only imagine what was going

---

[466] The Soldier's Hill estate was comprised of over 60 acres and in 1/4 acre lots as standard, it could have possibly amounted to almost 500 lots if 1/8 acre lots were also included. See map below.
[467] See *Ballarat Rate Assessment Books* VPRS 7260/P0002/2 – Ballarat East border ran along Havelock Street (far right) see VPRS 4771 P0002 Item 85 *Ballarat and Ballarat East Town Allotment Survey*
[468] *The Star (Ballarat)*, 'Municipal Council West', Thursday, 22 October 1857, 2

through their heads and the conversations as they began operations. What do we do now? - and where do we begin? - would most certainly been the main topic in that first foundation meeting. It was thus out of such questions that one of the first actions was the motion to authorise the Town Clerk to request copies of bylaws from the councils of Melbourne and Geelong which would then be used as a guide for drafting their own.[469] This became the task of Chairman James Oddie, and Councillors Stewart and Bolger.[470] However, the main challenge to the council was understanding and accepting the level of authority that they were able to exercise.

Around this topic, there was a great deal of assumptions and misinformation that tended to overstate their actual legislative powers. One of the most controversial held had to do with unalienated lands within the town boundaries. The perception held by the first council was that they should have full jurisdiction over all unsold land within the municipality and particularly the proceeds of same within, an expectation shared by many Victorian municipalities in the 1850s. This perception was held firstly because, in the drafting and passing of the Municipalities Act, it was proposed by Mr Harrison of the Legislative Council that the new municipalities could be partially funded by the sale of crown lands within the borders. This would then supplement the small grant allocated to them from the budget of 1855 and the comparatively small allocations in the forward estimates. Thus, one of the first actions was to write to the Colonial Secretary to clarify the matter as noted in the council minutes.[471]

---

[469] VPRS 13007 P0001 *Council Minutes 28 Jan 1856*
[470] VPRS 13007 P0001 *Council Minutes 31 Jan 1856* – these copies were received in late Feb along with other procedural guides -see Minutes 22 February 1856
[471] VPRS 13007 P0001 *Council Minutes, 28 Jan 1856*

Starting With Nothing
This was a matter of the highest importance as the council was beginning without funding. Even though the grant had been promised the previous year, its approval and allocation by the government in Melbourne continued to be delayed. Therefore, the lack of clarity on the lands question by the Colonial Government, which to the new councillors was a matter of urgency, could be better described as a 'paralysis of decision-making.' In their minds, the sale of land would have been an easy solution to the lack of a commencing operating budget while the promised £7500 grant eventually arrived after its interminable passing through the various levels of bureaucracy.

The 'ridiculous oversight' of encouraging the creation of new municipalities without any immediate funding, was not lost on the *Geelong Advertiser*. The editor's biting commentary, however, fell on deaf ears as parliamentary debates that should have been attending to it were bogged down with other matters such as implementing the ballot for the new assembly. As he argued: 'Other matters demanding 'careful consideration and originality' in the 1854 Act should have been more important' such as the fair apportioning of public works funding on respective populations, and the revenue from the sale of public lands apportioned to public works should also directly benefit the respective district to 'destroy the vice of centralization'. [472] This was taken up by most of the new municipalities and led by Sir George Verdon in the next year, strongly supported by the Ballarat Chairman James Oddie. Thus, as the *Geelong Advertiser* pointed out, especially concerning Ballarat, 'how is the Ballarat Corporation to be set up and maintained?'[473]

---

[472] *Geelong Advertiser and Intelligencer*, Wednesday 19 December 1855, Legislative Council December 18, 2
[473] *ibid*

Minutes of Meeting of the Municipal Council of Ballarat

Held at Baths Hotel on Friday 15th February, 1856

Present
1. The Chairman Jas Oddie Esq.
2. Councillor Jas Stewart M.D.
3. " Patr Bolger
4. " J. P. Carver
5. " Robt Muir

Absent
Councillor A. P. Rowden Esq.

Business

1st The Minutes of the Meeting held on Tuesday the 12th February were read and confirmed

Correspondence read

1st A letter from Councillor Bullock giving a just and reasonable excuse for his absence

2nd A Letter from the Manager of the Bank of Victoria referring to the loan required by the Council and informs the Council he is fully prepared to advance the sum by an over draft on an account current at the rate of eight per cent on the daily balance the Members of the Council personally guaranteeing the amount of such overdraft to the Bank (Accepted)

Copy of extract from Council Minutes noting personal guarantees for initial commencement loan 15 February 1856, VPRS 13007 P0001

Establishing Local Authority 223

Where the money was to come from did not appear to be the concern of the government. However, the new councillors were not deterred. As an indication of their sense of purpose, all unanimously agreed without any delay, to guarantee the establishment of the Council with their own finances.

Extension of initial loan to commence council operations. Copy of extract from Council Minutes 19 February 1856, VPRS 13007 P0001

This was facilitated by taking out a loan offering personal guarantees by all seven councillors, to the Bank of Victoria for a line of credit for £500. Initially for the financing of the stationery, equipment and temporary chambers to be constructed on the land granted to them in Sturt Street. Government assent first had to be sought, and a letter was drafted for that purpose and agreement obtained.

This amount however was subsequently deemed insufficient and was extended to £1000 at the next meeting on 19 February.[474] However, this 'small' oversight was never mentioned to the Chief secretary as it appeared quite obvious that the matter was of little interest seeing it was not Government funds that were at risk. At the same time letters were written to the local representatives, Peter Lalor and J B Humffray in the Legislative Council asking how much the initial grants would be and when they would be made available.[475] An answer was received in due course from both MLCs that was both vague and lacking in detail advising that the monies promised 'would be at the disposal of the council in a month or two.'[476] This certainly was not enough confirmation for them to commence operations and only reinforced their decision to press ahead with the application for additional short-term finance while other measures were pursued.

In their rush and eagerness to begin, however, it is not surprising that mistakes were made and perhaps the biggest blunder by the inexperienced Councillors was in the valuation and rating of freehold land and tenements in the municipality. Initially a plan conceived by councillors Muir and Tulloch and Chairman James Oddie as members of the finance committee, it was hastily put into action but with no legal advice as to its validity as it was for six months only.[477] As this was ultimately the primary source of

---

[474] *Council Minutes 19 February 1856, VPRS 13007 P0001*
[475] *Ibid*, 31 Jan 1856
[476] *Ibid*, 12 Feb 1856
[477] *VPRS 13007 P0001 Council Minutes 28 April 1856*

Establishing Local Authority 225

income it was attended to quickly to get notices out and create an income stream as quickly as possible. Tenders for Valuators and collectors had already been completed in March with Benson's application being selected. Valuations followed almost immediately with most residents receiving their valuation notices by the end of March 1856[478] followed by the assessment notices on April 20.[479] The objective is easy to understand as it would result in a return of around £20,000 in a few months, significantly bringing forward the realisation of their plans for Ballarat.

However, it was not to be. The assumption of the Council that their ingenuity would be rubber stamped by the Colonial Administration in Melbourne was dealt a major setback. A letter received from the Treasurer's office asserted that proof of the Council's assessment and levy needed to be supplied before the first half of the promised grant of £7500 would be received.[480] A letter was drafted in reply confidently assuring the Treasurer that all was in order and that all measures had been taken as requested. This included notices for a six-monthly rate of two pounds and ten shillings per centum which was ready to be collected on the word of the Treasurer.

However, just over two weeks later the Treasurer's reply was received dealing a huge blow to their plans. According to the letter, a rate levy for six months was not legal or constitutional, dashing plans for the expected influx of funds.[481] This precipitated a special meeting on the Friday following the usual meeting on the Wednesday where the letter was read and discussed. It was unanimously moved and seconded that the rate be immediately rescinded, and a new assessment be raised for the amount of five pounds per centum on all assessable properties. At the same time, the Council also decided to put to rest speculation on the issue of

---

[478] *ibid* 26 March 1856
[479] *ibid* 6 June 1856
[480] *ibid* 14 May 1856
[481] *ibid*, "Special Meeting" 6 June 1856

Establishing Local Authority 226

the future of Ballarat West and the mockery of it being merely a 'parchment township' as coined by the Ballarat *Times* in 1855.

With the increasing speculation from 1855 that mining would take precedence over the township clarification had been quietly sought from the Surveyor General on the powers and responsibilities of the Council. Members aligned with Thomas Bath and his 'Ballarat South' faction were ambivalent on the issue hedging their bets on a royalty windfall considering that much of the mining activity appeared to be contained in that area. As some mining enterprises were already operating in Ballarat South and towards Sebastopol and some speculative shafts had already been sunk along Lydiard Street South, a quiet approach had been made to the Government on the issue. The precipitating factor, however, was the increasing mining activity just inside the municipal boundary on the Yarrowee River encroaching onto the main road and obstructing traffic.

A motion was put forward by Councillors Muir and Tulloch to have this resolved once and for all with a ruling from the Governor.[482] However, traffic and safety were not the first priority of the Councillors. Rather it was an attempt to disrupt the growing threat to the township traders from the increasing number of commercial establishments on Government land with their lower capital costs, on the eastern side of the river where mining was being conducted. The intent was to have them move their business into the township to allow mining to continue unhindered across the flat and to ensure Ballarat West remained the centre of commercial activity into the future, and of course to maximise rate revenue. It was also an attempt by the freeholders in the township, who were developing a sense of pride in their neat, planned and regulated environment as well as in their newly endowed status, to impose the same order on the diggings population and eliminate

---

[482] *Ibid*, 4 June 1856

the chaotic ghetto developing on the town fringes with the mining activities.

Main Road & the Municipality Streets

This was based on reasonably solid evidence from the Resident Warden, Mr James Daly, whose advice was that the land was auriferous and that an enquiry would be necessary to determine whether the land in question could be sold.[483] Settling the fate of Main Road had been a major objective from the very beginning of the municipality and had been the subject of several initiatives to have the occupiers removed or relocated onto land in the township as either tenants or freeholders like themselves. In a long meeting on 2 April 1856 the position of the Council was made abundantly clear in correspondence to the Surveyor General on the proposal that the Main Road sales as proposed by Haines in 1855, would be detrimental to the appearance of the Township and rather prophetically noted that it could well become a catalyst for a future division between the mining and Township populations. It was thus moved, as the minutes record, that the Chairman be requested to officially notify the objection of the Legislative Council on three grounds:

1. That the sale of these lands will be a great injustice to the residents of the Township over whose interest it is our duty to watch.
2. That the whole of the land being more or less auriferous the sale of it must complicate very much, the question of mining on private land and would probably lead to a future collision with the mining population.
3. That although the Council would regret to see the present occupiers of stores on the Main Road Reserve put to any unnecessary loss, they at the same time protest against any part of the said Reserve being given as freeholds to the parties who have encroached upon it and thus making permanent the present unsatisfactory state of the said road it being now as unfit by its narrowness for the traffic passing

---

[483] Ibid, 25 June 1856

over it as it is by its insalubrity for occupation as an extension of the Township.

This was an issue that smouldered like embers that could not be extinguished for much of the year despite increasingly desperate attempts to drum up support and compliance with their wishes. One of the last desperate measures was a petition to the Government initiated by Messrs Moore and McLaren partners of local wine and spirit merchants Moore & Dunn and Tulloch & McLaren (Tulloch the Councillor) to refuse the renewal of the liquor licenses of the traders on the flat. The object was to compel them to remove their premises to the Township. A £5 reward was offered in the *Star* on Saturday 4 October for anyone obtaining signatures to that effect and leaving the petition with any store on the Main Road.[484]

> **£5 Reward.**
>
> WHEREAS a Memorial has been presented to the inhabitants of Ballarat Township, for their signatures, by Messrs Moore and M'Laren, the first of the firm of Moore & Dunn, and the latter of Tulloch & M'Laren, praying the Government to refuse the renewal of the wholesale wine and spirit licenses for next year to the merchants on the Flat, with the object of compelling them *nolens volens* to remove the premises to the Township.
>
> The above reward will be paid to any person obtaining
>
> **A copy of said Memorial with Signatures,**
>
> And leaving same at any store on the Main Road.
>
> By order of the
> CENTRAL COMMITTEE.

However, while this matter remained unresolved, their own patch on the western plateau was finally given the security that the council had been seeking, putting to rest the endless speculation by prospectors and those seeking to profit from their activities.

---

[484] *The Star* (Ballarat) Saturday 4 October 1856 page 4 (advertising)

Official notice came comparatively quickly providing official confirmation that they 'were the protectors of the public Streets' however, with the power of discretion on matters on public convenience.[485] This written confirmation was timely, reinforcing previous decisions made on such matters which were beginning to become more insistent. The latest had been just a fortnight earlier when a deputation from a newly formed mining company had approached the council regarding their intention to sink a shaft in Dana Street. The council responded that their responsibility was to watch over the streets for the public benefit and to grant permission would be to set a precedent that others would follow anywhere they liked in the township.[486] This

Extract from Council Minutes 6 June 1856 on clarification from Colonial Government on the jurisdiction of the Council regarding mining and integrity of the streets and private property

---

[485] VPRS 13007 P0001 *Council Minutes 25 June 1856*
[486] *Ibid, 6 June 1856*

confirmation came reinforcing actions already taken on this matter a fortnight earlier.

Income & Expenses First Half Year

```
Abstract of Revenue and Expenditure of the Municipal Council of
           Ballarat, half-year ending 16th July, 1856.
                    REVENUE              £    s.  d.
    By Goverment grant      ...    ...  3750   0   0
    By fines at Police Court ...   ...    40   0   6
    By rent       ...    ...    ...  ...   44  18   0
                                        ─────────────
                                        £3834 18   6

                  EXPENDITURE.            £    s.  d.
Salaries—Town Surveyor    ...   ...   ...  137   6   6
   „     Town Clerk  ...   ...   ...   ...  129  15  10
   „     Town Inspector   ...   ...   ...   64   7   8
Public works, streets, &c.   ...   ...   ...  363   5   2
Building Council Chambers, cottage, seats, &c. ... 662 15  0
Printing and advertising    ...   ...   ...   70   2   0
Stationery     ...   ...   ...   ...   ...   15   3   0
Preliminary expenses for Municipality   ...    9   3   0
Design for Corporation seal   ...   ...   ...   5   0   0
Office furniture   ...   ...   ...   ...   ...  38  12   8
Insurance of Council Chamber   ...   ...   ...  20   2   0
Valuation of assessable property   ...   ...  150   0   0
Incidental expenses   ...   ...   ...   ...   19   7   0
Interest on overdrawn account   ...   ...    10  13   6
                                        ─────────────
                                        £1695 13   5
              Balance on hand      ...  2139   5   1
                                        ─────────────
                                        £3834 18   6

              JOSEPH COMB, Town Clerk.
    Audited 9th August.
    M. Elliott,  }
    Wm. Moore,   }  Auditors.
```

Extract of the half-yearly report as published in the Ballarat Star 14 August 1856

Establishing Local Authority

At the end of January 1856, the only income the Council were expecting was the application fees for the position of Valuator, placed at £75 each.[487] With two to be appointed, the Council would begin operations with a total of £150.[488] This was to be more than taken up by the salaries of the appointed officers. The town surveyor, yet to be appointed was to receive £500 P A[489] and the temporary chambers also to be erected would take another significant slice.[490] Estimates for the erection of temporary council chambers on the land granted to them in Sturt Street were in the vicinity of £500[491] and due to their foresight, all this was more than covered by the overdraft account at the Bank of Victoria, secured by their personal guarantees.

The Inspector of Nuisances position, to which Mr Dimant was appointed, also attracted a yearly salary of £100.[492] However, once operations began from February 1856, Mr Dimant was arguably the most hard-working officer of the new council. The four years of inattention of the Goldfields Commission had accumulated a log of sanitary issues that were pressing for immediate resolution to make the township a more liveable and civilised environment. The first order was to ensure that the streets were transformed into places of order.

The Star reported on the changing appearance of the town in their 'Local Intelligence' on Thursday, 18 September 1856:

> There is a somewhat go-ahead spirit manifesting itself in the Municipality; but whether or not it be due to the congenial influence of the estimable corporation is beyond our skill to determine. The streets are gradually being laid out and formed, with here and there bits of kerbing and paved ways for entrance to yards or other places off the main streets.

---

[487] VPRS P0001 *Council Minutes 31 January 1856*
[488] *ibid,*
[489] *ibid*
[490] *ibid*
[491] VPRS P0001 *Council minutes 12 February 1856*
[492] VPRS P0001 *Council minutes 31ˢᵗ January 1856*

The article goes on to mention the new additions like the Dana Street school, the hospital, Council Chambers, the Wesleyan School, 'post and public offices ... highly creditable efforts of enterprise ... worthy of the importance and renown of "old Ballarat." Possibly, without even realising it by referring to 'old Ballarat' the *Star* had already acknowledged an important turning point from a mining camp to a permanent city, professionally managed with a plan for the future. Although it seems that there was some way to go before the Council would enjoy widespread acclamation for the revolutionary changes they had set in place.

13. Challenges and Achievements 1856-1857

Bylaws & Enforcement

To attract praise from the media in such a short time was a reflection of the competency, commitment, and hard work of those elected and employed. It recognized the fact that they took their roles seriously and were not overwhelmed by the enormity of the task in front of them. They had gotten on with things from day one in a logical manner with a clear sense of priorities which were set during bi-weekly meetings and methodically acted upon. Over the year therefore, the most pressing infrastructure projects were securing permanent premises, waste management, securing a reliable water supply, establishing a central marketplace and developing the streets of the town, all essential developments for a growing regional centre. After the lack of interest in civic affairs under the previous administration of the Goldfields Commission and the Central Roads Board, the task was to transform Ballarat from a goldfield into a regional town.

A prime problem was traffic management. The coach company of Calvert Covington & Williams had been in the habit of parking their vehicles on the footpaths when they were waiting or not in use, obstructing foot traffic and so increasing the potential for serious accidents. A circular letter was thus drafted and circulated for all such vehicles to keep the footpaths unobstructed forthwith and to be strictly adhered to.[493] However, this new and regulated way of doing things was not always well received and was resisted by all agencies of the old regime as well as many of the residents. The first signs of this reluctance to change were encountered by the newly appointed inspector of nuisances Alexander Dimant.

---

[493] VPRS 13007 P0001 *Council Minutes* February 5, 1856

The council received a letter of complaint from the inspector complaining that both the residents and the law were refusing to recognise his authority. Matters had been brought to a head when he issued and enforced notices on H Foster Esq. for dumping rubbish within ten yards of the Post Office – an obvious and flagrant provocation. The local magistrate, Captain Vignoles, however, dismissed the charges because a manure depot had not been appointed. [494] The council responded swiftly by commissioning a number of prohibition boards to be placed in prominent positions banning such behaviour, which were clearly also a violation of even the earlier Management of Towns Act under which the township had been maintained. They then began the task of locating a suitable place for a manure and rubbish depot.[495] At the next meeting, it was proposed that a bylaw be drafted to regulate 'the disposal of night soil and other offensive matters.'[496] The preference of the council was this could be achieved by locating the dump site outside of the municipal boundary. However, as this plan was not approved by the Surveyor General and so a location on the northeastern boundary near Black Hill was agreed upon not far from a subsequent site on the northeast side of Black Hill that existed into the 1970s.[497]

Just as important as the rubbish dump was the integrity of the water supply as the use of the swamp by an increasing number of businesses was posing a significant risk to the health of the town. Among those establishing themselves there were a dairy, a lemonade factory and a bone-boiling plant on the north side as reported to the council by the newly appointed inspector on 26 February.[498]

---

[494] VPRS 13007 P0001 *Council Minutes* 22 February 1856
[495] *ibid*
[496] *Ibid*, 26 February 1856
[497] VPRS 13007 P0001 *Council Minutes* 29 February 1856
[498] VPRS P0001 *Council Minutes* 26 February 1856

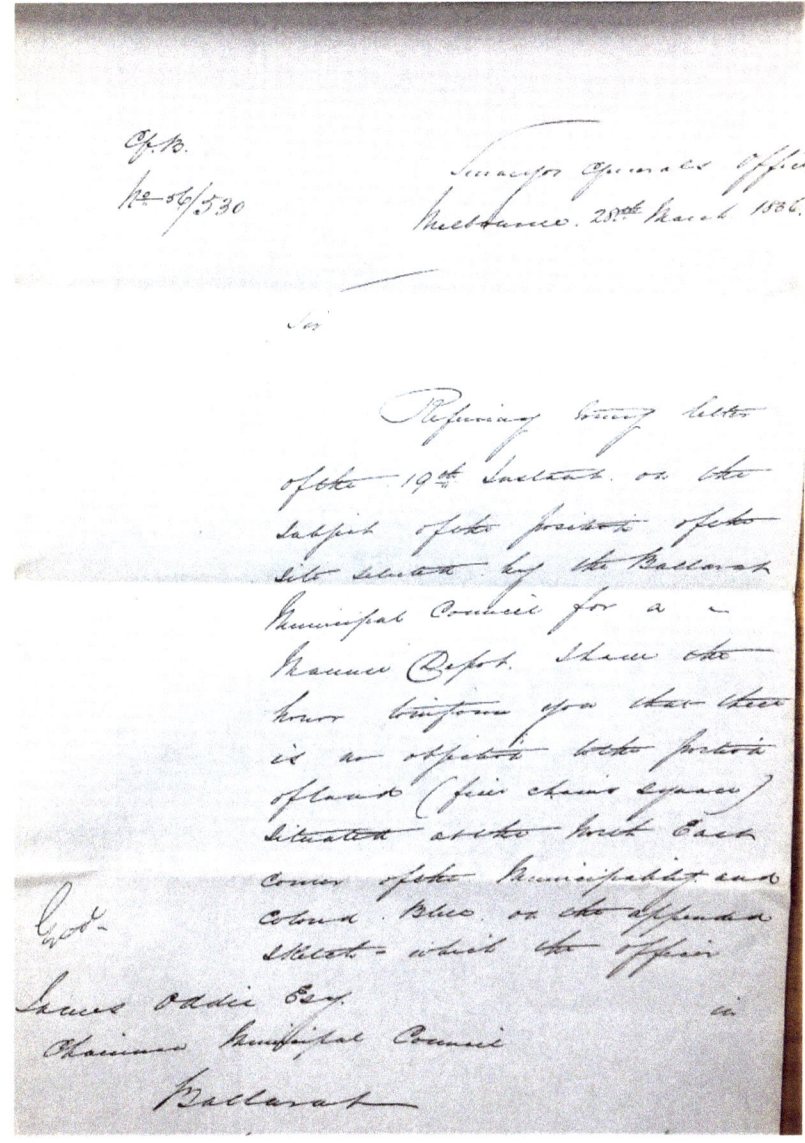

letter by Chairman James Oddie dated March 28, 1856, to the Surveyor General regarding the site for the manure dump on the northeast boundary of the Municipality: Public Records Office VPRS 2500 P0000/1 Letters Inward January – December 1856-1857

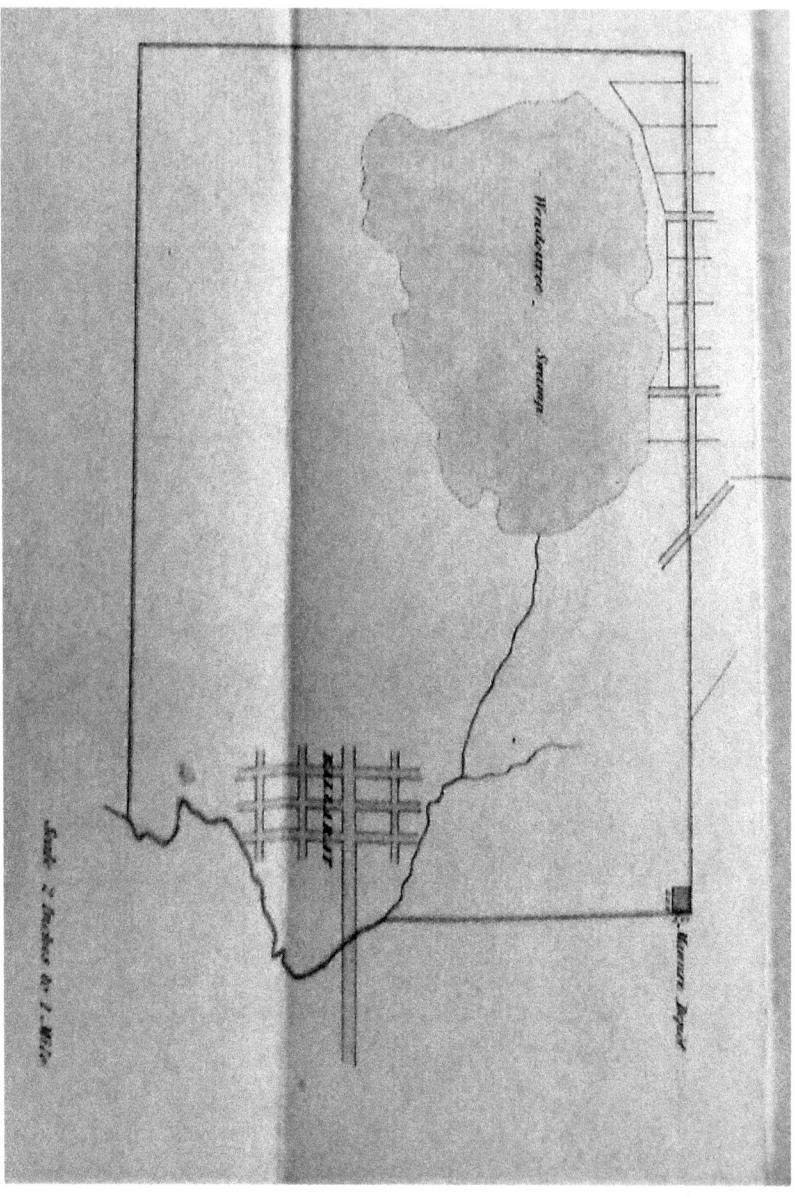

Sketch of manure dump location that accompanied the letter by James Oddie to the Surveyor General June 28, 1856: Public Records Office VPRS 2500 P0000/1 Letters Inward January – December 1856-1857

Challenges & Achievements 1855-1857 237

Lithograph of the north side of the swamp with the perimeter road (now fairyland?) 1856-1859 with established businesses nearby. A motion was raised in council on 26 December 1856 for a fence (bottom right?) to keep wandering cattle from entering the swamp at the request of Inspector Dimant: from the collection of Federation University Australia Art Collection Object registration A00466.

The latter was of particular concern due to the ongoing problem of carcasses being dumped into the water or animals drowning after getting stuck in the mud. The dairy was equally concerning with the cattle also defecting nearby and causing contamination. Another serious matter raised by Inspector Dimant was the encroachment of landowners with tents and stabling onto the swamp reserve, increasing the likelihood of further contamination noted in the same report. As a result, a bylaw was proposed to protect the swamp from such incursions.[499]

Water Supply

This spurred the council into action in not only preserving the integrity of the water source but also to endeavour to exert direct control over the whole vicinity of the swamp and the surroundings.[500] The result of this was the granting to the municipality of the Police Paddock on the north side on April 23 1856 which would be reserved for public gardens,[501] and approval on April 2 1856 for a road around the perimeter which was deemed necessary for effective policing and surveillance.[502] The use of the swamp and all the land immediately around its perimeter being reserved for the public was also becoming a matter for public discussion as a letter to Mr Humffray on April 27 1857 indicates.[503] This change of managers from the easy-going days of the Goldfields Commission however, however, did not come without resistance from those residing in the vicinity of the Wendouree Swamp. With the priority of the swamp as a water source it was an issue that was an urgent but often disputed one during the next few years as various solutions were entertained.

It was first raised by Councillor Muir on March 13 1856 and discussion continued throughout the year without resolution.[504] The government, through the Surveyor General's unsolicited advice, suggested that they raise the level of the swamp three feet employing a dam across the creek, presumably Gnarr's Creek, at the eastern end of the swamp to create a larger and more secure

---

[499] VPRS 13007 P0001 *Council Minutes* 26 Feb 1856 29 Feb1856, 13 March 1856.
[500] *Ibid* 14April 1856 & 23 April 1856.
[501] *Ibid*,11June 1856
[502] For approval for road around the swamp and Police Paddock see council minutes 14/5/1856, 23/4/1856
[503] *The Star* (Ballarat) Saturday 2 May1857 2, The Wants of Ballarat.
[504] VPRS P0001 *Council Minutes* 13 March 1856

water supply.[505] However, by July 3 1856 this was still in dispute as the minutes indicate, with the town surveyor finally instructed to complete a survey to raise the level two feet.[506] This was finally acted upon a fortnight later with a tender accepted from Evans & Barker for £30 for 'making a dam and embankment across the outlet at Yuille's swamp.'[507] This exercise of authority however was not welcome as once constructed it was partially destroyed within a few weeks by persons unknown.[508] The finger however could be fairly pointed at a Mr Graham a local land owner who refused to sell his abutting land to the Municipality but rather had requested compensation from the council for flooding caused by the dam.[509] He, along with other owners, also lobbied through Mr Cummins, a candidate for the 1857 council election, that they should have their own man on the council[510] and like Robert Smith, another potential candidate, wanted a well-maintained road to the swamp to be created to allow 'free access to the water.'[511]

By the end of August, a not-so-subtle appeal to the public was made informing them of the progress of the water supply with the publication of his detailed report made to the public by the town surveyor Samuel Baird.[512] This report is very illuminating showing the difficulties in supplying a growing town with fresh water. As it indicates, water was a vital resource for the district and its supply generated a great deal of commercial activity and traffic which

---

[505] *Ibid* 9 April 1856
[506] *ibid* 3 July 1856
[507] Council minutes 15/7/1856 as published in *The Star* (Ballarat) Wednesday 16 July 1856, Municipal Council, 3
[508] Council Minutes 13/8/1856 as published in *The Star* (Ballarat) Thursday 14 August 1856 Municipal Council 2
[509] Council Minutes 10/12/1856 as published in *The Star* (Ballarat) Saturday 13 December, 1
[510] *The Star* (Ballarat) Wednesday 14 January 1857, 2, The Municipal Election.
[511] ibid
[512] *The Star* (Ballarat) Saturday 30 August 1856, 4, Ballarat Water Supply. Report upon the most desirable means for obtaining the necessary supply of water to the township of Ballarat

would be adversely affected by the introduction of more modern and efficient means of supply.

Extract from the Ballarat Star Saturday 30 August 1856 showing part of the Water Supply report by Town Surveyor Samuel Baird.

ABSTRACT.

	£	s.	d.
Embankment, complete	606	6	0
Pipes	4029	16	0
Laying and jointing do	986	18	0
Fire plugs	150	0	0
	£5773	0	0
Add ten per cent. for contingencies	577	0	0
Total	£6350	0	0

In making out a return of the probable revenue arising from the consumption of water, I am quite aware it can only be approximated to at this season of the year; during the summer months a more correct return could be made by calculating the number of carts employed, and checking the number of times each cart is loaded; but in the absence of such information, and assuming that 15,000 are supplied form the Swamp, and allowing five persons as forming a family, and each family to consume only one half load per week at sixpence per half load will give a revenue of £75 per week, or £3,900 per annum, and allowing £600 per annum, for working expenses, will show a clear revenue of £3,300 per annum.

Or, assuming that 10,000 persons are supplied from the waters of the Swamp, and each person to consume two gallons per day, will give a return of £3,650 per annum,—less working expenses £600,—will give a return of £3,050 per annum.

It may be fairly estimated that in proportion to the reduction in the price of cartage, by having the terminus of the pipes, to supply carts, in Lydiard-street, that the quantity consumed by the public will be considerably augmented.

The existing method of supply was by way of water carts supplying water at sixpence a load on average to 3000 residential premises per week as well as hotels consuming 300 loads per week. Once controlled by the municipality, the revenue thus generated was expected to be £3,300 per Residents in Ballarat East would have access by way of a standpipe for water carts to be erected at the lower end of Sturt Street with a carters' terminus in Lydiard Street.[513] In this matter, the Surveyor General was more than willing to assist with a grant or a loan upon receipt of a prospectus indicated to Councillor

---

[513] *Ibid*

Stewart in a recent conversation.[514] This would also improve things immensely for those relying on carted water as the road to the swamp was often impassable and less than adequate as Councillor Robert Smith pointed out in his election speech in January 1857.[515]

By early September 1856, the council were less confident about the timeliness of government assistance, concerned about fires over the approaching summer and the guarantee of a constant supply of water declaring that they would be taking matters into their own hands.[516] This the Council did the following week, passing a bye-law to assume full Corporation control of the waters in the swamp as well as any private pumps and storage facilities in its immediate vicinity with due compensation paid.[517] In the meantime, an official approach to the Chief Secretary would be made for a grant of £10,000 to carry out the recommendations of the Town Surveyor.[518] Unfortunately, correspondence received in October from the Chief Secretary stated that any funding would have to have the sanction of the Legislature in the same manner as Melbourne and Geelong water supply funding.[519]

Thus, as the 1856 summer arrived, the matter remained in limbo. This was due in part to a lack of funds having only assumed full control of the water and the pumping and storage equipment from September. In the short term, it was also due to the lack of timeliness and indifference of the government in responding to requests for capital works funding[520] along with the unwillingness

---

[514] Council minutes 23/7/1856 as published in *The Star* (Ballarat) Thursday 24 July 1856, 2 Municipal Council.
[515] *The Star* (Ballarat) Monday 12 January 1857, 3, Meeting at the Swan Hotel.
[516] Council minutes as published in the *The Star* (Ballarat) Thursday 4 September, 2
[517] Council minutes 10 September 1856 as published in *The Star* (Ballarat) 11 September 1856, 2
[518] ibid
[519] Council Minutes 22 October as published in *The Star* (Ballarat) 23 October 1856, 3
[520] Council minutes 6 October 1856 as published in *The Star* (Ballarat) 9 October 1856, 3

of Mr Lalor to act on their behalf in the matter.[521] Councillor Muir thus proposed that there was little hope for any assistance from Mr Lalor and that a deputation be sent to Melbourne to directly lobby members of the Government. After a heated argument which ended in an enraged Mr Oddie walking out, it was decided that Councillors Muir, Tulloch and Carver would represent them on the matter.[522]

With nothing resolved in the new year, business premises nearby began making applications to the Council to lay their own pipes directly to their premises with the first approvals given to Mr Baird for his water mill and Hassell & Monckton's Flour Mill on February 4 1857.[523] By February 1857 matters took a positive turn with advice from the Commissioner for Public Works that the grant would not be made but that instead, a bill would soon be introduced to the Legislature allowing public bodies to borrow for essential works such as a water supply.[524] This began a new phase in the project with approaches being made immediately to local Banks to mortgage the rates and to issue debentures.[525]

Unfortunately, as 1857 progressed unity became compromised with the formation of the Eastern Municipality and a more ambitious proposal espoused by the Eastern Chairman W B Rodier to bring water from Warrenheip. This would be sufficient to supply the whole district well into the future allowing for population growth and economic expansion in the farming sector.[526] It was a far-sighted idea that was widely backed throughout the district and

---

[521] Council minutes 2 January 1857 as published in *The Star* (Ballarat) 3 January 1857, 2

[522] Council minutes Friday 9 January as published in *The Star* (Ballarat) 9 January 1857

[523] Council Minutes 4 February as published in *The Star* (Ballarat) 5 February 1857, 2, The *Star* (Ballarat) Thursday 31 July, 2, The Flour Mills

[524] Council Minutes Wednesday 18 February 1857 as published in *The Star* 19 February Thursday 1857, 2.

[525] Council Minutes Wednesday 25 February as published in *The Star* (Ballarat) Thursday 26 February 1857, 2

[526] *The Star* (Ballarat) Tuesday 25 August 1857, 3, Water Supply to Ballarat,

had the support of the local member of the Legislative Assembly, J B Humffray. Many had grown cold on the long-term viability of the Wendouree Swamp based on the reports of local squatters and land owners Learmonth and Waldie, district residents from the 1830s. Both had recounted extended dry periods in the 1840s and one occasion where Waldie was able to easily ride his horse over the hard-dried lakebed.[527]

Nevertheless, the Wendouree swamp project's most ardent advocates, Chairman James Oddie, Councillors Muir, W C Smith and local builder Robert Smith persisted despite the controversy erupting all over the district. Chairman James Oddie, since parties in the east were proposing another project, believed that problems with a future dry spell could be solved by barring those on the eastern side of the river access to the pipes once installed. After 'warmly objecting' to the Chairman's solution, a motion was passed at the end of June 1857 postponing the scheme.[528] Nevertheless, aggressive proponents of the Wendouree Swamp scheme, after a 'very angry' exchange led by the Chairman, Cr. Tulloch and new convert to his opinion W C Smith, soon had their way and tenders were called and accepted for the supply of pipes on Thursday July 16. This they did in defiance of a request by J B Humffray the member for North Grenville, to postpone the project until the Eastern proposal was fully considered.[529]

This final act unfortunately became a declaration of war between Ballarat West and the much larger but less affluent population of Ballarat East who took the fight to their Western colleagues. A loophole was exploited early in 1858 by the new eastern municipality to make use of the government-owned Main Road

---

[527] *The Star* (Ballarat) Monday 12 April 1858, 2 Water Supply
[528] Council Minutes Tuesday 23 June 1857 as published in *The Star* (Ballarat) Wednesday 24 June 1857, 3
[529] Council Minutes Wednesday 23 July 1857 as published in *The Star* (Ballarat) 24 July 1857, 3

and Sturt Streets to gain access to the proposed western water pipes. This action was facilitated by passing their bylaw to rescind the western ownership of the water in the Swamp in February 1858.[530] This effectively forced a stalemate resulting in the issue being taken out of the hands of the warring municipalities by the Legislature in Melbourne. Thus, on petition by Ballarat East councillors,[531] discussions began with J B Humffray's motion on Friday 21 1857[532] on the formation of a separate commission for sewerage and district water supply.[533] Unfortunately, delays continued as local Ballarat members Lalor (Ballarat West) and Humffray (Ballarat East) opposed each other on the issue with Lalor declaring he 'would oppose and delay the eastern project to the utmost of his power and if possible defeat it.'[534]

Accounting & the Streets

Of equal importance with the water supply, was the setting up of systems not always seen by the public, of accountability, planning and oversight. Unlike the old regime riddled with endemic inefficiencies, it was the hard-won local autonomy that was behind the 'go-ahead spirit.' Memories of the Eureka rebellion remained fresh and well-watered for some time after. Fuelled by the Royal Commission and its findings, a trove of material was readily available for the press and reformist politicians. Allegations of waste, financial mismanagement, corruption and largesse brought against the Goldfields Commission in 1854-1855 thus continued to feed the fires of reform amongst the mining population. There

---

[530] *The Star* (Ballarat) Monday 1 March 1858, 3, Ballarat East Water Supply

[531] *Petition Chairman and Councillors of Ballarat East against monopoly of water* Original Papers Tabled in the Legislative Assembly VPRS 3253/P0000/49 Letters inwards, Surveyor General

[532] *The Star* (Ballarat) Monday 24 August 1857,2, Proceedings in Parliament, Legislative Assembly, Friday 21 August 1857,

[533] *The Star* (Ballarat) Tuesday 4 August 1857, 2, Municipal Differences; 1

[534] *The Star* (Ballarat) Monday August 24, 1857, page 2, Proceedings in Parliament, Legislative Assembly, Friday August 21, 1857

were also allegations in Melbourne of mismanagement of most other Government agencies. The accusing fingers all pointed at the hapless Auditor-General Childers over the imprest system of funding government expenses as the major contributing factor.[535]

It is no surprise therefore that at Ballarat with the commencement of operations, matters such as this were taken very seriously with the Chairman taking a personal interest in expenditure on public works.[536] With no rate income yet received, the Council was dependent on the unfulfilled promise of an initial £3750 grant, half of the total £7500 promised in the initial legislation. Nevertheless, even though every penny was as important as the pounds, the council were not deterred in performing the role it had been elected to fulfill. Not shying away from the first real test of their effectiveness they decided to tackle the most obvious and most discussed - the township streets which were in a dreadful and dangerous state.[537] Contractors Martin & Scott had been engaged to do the first stage of the work of improvement of those not yet constructed as per the original survey of 1852. Unfortunately, they were not proving to be either quick or efficient being used to the ways of the old administration.

Having never served in this capacity before it was only to be expected that errors of judgment would occur. In this case, although of a technical nature, they could have had serious consequences if the work was not done according to the contract. Accusations were directed by Councillor Carver at the Chairman for not having obtained financial securities for the contract which represented a significant portion of their first budget.[538] By October £4000 had been well exceeded with a final and

---

[535] Geoffrey Serle, *The golden age, a history of Victoria, 1851-1861*, pp188-191
[536] Council minutes, 15 July 1856, 24 July 1856, 31 July 1856, 14 August 1856, 4 September 1856, 11 September 1856, 2 October 1856, as published in the *Star* the following day. By October a more compliant attitude is detected in relations between Martin & Scott and the Council.
[537] See fig 27 for a view of Lydiard Street North in 1855
[538] *Ibid*

unanticipated request made by the contractors for £705.[539] The lack of oversight was of great concern also due to the personal guarantees given by all seven councillors to the Bank of Victoria. However, the error was quickly rectified with Mr Oddie taking a personal interest in ensuring securities were obtained and the work was completed. The activities of Martin & Scott were scrutinised at almost every council meeting throughout 1856, and a system of penalties was set in place as an incentive to complete the work. Any progress payments were not released until conditions were met and with the additional use of their surveyor, close monitoring and daily reports of the work were possible.[540] This brought a big improvement to conditions in the centre of town over the previous years, very evident in pictures of Lydiard Street from 1855 to 1858.

Political Factions and Market Square

With the transformation of the streets a work-in-progress, local democracy was proving a much tougher skill to master. The proposal for a marketplace was first raised at the council meeting on 26 February 1856. It was to be in a reserve of four acres 'for the mutual benefit of both the township and the diggings.' The reserve was to have a frontage on Mair 'road' opposite the Government

---

[539] See Appendix XI page 212 for a record of the expenditure on this contract detailing the extent of the works

[540] *Ballarat Star*, 24 July 1856, Council Minutes 23 July 1856

Camp and extend in a straight line to another frontage below the church reserves on Dana Street.[541]

Lydiard Street 1855, from the collection of the Ballarat Historical Society Catalogue 232.80

Lydiard Street North 1857: Photo/coloured line engraving: S T Gill 1857 and J Tingle se: titled *Ballarat Post office & Township from Government enclosure*. Ballarat Historical Society Collection Images Catalogue No 321.79

---

[541] VPRS 13007 P0001 *Council Minutes 26 February 1856*

Lydiard Street South looking north 1858, after two years under municipal government, From the collection of the Ballarat Historical Society, B/W lithograph by S. T. Gill titled *Township of Ballarat from Bath's Hotel*, Catalogue No 531.81

However, a multiplicity of stakeholders turned this into a political football exposing the competing interests of the district which fell into three broad categories. The first was the agricultural district to the west of Ballarat which included leading figures in Ballarat West such as Thomas Bath.[542] and Muir Brothers both with large and productive farms in the Dowling Forest and Burrumbeet district to the northwest. The second were the eastern miners and traders whose main concern was access, and third were those with an eye for capital gains such as those who owned or intended to purchase land and properties nearby. All at some stage sought to influence the Ballarat West councillors to some degree.

After concerns over water in the original location, a smaller location nearer to the Unicorn Hotel on Sturt Street was selected but that also was rejected due to concerns by Taylor the surveyor

---

[542] *Geelong Advertiser and Intelligencer* 24 January 1856, Ballarat, 2; *The Star* (Ballarat) 12 August 1856, Local Intelligence, Agricultural Progress, 3; *The Star* (Ballarat) Friday 26 February 1858, Insolvent Court

that it would be too intersected with roads to be suitable.[543] A third option on the corner of Mair and Doveton Streets had been approved by a majority vote of the council after poorly attended public meetings early in 1856 and was subsequently given government sanction. However, after being confronted with a petition signed by 200 angry ratepayers against the Mair Street site, Councillor Muir felt obliged to carry the matter further.[544]

It was thus found that the decision in favour of Mair and Doveton Streets had been carried with only three councillors and the Chairman present without exploring other options. It was understood that the site was selected as it was a provision on the original plan. The other site was at the stone quarry on Sturt Street North, just past the hospital. It was, argued Cr. Muir, perfectly suited as it was the road used by the majority of district farmers into Ballarat as well as being central to the residents.[545] It was also well-suited, he argued (ambiguously) as none of the councillors owned land there and so could not be accused of partiality.[546]

The site in Sturt Street was therefore chosen by a ballot that took place during the week at the council chambers with the stone reserve in Sturt Street receiving overwhelming endorsement by 115 to 73.[547] The Council then moved to amend the request for the market reserve to be changed in accordance with the ballot and a petition drawn up for His Excellency's consideration.[548] At the same time, it was also moved and carried to request that quarrying

---

[543] *The Star* (Ballarat) Saturday 19 July 1856, The Market Place, 2
[544] *Ibid*
[545] *ibid*
[546] *ibid*
[547] *The Star* (Ballarat) The Market Place, Saturday, 26 July 1856.
[548] Council minutes Wednesday 13 August 1856, as published in *The Star* (Ballarat) 14 August 1856, 2

cease at the Sturt Street site immediately as blasting was endangering nearby residents and their homes.[549]

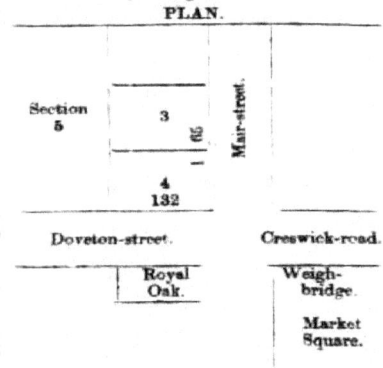

Advertisement in The Ballarat Star Monday 9 March 1857 with location of Market Square and weighbridge

However, this would not be the end of the matter as it was quite apparent that well organised interest groups were following a strategy that suited their own interests. [550] While the convenience and safety of local residents was used as a powerful justification for the new location by councillor Muir and his supporters[551], a far more powerful reason was employed by those in opposition.

A letter to the Editor of the *Star* appeared on 31 July advising that a rich quartz reef ran through the land and should be reserved until adequate technology could be obtained to work it.[552]

---

[549] Council minutes 31July 1857

[550] An even-handed letter to the editor by "A Ratepayer", accused one or two individuals, Cr Davies and Cr Carver who were very vocal in their opposition with Carver asserting that he was responsible for his ward (which extended to Main Road) and his alone. *The Star* (Ballarat) 19 July 1857, page 2 and *The Star* Open Column, To the Landowners and Rate Payers of Ballarat Township, 3

[551] *The Star*, (Ballarat) Tuesday 19 July 1856, The Government Quarries on the Township, 3

[552] *The Star* (Ballarat), Quartz Reef, Township, Ballarat, 3.

However, it was clear that the reef did not have the sanction of the Local Miners Court as their hand on this occasion was conspicuously absent. Nevertheless, Councillor Carver accused the Chairman of partiality and irregularity in voting twice on crucial matters to do with the south side of Sturt Street.[553] Carver, as a competitor with Oddie in the land sales business, as the above advertisement indicates, was clearly supporting northside and eastern constituents who owned properties near the Mair Street site.[554] Additionally, for convenience and moral justification, he also supported diggers from outside of the municipality who wanted easy access to the market. The press was employed by the rival parties to support their positions.

The most creative measure was a letter conveniently produced by Councillor Muir to the *Star* at the height of the dispute by a Crichton Strachan, accusing the Council of 'cool indifference' to his many approaches over the 'dangerous' quarrying methods employed by the roads contractors.[555] This was later raised by Mr Robert Smith as 'irregular' as he gave his speech for election to the council in January 1857.[556] In the end, it appears that time and the impending rollout of the rail throughout the colony were the deciding factors. As 1856 ended there was still no decision and with a growing rural industry, a market was desperately needed as farmers and sellers of agricultural produce were seeking a secure site to do business. As a short-term solution, Councillor Carver moved that they make use of the council hall as a weekend grain exchange.[557] To make matters even more urgent, the operator of the existing weighbridge, Mr Joseph Tait, had complained to the council that the existing machinery was 'useless' and he would have

---

[553] *The Star* (Ballarat) Wednesday 14 January 1857, The Municipal Elections, 2
[554] Ibid,
[555] *The Star*, (Ballarat) Tuesday 19 July 1856, The Government Quarries on the Township, 3
[556] *The Star* (Ballarat) Wednesday 14 January 1857, The Municipal Elections, 2.
[557] *The Star* (Ballarat) 13 December 1856

to repudiate his contract.[558] This matter had proven to be an unqualified disaster with £389 spent on installation and maintenance and only £13 realised from the lease and operations for the first six months of operation by the council.[559] It thus merely continued to serve the interests of Thomas Bath, who continued his monopoly over the only local weighbridge situated on his property adjacent to Bath's Hotel on Lydiard Street.

Nevertheless, over time, no decision was the best decision as the Market issue intersected conveniently with intense debate over the proposed rail from Geelong and Melbourne. It all ended in a coup for Ballarat West and the 'North-siders.' This was due to the unfavourable terrain in Ballarat East forcing the route into Ballarat to skirt around the base of Mount Warrenheip and into Ballarat West at the southern end of Soldier's Hill.[560] The new council was a prime mover in the endeavour as they first proposed to discuss the possibility of forming a line between Geelong and Ballarat in May 1856. This was first moved and seconded by councillors Carver and Stewart as a matter of urgency as the council minutes of 28 May 1856 reveal:

> That a committee of the whole council be formed with the chief merchants on Ballarat and communications be opened immediately with the Corporation of Geelong and that the members of the Council forming the deputation to the Surveyor General bring the matter before him.

This action was likely inspired by the recent failure of a private consortium in Geelong at much the same time due to the proposal for a bill for a government-owned rail line being presented to the

---

[558] *The Star* (Ballarat) Thursday 26 February 1857, Municipal Council.
[559] Income and receipts statement published for the first 6 months of 1856 in *The Star* (Ballarat) Thursday 12 February 1857, 3
[560] *The Star*, Ballarat, Thursday 18 September, The Railway Route, 2

Legislative Assembly.[561] Government control was also strongly supported by Peter Lalor, the member for North Grenville, as he explained his position after the failure of the Melbourne, Mount Alexander and Murray River Company to deliver anything at all after three years of operation.[562] Such a development had been under discussion from February 1856 particularly by the press in consideration of the booming coach patronage between Geelong and Ballarat and the Western District.[563] By July the beginnings of a coordinated scheme were emerging with a line from Geelong to Ballarat via Anakie and another from Melbourne to Ballarat in the planning stages.[564]

Thus, securing a decision on the Marketplace was viewed according to Councillor Carver as the single defining issue in the election of the new Councillors in January 1857.[565] Nevertheless, with the council still deadlocked on the matter it was proposed that as it was urgently needed, the weighbridge modifications would go ahead to ensure revenue was collected[566] as the weighbridge at Bath's hotel was always there as another competing option. This is because of a growing monopoly known as the 'south side.'

The principal mover among this group was Thomas Bath, owner of significant property on the south side of Sturt Street. As one of the original owners of four half acre lots he controlled the fate of subdivisions around the Town Hall as well as owning Bath's

---

[561] *The Geelong Advertiser and Intelligencer* Monday 7 July 1856, Railway to Ballarat, 3

[562] *The Star Ballarat*, Thursday 25 September 1856, Mr Lalor's meeting, 2

[563] *The Geelong Advertiser and Intelligencer* Saturday February 2, 1856, Ballarat, page 2

[564] *The Age* Melbourne Wednesday July 30, 1856, Railway Groups page 3, Petition Citizens of Ballaarat Direct rail line Melbourne to Ballaarat January 1857, original papers tabled in the Legislative Assembly VPRS 3253/P0000/37

[565] *The Star* (Ballarat) "The Municipal Elections", Wednesday 14 January 1857, 2, in his election speech Mr Carver stated that the Market Square seemed to be the test of qualification.

[566] Council minutes, 18 February 1857 as published in *the Star*, Thursday 19 February 1857, Municipal Council, 2.

Hotel, the most prominent establishment of its kind in Ballarat – also on the south side of Lydiard Street.

Vindication for Councillor Carver: the marketplace on the corner of Mair and Doveton Streets in 1866 with the Borough Weighbridge centre and the recently completed railway station in the background: State Library Victoria, Series / Collection A.V. Smith photographs of Ballarat and district.: Market Square ca 1866

The South side was where the mining activity appeared to be moving in 1856 and it was where the majority of funds were being spent by both the government and the public, the most immediate being the Golden Point access road and bridge. Specifically, the Gaol and Court House had been the object of intense lobbying for Government sanction for land and funds and were viewed by many with great approbation as they appeared to be for the exclusive benefit of hoteliers and land owners in Lydiard Street South.[567]

1860's Panoramic view of Lydiard Street South in Ballarat. The view shows the former Ballarat Supreme Court (later the Ballarat School of Mines), the Lydiard Street Wesleyan Church (later the Ballarat School of Mines Museum), the site of the Ballarat School of Mines Botanical Gardens, George Smith's Nursery, Ballarat Gaol. From the collection of Federation University Australia Historical Collection (Geoffrey Blainey Research Centre) Federation University E J Barker Library, Mount Helen Victoria, Object Registration 04258 –

During 1856 Bath and his clique had become dominant with the inclusion of council Chairman James Oddie who also owned land on Lydiard and Dana Streets. So much so that by the elections for 1857, private meetings were held at his hotel in Lydiard Street with anti-monopoly candidates locked out. W C Smith, a later chairman, mayor and member of the Legislative Assembly was one of those

---

[567] *The Star* (Ballarat) Tuesday 23 September 1856, To the Editor of the Star (by an Uninterested Burgess) presumably Councillor Carver

who found themselves out in the cold.[568] At the same time, Councillor Carver was deposed as an outspoken opponent of the South Side.[569] As the local Government Land Agent he was also likely, by the petty campaign by Oddie and inspector Dimant over his water closet during 1856 and 1857, viewed as a business rival of Chairman James Oddie a prominent private land agent himself.

Ballarat East Link Road & Telegraph

Attracting much less controversy was the proposed link between the diggings in Ballarat East and the developing areas of Ballarat South and Sebastopol. It provided essential access between the east and the south. But, more importantly for Ballarat West and its competitive advantage, it offered a bypass from the commercial district of Ballarat East and would 'be most advantageous to developing the trade of Ballarat.'[570] After much discussion on the matter it was agreed by all council members that this would be facilitated by extending Eyre Street to Golden Point and building a bridge across the Yarrowee River with joint funding coming from the Public Works budget and the council rates.

Verbal agreement from the Colonial Government was obtained by Chairman James Oddie while in Melbourne attending the Municipal Delegates conference that they would assist with fifty percent funding of the expense.[571] By the end of 1856 the *Star* so described it:

> ... the formation of the new road across the flat, from Armstrong Street to Golden Point, the aspect of the locality is greatly changed from its position six months ago. Already a street has sprung up on the Golden Point side leading from the bridge to Old Post Office Hill, and shops and hotels and private houses are pretty numerous ... there are the crushing works of

---

[568] *The Star* (Ballarat) Wednesday 14 January 1857, The Municipal Elections, 2
[569] ibid
[570] VPRS 13007 P0001 *Council Minutes*, 6 March, 1856
[571] *The Star* (Ballarat) Thursday 14 August 1856, Municipal Council, 2

Challenges & Achievements 1855-1857

Messrs Black on the north side of the road and on the south a continuous line of dwellings and stores.[572]

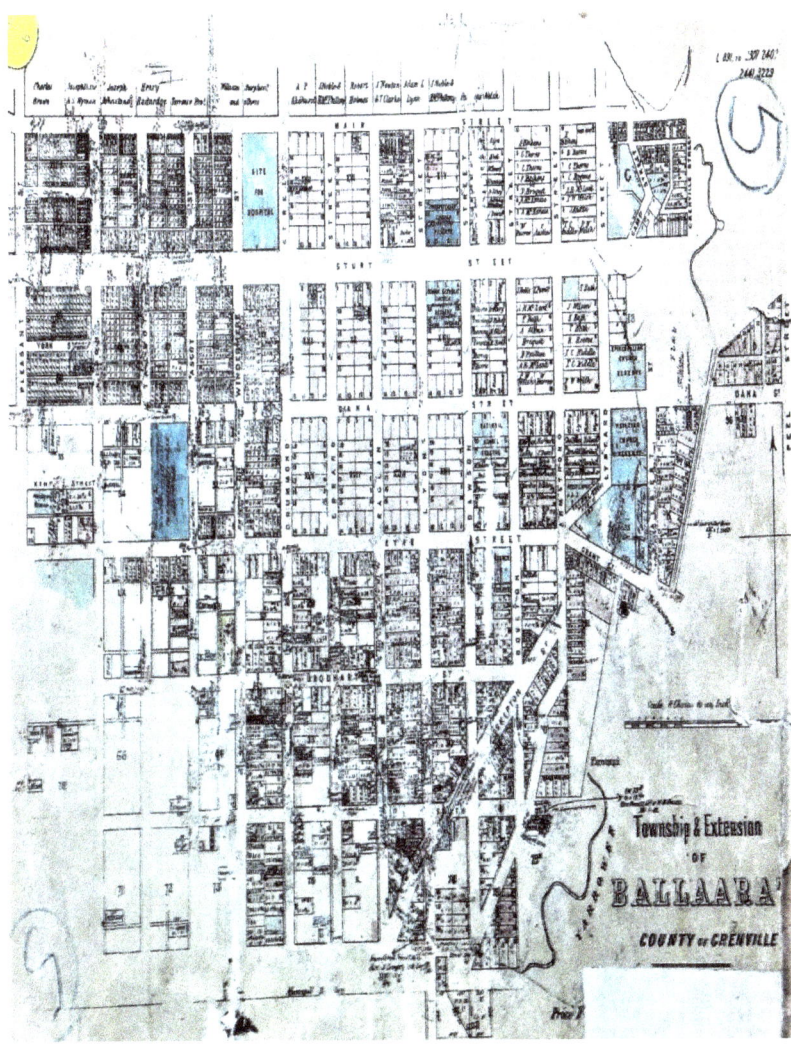

1856 plan of township and extension before the Yarrowee River bridge (previous page) – note reserved land in blue – churches left and right on Dana Street and court & Gaol precinct on LHS of Grant Street – (all still existing 2025) Public Records Office VPRS 2500 P0000/1 Ballarat Municipal Council Letters Inward January – December 1857

---

[572] *The Star* (Ballarat) Saturday, 17 January 1856, Local Intelligence, 3

1870 photograph with a view of Eyre Street extension to Golden Point and bridge over the Yarrowee top left with School of Mines, courthouse and Gaol centre top and immediately right. Photograph – black and white – Lydiard Street South, Ballarat 1870– VictorianCollectionsDSCN2315.JPG
https://victoriancollections.net.au/items/59b1dc2621ea671de4ccf4dd

It proved to be a far-sighted decision continuing to be the major link between east, west and south Ballarat current at the time of this book in 2018.

The year 1856 thus concluded turning the final page on the old era. A new age had begun with Ballarat linked on all sides with a system of roads, order established in the town's streets, organised waste services and bylaws in place to regulate buildings and living conditions. To complete the transition, on Wednesday 3 December 1856 the year concluded with the arrival of the telegraph. It thrust Ballarat West from the old personal, word-of-mouth age into the modern age of 1857 with the flick of a switch. In the spirit of improvisation that characterised much of that era, the *Star* reporter described it:

> There being no accommodation ready at present, the spot selected was the last post near the Unicorn Hotel in the Township. A wire was carried from the post to a small testing machine placed on a stump at its base, and thence – to secure moisture – carried to the stream adjoining, which runs from Mr Bath's claim. For a considerable time, no notice was taken of the repeated attempts of Mr McGowan to obtain a 'hearing' ... About half past eight however, a responsive – click – click – was obtained ... Mr Humffray who was at the Melbourne station, then transmitted the following remarks to Mr McGowan – "The establishment of the Electric Telegraph between Ballarat and Melbourne is a far more pleasing event to celebrate on the anniversary of the 3rd of December than stockades and massacres." – Yours faithfully, J B Humffray.

"The establishment of the Electric Telegraph between Ballarat and Melbourne is a far more pleasing event to celebrate on the anniversary of the 3rd of December than stockades and massacres." J B Humffray.[573]

Conclusion

J B Humffray's statement when the telegraph was connected, exactly two years after the Eureka Stockade, sums up the values and the vision of the 1850s generation at Ballarat. It was one of embracing the modern world with technology and civic infrastructure suitable for a modern urban community. It also shows how far the Ballarat community had moved in just eighteen months since 1854 and the removal of the Goldfields Commission. Such progress, as this book has argued, was due to the establishment of municipal government. Finally integrated into the civic fabric of colonial society, the council was able to focus on the needs of the public and the growing community. By offering a new governing body it also provided healing and hope for a progressive future after the traumatic events of 1854.

This was largely due to the calibre of people that emerged out of British social and political turmoil in the mid-nineteenth century as industrialization and urbanization exposed the need for a better local government system. With the influx of these educated, and literate artisans, the Australian colonies underwent a similar transformation as they harnessed the indiscriminate opportunities of the gold resources. Their pioneering efforts, as they did in Britain, dragged a society that had been based on a pastoral political economy, into the modern age, establishing modern rational systems of local and colonial government and new forms of industry.

On the goldfields, this transformation was particularly acute, due to the Government's ongoing attempt to maintain a pastoral

---

[573] The *Star* (Ballarat) 4 December 1856

hegemony over the vast and sparsely populated inland regional areas. The delusion that this could be maintained by keeping these areas separate from established civic society ignored the changing social and economic conditions in Britain and in colonial Victoria, particularly with the discovery of gold and the movement of the large numbers of people affected. Thus, by denying the establishment of the same forms of civil government experienced elsewhere in Victoria, the miners' increasing demands for equality with the rest of the colony ended at Eureka and their eventual integration initially through municipal government and the later colonial voter franchise.

This was achieved by Geoffrey Serle's 'morally enlightened elite'[574] – the generation that came after Chartism, outraged at the ongoing structural inequality of the political and cultural systems back home. It was a young generation steeped in the values of utilitarianism, free trade, liberalism, the civic gospel of George Dawson and the civic application of science and technology. The elected members of the first council such as Chairman James Oddie, Robert Muir, and Dr James Stewart along with local parliamentary representative J B Humffray were shining examples of this generation. Many came on the promise that a fair and commercial society was able to be realized in the colony of Victoria. It was also based on the determination that the flaws of the British system - the entrenched monopolies and institutions that had displaced them, would not intrude into their chosen home. Fundamental was the liberal belief that taxes should be a guarantee of public well-being as well as political representation.

This idea, as David Goodman reminds us, was based on a belief in a 'social contract' based on the 'egalitarian genius' of the British constitution, confident that trial by a jury of one's peers was a sure defence against tyranny. Through the application of 'equal knowledges' – it was, as many new British municipalities and local

---

[574] Geoffrey Serle, *From deserts the prophets come*, Heineman Melbourne, 1973, p25

residents discovered, the bulwark that established their validity in the mid-1800s.[575] It was expressed visibly in daily life through the ability to participate in local government and the creation of solutions to the problems of urbanization, replacing the old methods and solutions of days gone by.[576] This is how the diggers expected life should be in the colonies far away from the power of the aristocracy, the church and the remnants of the old feudal institutions that continued to resist the onset of progress and modernity.

However, this expectation was dealt a blow on the goldfields which effectively operated as a different social system, quarantined by government policy from the rest of society. Thus, in the eyes of the Goldfields population, the management of the district by the Goldfields Commission with its marauding police troopers and the assumption of guilt, had taken a step backwards into tyranny and disorder. Diggers were treated as aliens existing in an ambiguous state separate from the protections and order of civic society enjoyed elsewhere away from the goldfields.

This occurred despite the Government being warned in official reports, by public commentators and the diggers themselves very early in the gold rush era, that the goldfields policy could lead to all sorts of abuses. However, warnings were ignored and human rights abuses and opposition to them gathered momentum. Under Commission control, conflict, disorder corruption, waste and the squandering of local taxes flourished. Epitomised by the Bentley Hotel affair at Ballarat in 1854, the ongoing mismanagement triggered a furious backlash from the mining populations across the colony culminating with the Eureka rebellion and the removal of the Goldfields Commission. However, its removal only completed half of the solution, with its greatly reduced replacement operating merely another department among many

---

[575] David Goodman, *Goldseeking: Victoria and California in the 1850s*, Allen & Unwin St Leonards NSW 1994, p85
[576] *Ibid*, p75-77

others. Having lost its dominion over the diggers, it fell to them to establish their own local self-governing body as there would be little assistance from the government in making the transition to civil government.

Nevertheless, the colonial government had finally come to terms with the fact that Ballarat was a permanent urban centre with emerging industries sufficient to support an ongoing population. This was acknowledged in its inquest into the Eureka rebellion and its causes, citing a lack of local self-government as a major factor. It was also recognized locally early in 1855 after the Goldfields Commission had been disbanded and most of their police oppressors had been dismissed or deployed elsewhere. With no local government, crime quickly became a problem highlighting the urgent need to establish a local self-governing body. Fortunately, such an eventuality had been recognized well before Eureka by progressive politicians and officials of the same ilk as the diggers in Melbourne who had initiated the process of extending local government to the regional gold mining centres. Begun over a year before, it was considered to be an essential element in developing the economic prospects of the colony. By 1855-57, as Quaife pointed out, the time was right for its application in regional Victoria, as the call for political rights among the previously itinerant diggers, was also becoming the call for social progress of 'jobs, roads, and bridges.'[577]

The seeds of these dramatic social and political changes, however, had been sown even earlier, in January 1852 when the township was first surveyed and private lots made available. An investment was made by those early purchasers like T C Riddle from Geelong and early arrivals like Thomas Bath and James Oddie, who saw a bright future for the region. It wasn't long in the Ballarat township, that other developments occurred soon after the

---

[577] G R Quaife, 1967, 'The nature of political conflict in Victoria 1856-7', p221-230

first survey - a permanent post office, hotels, and commercial buildings such as banks, a land office and surveyor and other legal and government offices. However, with the Goldfields Commission effectively the regional Government, the two-regime solution of the governors existed in plain sight. It created a social divide - one defined by private ownership and the other tenancies or leaseholders under direct Government control, both subject to different sets of legislation. This would form the basis of a life-or-death struggle for the township and local self-government during 1855.

In this hiatus period, various mining interests sought to maintain the local hegemony over the land and the culture of *laissez-faire* that had prevailed under the Goldfields Commission. However, as all players painfully discovered with the Eureka rebellion, conditions had fundamentally changed requiring the application of better organized capital, technology and more cooperative social arrangements. There would be no going back to the unfair competitive arrangements that flourished under the old administration. Thus, with people like James Baker and the implementation of fair access to the resources with ideas like the frontage system, the capital-intensive resources of Ballarat South were able to be fully developed. This provided a massive boost to the local economy and made possible the establishment of a municipal government with the huge extension of the Ballarat urban area southwards with an exponential boost in population and rateable properties.

However, from the perspective of the present day, it is clear that once attained, local government in the mid-1850s in colonial Victoria was a far cry from the local self-government proposed by British commentators and activists such as Joshua Toulmin-Smith. There were no provisions in the Act for local policing, and limited power to raise funds for much-needed infrastructure, both fundamental and ongoing deficiencies in the Local Government

Conclusion

system highlighted by David Dunstan from its inception.[578] Nevertheless, public order was restored quickly under the Municipal Government, as many of the tasks carried out by the police such as surveillance, licensing, permits and regulation were assumed by the Council. A great deal of credit for this must be given to Alexander Dimant the town Inspector of Nuisances and his diligent attention to detail.

However, as the Central Government pointed out, police protection was very costly for such a widely dispersed population. Further, it reminds us that in Britain and even more so in the Colony of Victoria, the transition to modernity was based on the capacity to pay for the necessary infrastructure leaving many local communities dependent on outside sources. Thus, while British Chartists and Liberal reformers achieved early Local Government power after 1835 and often through protracted legal action, eventually, as Fraser and Hennock[579] point out, it fell to the Tories with their political and financial resources to achieve real progress with necessary sanitary and infrastructure progress in the cities. Likewise, in Victoria at Ballarat beginning with a base of only 595 rateable properties in 1856, the financing of large capital works could only be achieved with assistance from the colonial treasury.

Nevertheless, with the equity of property now available for a large group of eager entrepreneurs in Ballarat West, this did not stop the new councillors from seeking direct forms of financing for the water supply at the swamp, an enterprise that ended in bitterness and local division between east and west and ultimately in the hands of the Colonial Government. Notwithstanding, it was no coincidence that the founding members of the Ballarat West Municipality were all men of commerce who saw municipal government as a vehicle for business opportunities through the

---

[578] David Dunstan, *Governing the metropolis: politics, technology and social change in a Victorian city: Melbourne 1850-1891*, 1984, pp 23-41

[579] Derek Fraser, *Power & authority in the Victorian city* 1979; E P Hennock, *Fit and proper persons: ideal and reality in nineteenth century urban government*, 1973

Conclusion

aggressive lobbying for government funds for roads, public buildings, rail and telegraph. Although initially heavily dependent on capital grants from the colonial treasury, in the eyes of J B Humffray and the leaders of Ballarat West, this was justified by the unfairly distributed revenue collected since gold discovery in 1851. This point was strongly advocated by the hitherto unrecognized efforts of local politician J B Humffray[580] elected in 1856, who worked tirelessly to satisfy the political demands of the miners' charter in 1854 and to implement the miners' program of modernization and decentralization as described in the *Age*.

Despite factionalism that emerged over the creation of public assets, the first councillors put the Council and the municipality first, at least during the first twelve months with their personal guarantees a declaration of their faith in the new governing body. The first twelve months were a steep learning experience as they fought hard with recalcitrant lawyers, miners, officials squatters and the easterners, to establish their authority and maintain the integrity of the town, its assets and its municipal boundaries.

They created a model of management that involved consultation and the strategic placement of members such as Cr Muir as Chairman of the District Roads Board and others in the Chamber of Commerce as an ambitious program was drafted and enacted for Ballarat West and the district as a whole. While the limitations of local powers were not originally fully comprehended, the founding members were committed to a program of progress and development to maximise local prosperity. This overlooked function of municipal councils as argued by Bligh & Grant and Power et al, is exemplified in the role that the Ballarat West councillors played in the district in 1856-7 by creating roads, a water supply, the marketplace and facilitating arrangements for the telegraph, rail and other infrastructure projects like the court house

---

[580] Diane Langmore, 'Humffray, John Basson (1824-1891)', *Australian Dictionary of Biography*, Volume 4, (MUP) 1972

Conclusion

and their own Town Hall. [581] Just as importantly, this study has also uncovered the unheralded contributions by previously unknown community leaders such as Robert Muir, and J B Humffray in that foundational period of 1855 – 1857 for Ballarat West as they made the transition from tyranny to becoming an important and integral part of the new colony of Victoria.

---

[581] Bligh Grant & Joseph Drew, *Local government in Australia: history, theory and public policy*, 2017; John Power, et al, 'Overview of local government in Australia', 1981

BIBLIOGRAPHY

Primary Sources

Newspapers

Adelaide Times
The Age (Melbourne) 1853 – 1857
The Argus (Melbourne) 1855 – 1857
Bathurst Free Press and Mining Journal 1851
Bell's Life in Sydney and Sporting Reviewer, 1851
The Bendigo Advertiser 1855 – 1857
Colonial Times, (Hobart) 1855
The Cornwall Chronicle (Launceston)
The Empire (Sydney) 1851
The Geelong Advertiser and Intelligencer 1851 – 1857
Goulburn Herald and County of Argyle Advertiser 1851
The People's Advocate and New South Wales Vindicator
The Maitland Mercury and Hunter River General Advertiser 1851
The Melbourne Daily News 1851
The Mount Alexander Mail 1856 – 1857
The People's Advocate and New South Wales Vindicator 1851
The Portland Guardian 1855 – 1856
Rockhampton Bulletin, February 1874
The Sydney Morning Herald 1851-1855
The Star (Ballarat) 1856 – 1874
The Tasmanian Colonist
The Times (Ballarat) 1855

Public Records

VPRS 8168 P0005 FEAT 665A *Ballarat First Survey 1852*
VPRS 8168 P0005 FEAT 553: *Plan of Ballarat Township Reserve in the District of Grenville 1856*
VPRS 13007 P0001 *Council Minutes 1856 - 1857*
VPRS 8168 P0005 GF5: *survey map Ballarat South 1855 – 1857*
VPRS 8168 P0005 *Historic Plan Collection CN94: Soldiers Hill Ballarat 1859*

VPRS 2500 P0000/1 *Ballarat Municipal Council Letters Inward January December 1856-1857*
VPRS 7260/P0002/1 *Ballarat Rate Assessment Books 1856 – 1857*
VPRS 7260/P0002/2 *Ballarat Rate Assessment Books 1857 – 1858*
VPRS 4066/P Unit 1, November no 69 *Ballarat Reform League Charter*
Surveyor General's Office. (1855). *Township & extension of Ballaarat, County of Grenville [cartographic material] / Surveyor General's Office, Melbourne, Dec. 20, 1855, J. Jones, Lith.* Melbourne: Surveyor General's Record
VPRS 3253/P0000/37 *Petition: Citizens of Ballaarat Direct rail line Melbourne to Ballarat, January 1857*, Original Papers Tabled in the Legislative Assembly
VPRS 3253/P0000/49 *Petition: Chairman and Councillors of Ballarat East against the monopoly of water* Original Papers Tabled in the Legislative Assembly
VPARL 1853 – 54 No31 *Statistics for the Colony of Victoria*, page 39, *Argus* (Melbourne) Thursday 22 July 1852
VPRS 1095 P0000/5 1852/2760 *Petition To La Trobe and members of the Executive Council, from the Gold Diggers and others residing at the Bendigo Goldfield.* 2 July 1852
VPRS 2500/P0000/Unit 91/ Circular 53/H6971 19 September 1853, *Chief Commissioner Melbourne to officers in charge of police on the goldfields respecting their position in relation to the Resident Commissioners*
VPRS001189/P0000, Units 83-91, *Goldfields Commission correspondence & reports*

Government Reports and Gazettes

VPARL1854-55NoA76p[1] *Report of the Select Committee of the Goldfields together with the Minutes of Evidence and the Appendix*, 1 November 1853, Parliament.Vic.gov.au/papers/govpub/]
Report from the Commission Appointed to Inquire into the Condition of the Goldfields, to His Excellency Sir Charles Hotham, K, C, B, Lieutenant Governor of the Colony of Victoria etc, First Published 1855 by Argus office, Melbourne, introduced and edited by Hugh Anderson, Red Rooster Press, Melbourne
Victoria Government Gazette No. 86 Tuesday, September 4, 1855
- No. 97, Tuesday October 2, 1855
- No 127, Tuesday December 18, 1855
Ballarat (Vic.). Council. *City Council of Ballarat: the mayor's special report,*

25th anniversary, 1881, Ballarat 1881

Report from the Select Committee of the Legislative Council on a New Constitution for the Colony; together with the Resolutions and Proceedings of the Committee and the Draft of a Bill, Votes and Proceedings, Legislative Council (Vic) sess 1853-4, Vol 111, no Dl1, 15, 34

Secondary Sources

Anon, *Engineers and officials: an historical sketch of the progress of "health of towns works" (between 1838 and 1856) in London and the provinces: with biographical notes on Lord Palmerston, the Earl of Shaftesbury, Lord Ebrington, Edwin Chadwick, C.B., F.O. Ward, John Thwaites*. 1856. London: E. Stanford

Barber Brian, Municipal Government in Leeds, 1835-1914, in Derek Fraser Ed., *Municipal reform and the industrial city*, Leicester University Press, New York, 1982

Barrett, Bernard, *The civic frontier: the origin of local communities and local government in Victoria*, Melbourne University Press, 1979

Bate Weston, *Lucky City: the first generation at Ballarat 1851-1901*, Melbourne University Press, Melbourne, 1978

Beggs-Sunter, Anne, *Eureka and the Transformation of the Mining Industry in Mid-Nineteenth Century Australia*, Paper to the 8th National Labour History Conference, Brisbane, September 2003

Bennett, J, 'The London democratic association 1837-41: a study in London radicalism', in Epstein, J, and Thompson D, (eds.), *The chartist experience: studies in working-class radicalism and culture, 1830-1860*, MacMillan Press, London, 1982.

Berman Marshall, *All that is solid melts into air: the experience of modernity*, Penguin Books, New York, 1988

Berry Christopher, *The idea of commercial society in the Scottish Enlightenment*, Edinburgh University Press, Edinburgh, 2015

Blainey Geoffrey, *The rush that never ended: a history of Australian mining*, Melbourne University Press, Carlton, 1963

Bowman, Margaret, 'Local Government in Australia' in: *Local democracies: a study in comparative local government*, Margaret Bowman & William Hampton eds, Longman Cheshire, Melbourne, 1983

Bowman, Margaret, *Local Government in the Australian States*, Australian Government Publishing Service, Canberra, 1976

Briggs, Asa (1963), *Victorian cities*, Penguin Books, Harmondsworth UK 1968

Broome, Richard, *The Victorians: Arriving*, Fairfax, Syme & Weldon Associates, McMahon's Point NSW, 1984

Brown Lucy, "Chartists and the anti-corn law league", in Asa Briggs ed., *Chartist studies*, Macmillan, London, 1959

Cannadine David, *Lords and landlords: the aristocracy and the towns 1774 1967*, Leicester University Press, 1980
- *Class in Britain*, Penguin Books, London, 2000

Carboni Raffaello, *The Eureka Stockade; the consequence of some pirates wanting on the quarter-deck a rebellion*, Carboni Raffaello, Melbourne, 1855

Graeme S Cartledge, *A nineteenth-century Scot in colonial Australia: the adventures, misadventures and enterprises of an entrepreneur and pioneer in the eastern Australian colonies*, Local Research Publishers, Winter Valley Australia 2022

Lord Robert Cecil's Gold Field's Diary, with Introduction and Notes by Professor Ernest Scott, Melbourne University Press, Melbourne, 1935

Chambers J D & Mingay G E, *The Agricultural Revolution 1750-1880*, B T Batsford London, 1966

Chandler J A, *Explaining local government: local government in Britain since 1800*, Manchester University Press, Manchester, 2007

Chapman R J K & Wood Michael, *Australian local government: the federal dimension*, George Allen & Unwin, Sydney, 1984

Cobden Richard, 'Incorporate your Borough' in Ralph Roth & Robert Beachy, *Who ran the cities: city elites and urban power structures in Europe and North America 1750-1940*, Ashgate Publishing, Aldersgate UK, 2007

Connell R W and Irving T H, *Class structure in Australian History: Documents, Narrative and Argument*, Longman Cheshire, Melbourne, 1980

Cusack, Frank, Bendigo: a history, Heinemann, Melbourne, 1973

Dunstan David, 'A long time coming', in: Brian Galligan ed., *Local Government reform in Victoria*, The State Library of Victoria, Melbourne, 1998
- *Governing the metropolis: politics, technology and social change in a Victorian city: Melbourne 1850-1891*, Melbourne university press Melbourne 1984

Durkheim, Émile. *The Division of Labor in Society*. Free Press, [1893] 1964

Ellens J P, *Religious routes to Gladstonian liberalism: the church rate conflict in England and Wales 1832-1868*, The Pennsylvania State University Press University Park, Pennsylvania, 1994

Elliott Adrian, Municipal government in Bradford in the mid-nineteenth century, in Derek Feser ed. *Municipal reform and the industrial city*, Leicester University Press New York 1982

Epstein James A, *Radical expression: political language, ritual and symbol in England 1790-1850*, Oxford, New York, 1994

Charlotte Erickson, *Invisible immigrants: the adaptation of English and Scottish immigrants in 19th century America*, Cornell New York 1972

Fraser, D, *Power and authority in the Victorian city*, St Martin's Press, New York, 1979

- Municipal reform in historical perspective, in *Municipal reform and the industrial city*, Leicester University Press New York, 1982

Gascoigne John (with the assistance of Patricia Curthoys), *The enlightenment and the origins of European Australia*, Cambridge University Press, Melbourne, 2002

Gatrell V A C, 'Incorporation and the pursuit of liberal hegemony in Manchester 1790-1839', in Derek, Fraser ed., *Municipal reform and The industrial city*, Leicester University Press, New York, 1982

Goodman David, *Gold seeking: Victoria and California in the 1850's*, Allen & Unwin, St Leonards NSW, 1994

Grant Bligh & Drew Joseph, *Local government in Australia: history, theory and public policy*, Springer Nature Singapore, 2017

Griffiths, Peter, *Three times blest: a history of Buninyong and district 1837 – 1901*, Buninyong and District Historical Society, 1988

Peter Gurney, *Wanting and having*, Manchester University Press, Oxford, 2015

Hall Stuart & Gieben Bram eds, *Formations of Modernity*, Polity Press Cambridge 1992

Hamilton, Peter, 'The enlightenment and the birth of social science,' in Stuart Hall and Bram Gieben, eds., *Formations of modernity*, Polity Press Cambridge, UK, 1992

Hardy, J R, *Squatters and Gold Diggers, their claims and rights*, Sydney, Piddington, George Street 1855

J F C Harrison, 'Chartism in Leeds' in Asa Briggs ed., *Chartist studies*, McMillan London 1959

Hartz Louis, (1964), *The founding of new societies*, Harcourt & Brace Inc, New York

Held, David, 'The development of the modern state', in Stuart Hall and Bram Gieben eds., *Formations of modernity*, Polity Press, Cambridge UK, 1992

Hennock E P, *Fit and proper persons: ideal and reality in nineteenth century urban government*, Edward Arnold (Publishers) London 1973

Hirst John, *The strange birth of colonial democracy*, Allen & Unwin North Sydney, 1988

Hobbes T (1651) "Leviathan": reproduced from Held, D. *et al* (eds)

1983, *States & Societies*, Martin & Robertson Oxford, 1983

Hornby Frank AM, MSP, *Australian local government and community development, from colonial times to the 21st century*, Australian Scholarly Publishing, North Melbourne, 2011

Ince, Onur Ulas, *Colonial capitalism and the dilemmas of liberalism*, Oxford University Press, New York 2018

Irving Terry, *The Southern Tree of Liberty: the democratic movement in New South Wales before 1856*, The Federation Press, Sydney, 2006

Jenks Edward, *An outline of English local government*, Methuen & Co, London, 1894

Jones Ben T, 'Eureka Britannia: Civic republicanism and the politics of rebellion in the British world' in *Eureka: Australia's greatest story*, in David Headon & John Uhr (eds) The Federation Press Sydney 2015

Just P, *Australia, or notes taken during a residence in the Colonies from the gold discovery in 1851 till 1857*, Dundee, Durham & Thomson, 1859

Kelly William, *Life in Victoria*, London, Chapman and Hall, 1859

John Dunmore Lang, *Cooksland in North-Eastern Australia; the future cotton field of Great Britain: its characteristics and capabilities for European colonization, with a disquisition on the manners and customs of the aborigines*, Longman Brown Green and Longmans, London, 1847

Langmore Diane, 'Humffray, John Basson (1824-1891)', *Australian Dictionary of Biography, Volume 4*, (MUP) 1972

Laslett Peter, *The world we have lost – further explored*, 3rd edition, Methuen London, 1983

Lee Mike, *"Peterloo"*. Venice International Film Festival 2018. Venice Biennale. 16 July 2018.

McCracken Grant, *Culture & consumption: new approaches to the symbolic character of consumer goods and activities*, Indiana University Press, 1990

Neil McKendrick, John Brewer and J H Plumb, *The birth of a consumer society: the commercialization of Eighteenth-century England*, Bloomington: Indiana University Press 1982

Mackenzie W J M, *Explorations in government, collected papers*, MacMillan, London, 1975

MacIntyre Stuart, *A colonial liberalism: the lost world of three Victorian visionaries*, Oxford, Melbourne, 1991

Macintyre Stuart & Clark Anna, *The history wars*, Melbourne University Press, Melbourne, 2003

McNally, *Political economy and the rise of capitalism: a reinterpretation*, University of California Press, Los Angeles 1988

McNeill Judy, 'Local Government in the Australian Federal System, in: Brian Dollery & Niell Marshall eds. *Australian local government: reform and renewal*, MacMillan Education Australia, South Melbourne, 1997

Manning, Brian, *The English people and the English revolution*, Penguin Books Harmondsworth UK, first published by Heineman Educational Books 1976

Martin, A., 'Australia and the Hartz 'Fragment' Thesis' in *The Whig view of Australian history and other essays*, Melbourne University Press, Carlton, 2007

Mill J S, *Considerations on representative government*, first published 1861 The Floating Press Aukland NZ 2009

Melleuish, Gregory, 'A short history of Australian Liberalism' *Centre for Independent Studies – CIS occasional papers, 0155-7386; 74*, 2001

Molony John, *Eureka*, First published by Viking 1984, This edition, Melbourne University Press, 2001

D Morier-Evans, *The commercial crisis 1847-1848*, Letts & Son & Steer, London 1849

G A Oddie, Oddie, James 1824-1911, *Australian Dictionary of Biography*, Centre of Biography, Australian National University

Pickering, Paul, 'Who are the traitors? Rethinking the Eureka Stockade in: David Headon & John Uhr eds., *Eureka: Australia's greatest story*, The Federation Press, Sydney 2015

Power, John, Wettenhall, Roger and John Halligan, 'Overview of local government in Australia, in: *Local government systems of Australia (Advisory Council for Inter-governmental Relations Information Paper No 7)* Australian Government Publishing Service Canberra, 1981

D M Purdie, *Local government in Australia: reformation or regression*, The Law Book Company, Sydney, 1976

Andrew Reekes & Stephen Roberts, *George Dawson & his circle: the civic gospel in Victorian Birmingham*, The Merlin Press Dagenham UK, 2021

Rule John, *Albion's people: English society 1714-1815*, Longman Group New York, 1992

- *The Vital century: England's developing economy 1714-1815*, Longman New York 1992

Sandow, Mary, *The Town Hall Ballaarat 100 years*, Ballaarat City Council, 1970

Serle Geoffrey, *From deserts the prophets come: the creative spirit in Australia 1788-1972*, William Heinemann Melbourne, 1973

- *The golden age, a history of Victoria, 1851-1861*, Melbourne University Press, 1963

Schonhardt-Bailey Cheryl, *From the Corn laws to free trade: interests, ideas and institutions in historical perspective*, The MIT Press, London, 2006

Smiles Samuel, LLD., *Self Help, with illustrations of conduct and perseverance*, First Published 1859, Popular Edition, John Murray, London, 1897

Spring David, 'English Landowners and Nineteenth Century Industrialism', in *Land and Industry: the landed estate and the industrial revolution*, a symposium edited by J T Ward and R G Wilson, David & Charles, Newton Abbott, 1971

Spielvogel Papers, Vol. 1, Version 3 First published 1974, edited by J A Chisholm MBE

Sykes, Alan, *The rise and fall of British liberalism*, 1776 – 1998, Longman New York, 1997

Taylor Miles, *The decline of English Radicalism 1847-1860*, Clarendon Press Oxford, 1995

Marjorie Theobald, *The accidental town: Castlemaine, 1851-1861*, Australian Scholarly Publishing, North Melbourne, 2020

Dorothy Thompson *The Chartists: Popular politics in the Industrial revolution* Temple Smith London 1984

Thompson F M L, *English landed society: in the nineteenth century*, Routledge & Keegan Paul Ltd, London, 1963

Thornhill W, *The growth and reform of English local government*, Weidenfield and Nicholson, London, 1971

Turner H G, *A history of the Colony of Victoria from its discovery to its absorption into the Commonwealth of Australia in two volumes, Vol. II A.D.1854-1900* Longmans Green and Co. Melbourne, 1904

Verdon, Sir George Frederick, *The present and future of municipal government in Victoria*, Melbourne, W Fairfax & Co 1858

Ward J T and Wilson R G (eds.), *Land and industry: the landed estate and the industrial revolution*, David & Charles, Newton Abbot, Devon, 1971

Webb, Sidney and Webb, Beatrice and Ponsonby, G. J. *English local government. Vol. 5: The story of the King's highway.* Cass, London, 1963

William Westgarth, *The Colony of Victoria, its history, commerce and gold mining; its social and political institutions; down to the end of 1863*, Sampson, Low, Son and Marston, London, 1864

Joanna M Williams, *Manchester's radical Mayor, Abel Heywood, the man who built the town hall*, The History Press, Port Stroud, Gloucestershire UK, 2017

Withers W B, *History of Ballarat and some Ballarat reminiscences*, First Published 1870, Published in Ballarat by Ballarat Heritage Services, 1999

Theses

Beggs-Sunter, Anne, *James Oddie, (1824-1911) his life and the Wesleyan contribution to Ballarat*, MA Thesis, Deakin University, 1989
- *Birth of a Nation? Constructing and De-Constructing the Eureka Legend*, PhD Thesis, Department of History, University of Melbourne, 2002

Croggan Janice, *Strangers in a Strange Land*, Phd. Thesis, Federation University Ballarat, 2002

Cousen, Nicola, *Dr James Stewart: Irish Doctor and Philanthropist on the Ballarat Goldfields*, PhD Thesis, Federation University Ballarat Vic, 2017

Lewis R A, *Edwin Chadwick and the public health movement 1832-1854*, Phd. Thesis unpublished, University of Birmingham, 1949

Messner, Andrew, *"Chartist political culture in Britain and colonial Australia, c 1835-1860"*, Phd. thesis, UNE 2000

Quaife, G R., *The nature of political conflict Victoria 1856 – 57*. Masters Dissertation, Melbourne University, School of History, 1964

Michael Radzevicius, *Edward Gibbon Wakefield and an Imperial utopian dream*, Ph.D., University of Adelaide, 2011

Rootes, Grant, *A chaotic state of affairs? the permissive system of local government in rural Tasmania 1840 – 1907*, University of Tasmania, Hobart, 2008

Ruzicka E R, '*A political history of Tasmanian Local Government: seeking explanations for decline*' Phd., Thesis, University of Tasmania, 2016

Williams, Paul, *Colonial rebellions in British America, Canada and Australia, a comparative trans-colonial Study concerning their causes, outcomes and connectivity in the attainment of responsible government in Canada and Australia*, PhD thesis, Federation University, 2011

Periodicals

J V Beckett, 'The Pattern of Land Ownership in England and Wales, 1660-1880', in *The Economic History Review*, Vol. 37, No.1, (Feb 1984)

Cannadine David, Urban development in England and America in the nineteenth century: some comparisons and contrasts, in *The Economic History Review, New Series*, Vol 33, No 3 (Aug. 1980)

J P D Dunbabin, "British Local Government Reform: The Nineteenth Century and after", *The English Historical Review*, Vol. 92, No. 365,

(Oct 1977)

Gutchen, Robert M. 'local improvements and centralization in nineteenth century England', in: *The Historical Journal, Vol 4, No 1,* 1961

Jack Harrington, Edward Gibbon Wakefield, the liberal political subject and the settler state, in *Journal of Political Ideologies,* 20 (3)

Jordan D, "The political methods of the anti-corn law league", *Political science quarterly,* vol., 42, No 1, March 1927

Joyce Patrick, 'The factory Politics of Lancashire in the Later Nineteenth Century', in: *The Historical Journal, Vol. 18, No. 3 (Sept. 1975)*

Messner, Andrew, 'Land, leadership, and immigration: some problems in Chartist historiography', *The Historical Journal,* Vol 42, No 4, (Dec 1999)

Ogborn, Miles, 'Local power and State Regulation in Nineteenth Century Britain', in: *Transactions of the Institute of British Geographers, vol. 17, No 2* (1992) The Royal Geographical Society

Prothero J, 'London Chartism and the trades', in *The Economic History Review,* Vol, 24 No. 2 (May 1971)

Quaife G R, The Diggers: 'Democratic Sentiment and Political Apathy' in: *The Australian Journal of Politics and History,* Vol, 13, Issue 2 August 1967

Rubenstein W D, 'Elites and the Class Structure of Modern Britain', in: *Past & Present,* No.76 (Aug. 1977)

Sayer Derek, 'A notable administration: English state formation and the rise of capitalism', *American Journal of Sociology,* Vol. 97, No 5, (March 1992)

Shaw Albert, "Municipal Government in Great Britain". *Political Science Quarterly.* The Academy of Social Science. 4 (2)

Smith Julia, 'Land Ownership and Social Change in Late Nineteenth Century Britain' in: *The Economic History Review, New Series,* Vol. 53, No.4 (Nov 2000)

Sweet Rosemary, 'Freemen and independence in English borough politics c. 1770-1830', *Past & Present, No. 161, Nov. 1998*

Thompson E P, 'the moral authority of the English crowd', in the eighteenth century, in *Past and Present No. 50* (Feb 1971)

Thompson F M L, 'Land and Politics in England in the Nineteenth Century', in: *Transactions of the Royal Historical Society,* Vol 15 (1965)

William Van Vugt, Running from ruin? The emigration of British farmers in the wake of the repeal of Corn Laws, *Economic History Review,* 2nd ser XLI 3 1988

John Waugh, Framing the first constitution, 1853-1855, in *Monash University Law Review,* 1997, Vol. 23 (2),

Weinstein Ben, 'Local self-government is true socialism: Joshua Toulmin Smith, the state and character formation', *The English Historical Review*, Vol. 123, No. 504 (Oct.2008)

Wettenhall, R L, 'Towards a reinterpretation of Tasmania's local government history', *Journal of the Royal Australian History*, 67 1981 2

Pamphlets

Toulmin-Smith Joshua, *Local Self-Government and centralization: the characteristics of each; and its practical tendencies, as affecting social moral and political welfare and progress, including comprehensive outlines of the English Constitution*, John Chapman, London, 1851,

- *Local Self-Government un-mystified, a vindication of common sense, human nature and practical improvement, against the manifesto of centralism put forth at the Social Science Association*, London, 185

City Council of Ballarat: *the mayor's special report, 25th anniversary, 1881* Ballarat 188

INDEX

Agricultural workers
    redundancy & dispossession of, 21
Allday, Joseph
    & Birmingham Tories, 62
    Birmingham Chartist Alderman, 62
Allen, Mr
    & Ballarat 1855, 165
Allison, Dr, 197
    1856 Ballarat speech, 153
Anakie, 253
Anglican church
    a pillar of British society, 17
Anglicans
    & Ballarat West, 86
Anti-Corn Law League, 50
Anti-corn Law movement
    & Ballarat West, 86
Anti-transportation, 34, 35, 36, 105
    & Goldfields, 105
    NSW, 102
Aristocracy, 262
    & Australian colonies, 200
    19th century ownership of British towns, 17
Armstrong Street, 256
Armstrong, Commissioner, 125
    1st at Ballarat goldfield, 123
    assists diggers in locating gold, 126
    extends credit to diggers 1851, 126
    turbulent st meeting with Ballarat diggers Sept 1851, 125
Artisans
    & emigration, 22
    industrialization & loss of status, 20
Arts, the
    encouraged at Ballarat 1856, 205
Assimilation
    & Victorian diggers early 1850s, 28
    miners protest absurdity of 1851 policy, 115
Australasian League, 35, 102, 106
Australian republic
    1851 movement for, 35
Autonomy
    & UK local Gov't, 64

1840s Melbourne & NSW, 66
Victoria, 64
Baird, Mr
    Ballarat West water mill approval 1856, 242
Baird, Samuel
    & Ballarat water supply 1856, 239
    appointed Ballarat West surveyor 1856, 189
Baker, James, 205
    & Ballarat Industrial Institute 1856, 198
    & Ballarat South frontage system, 204
    & frontage system, 6
Bakery Hill, 171
Ballarat, 138
    & agriculture, 206
    & Cornish miners 1855, 177
    & permanent settlement, 186
    1852 population 6400, 131
    1854 mapping & roadworks by Goldfields Commission, 134
    1854 population 30,000, 132
    1855 law & order crisis, 161
    1855-7 East West division & 1855 municipal petition, 180
    1856 agricultural industry, 170
    a major market town by 1854, 54
    commercial need for municipality by 1854, 54
    Commissioner duties 1852, 131
    contrasted with Bendigo 1854, 54
    first survey, 23
    in 1854, 132
    in 1855, 168
    J B Humffray election celebration 1856, 153
    traders & mining 1854-5, 171
Ballarat Chamber of Commerce, 159
Ballarat Early Closing Association
    & James Oddie, 191
Ballarat East, 53, 185, 189, 197, 213
    & water supply 1856, 240

1857 Warrenheip water scheme for Ballarat district, 242
disorder under goldfields Comm, 81
Municipality est 1857, 82
rail connection, 252
recinds Ballarat West ownership of Swamp 1858, 244
viewed as undesirable for Ballarat West 1855, 181
Ballarat East Municipality, 242
creating urban order from 1857, 82
Ballarat Gold Diggers Association, 120
a forerunner of Ballarat Reform League, 148
demand for revenue s/be spent locally 1853, 146
Ballarat Goldfields
management of & Eureka Rebellion, 52
Ballarat Hospital, 232
Ballarat Industrial Institute, 198
Ballarat Municipality
1855 proposed extension, 179
competing petitions 1855, 178
meeting on petition for April 1855, 167
Ballarat North
& Gold Dept corruption 1855-7, 82
Ballarat Pioneers Association, 26
Ballarat Reform league
& Ballarat local gov't, 5
Ballarat Reform League, 159
demands immediate change of Goldfields admin Nov 1854, 155
list of demands Nov 1854, 148
press claims aims achieved Jan '55, 156
Ballarat Reform League Charter
& demand for local gov't on the goldfields Nov '54, 155
on tyranny, 155
Ballarat School of Mines, 199
Ballarat South, 192
& deep lead mining from 1856, 192
1856-7 extension, 214
occupation of proposed lots 1856-7, 214
Ballarat South Faction
& Ballarat expansion 1855-7, 226
Ballarat storekeepers
& origins of municipal gov't, 165
Ballarat Swamp

resistance to Council control of 1856, 238
Ballarat Times
& license fee, 188
Ballarat Township, 207, 263
& 1855 crime wave, 156
& civic leadership 1855, 158
& freehold 1855, 171
& gold deposits, 168
& mining, 171
& mining 1855, 175
1855 expansion, 151
1st survey 17 Jan 1852, 136
admin of immediately after Eureka Rebellion, 158
existence under threat from mining 1855, 174
future of goldfield discussed Jan 1855, 158
squatter-backed self-protection society 1855, 165
under different rules to Goldfields, 264
under Goldfields Commission authority 1852-1855, 136
Ballarat Volunteer Protection Society, 169
Ballarat Weighbridge
1855-6, 169
Ballarat Wesleyan School, 232
Ballarat West, 178, 252
& British non-conformist founders, 86
& bushfire concerns 1856, 241
& Central Roads Board 1856, 197
& entrepreneurial councillors, 81
& est of goldfield order after Eureka, 80
& farming 1856, 249
& jurisdiction in Main Road 1856, 213
& legal jurisdiction, 213
& limited powers, 266
& local factions 1856, 251
& local infrastructure investment, 80
& local squatters, 243
& no inaugural funding, 87
& North Grenville electorate, 207
& policing authority, 88
& post 1835 British Municipalities, 86

& progress, 266
& public works department dispute 1856, 213
& railway, 251
& relocation of Main Rd traders 1856, 227
& residential water supply & cost 1856, 240
& south side development 1855-7, 254
& the local monopoly 1857, 255
& water carts 1856, 240
1855 real estate, 169
1856 crackdown on leaseholding, 180
1856 enforcement of rubbish dumping 1856, 234
1856 grain exchange, 251
1856 rate book, 80
1856 water supply integrity, 234
1856-7 rate records, 25
1857 Council elections, 253
1857 doubts on Swamp's water supply reliability, 243
1st 1856 sale of town lots, 185
1st assessment notices, 225
1st Council elections Jan 1856, 187
1st Council meeting, 209
1st council of professionals & businessmen, 86
1st municipal meeting Jan 1856, 184
1st municipal weighbridge 1856, 252
1st valuations for 6 months only, 225
6 monthly rate scheme rejected, 225
a regional centre of commerce 1856, 168
Agricultural Society founded 1856, 194
application for valuators Jan 1856, 188
application for water supply grant 1856, 241
authority over streets confirmed 1856, 229
Ballarat Industrial Institute, 194
Ballarat Swamp & adjacent enterprises 1856, 234
Ballarat Swamp dam at Gnarr Creek 1856, 238
banks approached for water supply arrangem't Feb 1857, 242

based on ideals of a fair society, 25
bye-law assuming control of Swamp & water supply Sept 1856, 241
bye-law for night waste disposal 1856, 234
by-pass road & bridge linking Ballarat East 1856-7, 256
c/f with Ballarat East 1856-60, 82
capital grants, 266
Chamber of Commerce founded 1856, 194
commencement grant advancement, 245
commencement loan extended, 224
commercial competition with Ball't East, 226
competing municipal petitions, 5
conflict with East over water supply, 243
council candidates Jan 1856, 185
Council Chambers erected, 210
Dana St mining application denied, 229
Eastern attempts to influence, 87
enforcing municipality boundaries, 212
est of & individual rights, 154
existence threatened by mining 1855-6, 226
factionalism 1856-7, 266
faith of founders in Municipality, 266
farming, 251
financing infrastructure 1856, 265
fire brigade proposed Jan 1856, 185
founded by displaced Britons, 25
Golden Point access road and bridge, 254
Hassell & Monckton flour mill 1856, 242
Hospital foundation stone Dec 1855, 187
initial municipal expenses 1856, 231
inspector's appointment & salary, 231
library, 195
loan for commencing municipality, 221
local resistance to incorporation, 87
Market Square, 169
Market Square 1857, 253

market square proposed Feb 1856, 246
mocked as a 'parchment' township 1855-6, 226
municipal council & Soldiers Hill 1857, 219
municipal income for Jan 1856, 231
municipality as agent for progress, 5
municipality petition granted Dec 1855, 184
new court house 1856, 184
new rubbish depot 1856, 234
original market reserve site, 249
personal guarantees for municipality commencement, 224
Police Paddock granted 1856, 238
popularity with local diggers 1856-7, 80
public gardens reserve 1856, 238
railway project, 252
railway project 1856, 197
ratepayers 1856-7, 80
rates, 188
resistance to new traffic laws 1856, 234
sanitary issues 1856, 231
street development project 1856, 231
swamp perimeter rd 1856, 238
telegraph connected 3 Dec 1856, 258
the new Court House, 254
the new Gaol, 254
the South Side monopoly 1857, 253
town hall land application, 209
township streets project 1856, 245
traffic management bye-law 1856, 233
unified under Municipal Council, 81
valuation & rating errors 1856, 224
water supply, 265
water supply scheme postponed 1857, 243
weighbridge, 253
Ballarat West Municipality, 47, 265
& importance to the district, 266
& initial Gov't grant, 221
& Peter Lalor dissatisfaction 1856-7, 4
as a basis for local progress, 48
bye-laws drafted 1856, 220

commenced without Gov't funding, 221
est under 1854 Act, 47
establishment of, 88
local resistance to, 88
Bank of Australia, 213
Bank of NSW, 169
Bank of Victoria, 169, 192, 231
   & Ballarat West streets contract 1856, 246
   loan for Ballarat West commencement 1856, 224
Barrett, Bernard, 49, 52, 65
   history of Vic local gov't, 52
Barrow, 17
Bate, Weston, 49, 54, 193
   & Ballarat West, 189
   & Eureka Rebellion, 54
   & goldfields social integration, 55
   ommission of story of Ballarat West Municipality, 49
Bath, 17
Bath, Thomas, 255
   & Ballarat South faction 1855-7, 226
   & Ballarat transport terminus 1855, 169
   & goldfields enfranchisement 1855, 193
   & mining in Ballarat Township 1855, 176
   & regional farming, 248
   & South Side monopoly 1857, 253
   Lydiard St mining claim, 259
Bath's Hotel, 169, 176, 254
   & Ballarat West Council meetings, 209
   Ballarat Township future discussed Jan '55, 159
Bathurst, 98, 103
Batman, John, 27
Bendigo
   & Red Ribbon protests 1853, 144
   1852 petition, 140
   est under 1854 Act, 47
Bendigo goldfields
   & Fitzroy's 1851 economic stimulus, 104
Bennett, Jennifer
   London Democratoc Society Study, 20
Benson, Valuator
   1st Ballarat West valuations, 225

Bentham, Jeremy. *See* Utilitarianism
    & mass society, 73
    & utilitarian social solutions, 72
Benthamites
    & local government reform, 72
    & municipal government, 74
    individual & social happiness, 74
Bentley
    murder of, 158
    murder of, 148
Bentley's Hotel
    & social disorder under Goldfields Commission, 262
Binney, Mr
    & Ballarat 1855 law & order inquiry, 165
Birmingham, 62
    & freehold land, 17
    & need for 1850s public utilities, 63
    & the civic gospel, 61
    19th century legality of municipal charter, 84
    industrial revolution & social change, 13
Black Crushing Works, 257
Black Hill, 234
Blake, William, 77
Bolger, James Cr, 220
Bolger, P, 188
Bolton
    19th century legality of municipal charter, 84
Booley, Robert, 38
Bowman, Margaret, 46
Bradford, 85
    & post-reform dissenter influence, 62
    19th century local government, 90
Briggs, Asa, 78
Brighton (UK), 17
    owned by Duke of Devonshire, 62
Bristol
    pre-reform corporation, 60
British economy
    1840s downturn, 24
British Municipal Corporations Act 1835
    1st Gov't institution created for modern society, 71
British Municipal Government
    & urban transformation after 1835, 6
    as social reconciliation, 6
British municipalities
    as a political forum for 19th century lower classes, 47
Brown, Captain
    & Red Ribbon protests, 144
Building regulation, 14
Buninyong, 131, 132, 138, 171
    proximity to Ballarat goldfield, 98
Burke, Governor
    & Port Phillip settlement, 65
Burrumbeet, 248
Bush Rangers
    at Ballarat 1855, 163
    Ballarat gang arrested April 1855, 164
Butcher, W H
    & Ballarat telegraph 1856, 178
California, 103, 112
    an example of avoidable evils, 126
    gold & liberal transformation of, 116
    goldfields, 101
Calvert Covington & Williams coach company, 233
Campbell (MLC)
    Municipal Councils signal a new colonial era 1854, 140
Canada
    & Municipal Councils, 140
Canadian Creek
    & gold claims, 3
Cannadine, David, 16
Capitalism
    & British social change, 83
    & urbanization, 75
Carboni, Raffaelli, 207
Carr, Dr Alfred, 54
    & Ballarat Gold Diggers Assn, 120
    & Ballarat Gold Diggers Association, 145
    1853 miners protest committee, 133
    demands self-government for Ballarat 1853, 146
Carrington & Rollins
    Ballarat booking office, 169
Carver J S Cr, 188, 242
    & 1857 election, 253
    & Geelong Ballarat rail, 252
    & Town Hall as temporary grain exchange 1856, 251
    & water closet dispute, 196

accuses Oddie of partiality, 251
Oddie mismanagement accusation, 245
representing Ballarat East diggers, 87
voted out 1857 over Marketplace stand, 256
Castlemaine, 138
   & Miners Right 1857, 215
   & transition to civic government, 53
   & transition to civil gov't, 52
   contrasted with Ballarat, 54
   est under 1854 Act, 47
   history of, 53
Catholicism
   & Ballarat West, 86
Cavanagh brothers
   Vic 1851 successful diggers, 117
Cecil, Lord Alfred
   British PM, 26
   impressed by Victorian diggers, 26
Central Roads Board, 181, 210, 211
   & Ballarat Township, 158
   & land occupation 1856, 214
   Ballarat West dispute 1856, 211
Centralization
   & colonial Victoria, 139
   & Eureka Rebellion, 56
   & need for early goldfields admin, 67
   & Sir E Bulwer Lytton (UK), 68
   & Vic Goldfields Commission, 113
   & Western District 1851, 125
   a growing problem 1853 (Vic), 138
   British utilitarian attempts at, 75
   colonial NSW, 65
   colonial Victoria, 64
   UK legal battles against, 63
Chadwick, Edwin. *See* Centralization, *See* Utilitarianism
   utilitarian & Benthamite, 75
Chamber of Commerce, 266
   as an intermediary body with Gov't, 197
   founded Aug 1856, 196
Chambers of Commerce
   & municipal councils, 37
Chandler, J A, 59
Chapman V Rutter
   landmark municipalization case, 85
Charles 1st, 153
Charlie Napier Hotel (Ballarat), 161

Chartism, 16, 50
   & 1850s Birmingham municipality, 62
   & Ballarat West, 86
   & commercial society, 83
   & goldrush population, 261
   & influence on Ballarat Founders, 49
   & modernity, 20
   British failure of 1848, 90
Chartists, 95, 206
   & 1848 franchise failure, 28
   & local government, 90, 265
   & the People's Association, 119
Childers, Auditor-General
   & Goldfields Commission expenditure, 245
Chisholm, Caroline, 22
Church, the, 262
Civic Gospel, 261
Civic society
   & unintegrated population, 15
   Ballarat need for after Eureka, 67
   Capt John Harrison Bendigo goldfields, 119
   goldfields implementation as a solemn duty, 88
   unintegrated diggers, 28
Civil administration
   & Goldfields Commission, 53
Clarke, Andrew Surveyor General
   & Bendigo 1st survey, 53
   & new municipal corporations Act 1854, 138
   & regional Victorian towns 1851-2, 135
   Municipal Corporations a break from the past, 139
Clarke, Rev W B, 96
Clarke, W J 'Big'
   Ballarat district squatter & landowner, 206
Class, 25, 51
   & British political system, 51
   & goldfields, 95
   & James Oddie, 23
   land & middle classes, 51
   tenant farmers & independent artisans, 24
   UK upper class & adaptation to modernity, 16
Clow, Resident Commissioner

charitable works for needy miners, 133
Coach Service
   Geelong to Ballarat 1852-1855, 253
Cobb & Co, 169
Cobden, William, 14, 77, 78
   & Manchester municipalization, 77
Colonial Bank, 169
Colonial Bank of Australasia, 194
Colonial Government
   & Goldfields civic infrastructure, 265
Colonial Secretary, 220
Colonial Treasury, 136
Comb, Thomas, 188
   1856 Town Clerk, 180
Commercial society
   & feudal traditional government, 15
Commercial Society
   & local guilds, 83
   British unrealized expectations of, 90
   land & transition to, 51
Commercialization, 45
   & breakdown of Scottish feudalism, 11
   & emigration, 22
   & replacement of feudal world view, 71
   1840s farm consolidations in Britain, 24
   Adam Smith & Scottish philosophers, 9
   increased pace of from 18th century, 51
   James Hogg's lament, 12
Commissioner Armstrong
   impressed by Ballarat miners Sept 1851, 123
Conference of Municipal Delegates
   Victoria 1856 & 1858, 68
Conservative drag
   & Victorian Government policy 1851, 122
Constitution
   Victorian debate on from 1850, 28
Consumer revolution, 83
Convicts, 102
   & goldfields concerns, 101
   & license to dig, 104
   as separate from civil society, 95
   emancipated, 95

Cooksland. *See* Lang J D
Cope, Mr Lawyer, 205
Corn laws, 77, 206
Cornishmen
   at Ballarat 1855, 161
Cowie, James
   Geelong mayor, 37
Creswick, 162
Creswick Creek, 131
Crow Club, the, 164
Crown land
   & 1851-57 Ballarat East traders, 174
   & Ballarat municipal status, 180
   & Ballarat West house contruction, 215
   & colonial prospecting/mining status 1851, 121
   & UK mining policy, 110
   occupation of 1856-7, 214
   proceeds of & new Municipalities, 220
   sale of, 220
CSR. *See Robert Muir*
Cummins, Mr
   1857 Council candidate on Swamp issue, 239
Cusack, Frank, 50, 52
   & Eureka Rebellion, 54
D'Ewes, Police Magistrate
   & Eureka Rebellion, 158
Daly, James Acting Resident Warden, 214
   & Main Rd properties 1856, 227
Dana Street, 255
   & Church reserves, 247
Dana Street school, 232
Dana, Captain
   brutality turning people away, Ballarat Oct 1851, 127
   troop leader with 1st Ballarat Commissioner, 123
Dawson, George, 261
   & civic gospel. *See* Birmingham
De Toqueville, Alexis, 199
Decentralization
   & Municipal Corporations Act (Vic), 139
Democracy
   & 1851 policy of 'conservative drag', 122
   & replacement of Victorian Pastoralism, 29

& Vic policy of conservative drag, 114
local, 83
Dennys Lascelles
Geelong wool brokers, 37
Dennys, C J, 37
Denovan, William, 52
Department of Works
& resistance to Ballarat West gov't, 88
Victoria, 136
Depression
1840s, 22
Devonshire (Dukes of)
owners of Brighton, 62
Diggers
& 1855 social & political integration, 151
& desire for civic society, 31
1851 examples of desperate digging forays, 118
all considered felons, 54
Ballarat cooperation with harvest 1851, 127
Ballarat Goldfield & protection Oct 1851, 127
divisions amongst, 3
Diggers' Congress', 53
Digging syndicates
1851 Vic description of, 117
Dimant, Alexander, 195, 231, 256, 265
& Cr Carver dispute, 196
& enforcing new traffic laws 1856, 233
& swamp precinct health 1856, 237
1st town inspector Ballarat West 1856, 89
appointed Ballarat West council inspector 1856, 189
District councils
opposed by Dr Thompson Geelong Mayor, 36
District Police Magistrate
& Ballarat Township, 158
District Roads Board, 194, 266
1853 creation Victoria, 67
1st Ballarat elections 1856, 211
Ballarat West dispute 1856, 211
est in Ballarat District 1856, 67
opposition to Ballarat West 1856, 210
Doveton Street

& Market Square, 249
Dowling Forest, 248
Drew, Joseph, 45
Duffy, Charles Gavan, 192
Dunstan, David, 49
& local Gov't Victoria, 265
Durkheim, Emile
& anomie, 19
Eastbourne, 17
Economy
1850s effects of gold on, 103
British railway collapse 1847-8, 24
Dominance of aristocrats, 16
early 1850s Victorian, 27
Gov't anti-gold rush financial measures, 104
Edgbaston, 17
owned by Lord Calthorpe, 62
Elections
Ballarat West c/f with Victorian general 1856, 88
colonial Victoria 1856, 88
Electoral Franchise, 27
early colonial Victoria, 27
Port Phillip Chartists, 28
Elizabethan regime
& local government, 58
& poor laws, 11
Emerald Hill, 52
Emigration
& agricultural workers, 22
British solution for unemployed & displaced, 26
respectable gold-seekers, 22
to preserve social elites, 22
to reclaim lost independence, 24
Enclosure, 14
& commercialization, 21
Engels, Frederick, 14
portrayal of Manchester, 77
Enlightenment, the
& colonial Australia, 199
& diggers' values, 25
Entertainment venues, 132
Erickson, Charlotte
& British emigration, 22
Established Church, 200
Ethnicity
& goldfields conflict, 1
frontage system & rival solution, 5
Eureka, 53
& goldfields social change, 78

& physical force faction, 4
Eureka Hotel, 3, 148
   & corruption, 81
   & local corruption, 81
Eureka lead, 3
   & Irish, 148
Eureka Rebellion, 148, 244
   & constitutional principles, 157
   & creation of Ballarat municipal gov't, 79
   & goldfields social change, 79
   & municipal govt, 23
   & new Act for Municipal Corporations, 138
   & Peterloo, 77
   & resolving dispute between English & Irish, 204
   a culmination of 4 years of digger agitation, 130
   J B Humffray silenced by physical force faction, 4
   lack of civic government as a cause, 68
   Melbourne rallies 1854-5, 156
   telegraph connection 2 years after, 260
Eureka Stockade, 138
   the end of miners' campaign against the Gov't, 149
Eureka Stockade Movement
   & Ballarat South frontage system, 204
Evans & Barker
   Ballarat contractors 1856, 239
Ex-convicts
   Victorian fears of, 106
Eyre Street, 256
   illegal quarry dispute, 211
Eyre, acting Police Magistrate, 131
Fabianism
   modern municipal gov't & accusations of, 84
Factories
   & a new society, 11
   & urban chaos, 73
   19th century construction & labour demand, 13
   19th century pollution & environmental degradation, 14
   a better option than parish poor relief, 13
   as a 'barracks for industry, 13
   as a working family enterprise, 13
   labour needs met by declining agricultural workers, 13
   proliferation from late 1700s, 12
Factory hands
   & redundancy of independent trades, 21
Farming
   changes to from Tudor dynasty, 12
Farms
   commercial rationalization of, 21
Fawkner, J P, 27, 30
   & Municipal Councils, 140
   early diggers supporter, 111
Fellows, T H MLA, 201, 202
   & Toryism, 202
Feud
   J B Humffray & Lalor, 1
Feudalism, 58
   Scottish, 11
Fitzroy, Sir Charles, 96, 106, 129
   & 1851 immigration scheme, 144
   1851 economic measures, 104
Flood, Edward
   Sydney Mayor, 35
Foster, John Colonial Secretary, 138
   & anti-centralization measures 1853, 138
   & Miners Charter 1854, 148
   & New Constitution, 201
   & progress, 207
   & regional representation 1853-4, 135
   1855 explanations of goldfields administration, 154
Fourth clause
   & goldseekers, 110
Franchise
   absence of & Municipal Govt, 43
Franchise, the, 53
Fraser, Derek, 57, 74, 85
Fraser, Mr
   & Ballarat West affordable homes scheme 1850s, 193
Free market
   & local economies, 9
   & local government, 9
   & social instability, 9
Free market, the, 83
Free trade, 16, 261
   & 1851 Quartz mining tax, 115
   & J B Humffray, 201

& William Cobden of Manchester, 78
1840s success at expense of Chartists, 90
the British movement, 83
Freehold land
  idea of in Aust, 26
Frenchman's Lead, 204
Galloways, the
  Vic 1851 early successful diggers, 117
Gascoigne, John, 199
Geelong, 89, 95, 132, 241
  & civil government, 154
  & municipal council makeup, 87
  & railway to Ballarat West, 252
  1st local Gov't laws passed 1841, 66
  a centre of gold rush political activism, 31
  est of Modern Municipal Gov't, 71
  info sessions on gold seeking Oct 1851, 125
  legal & political reform movements, 119
  Mayor 1850s political activist, 30
  proximity to goldfields, 98
  rallies in support of Ballarat diggers 1854-5, 156
  staging point for 1851 digging syndicates, 117
Geelong Advertiser
  & Goldfields Commission, 113
Geelong Chamber of Commerce, 37
Geelong District Constitutional Committee
  Mayor Thompson president, 36
Geelong Municipal Council
  & political reform, 36
  est before colonial government, 47
Geological survey map
  Ballarat 1855-7, 175
George Hotel, 188
  fatal shooting 1855, 164
Gibson, W S, 125
  information sessions on Goldfields at Geelong, 125
Gillies, Duncan
  & miners' affordable homes scheme, 192
Gnarr's creek, 238
Gold
  & anticipation of social change, 115

& exchange rate, 103
& protection of pastoral & assoc industries, 115
& revolutionary change, 122
1851 competition NSW & Vic, 111
1851 economic measures due to, 104
1851 political circular on control of, 115
as a solution to transportation, 102
discovery of, 95
discovery of & liberalism, 27
discovery of managed by Gov't, 95
early NSW Gov't policy, 94
goliath nugget, 97
Gov't control of seeking & extraction, 97
Macgregor's disovery, 96
NSW discoveries, 96
NSW discovery proclamation, 96
NSW Gov't assertion of ownership, 99
NSW Gov't public gold-seeking instructions, 96
NSW public interest, 97
NSW resource management, 94
Vic discovery of as a civic duty, 110
Victoria pre-1851 gold rush, 110
Gold Acts
  enforcement of, 95
Gold buyers
  Ballarat, 169
Gold committee
  Victoria 1851, 38
Gold Department
  & Ballarat West 1856, 197
  & est of Ballarat West 1856, 210
  & land occupation 1856, 214
  & Main Road Traders 1856, 214
  & Soldiers Hill land development 1857, 217
  at Ballarat, 87
  pauses mining in Ballarat 1855, 175
Gold Diggers Association, 145
  & 1853 diggers protests, 145
Gold discovery
  NSW Gov't responses to, 105
Gold districts
  description of, 94
  separate from civic society, 94
Gold legislation
  & new constitution (Vic), 118

& unconstitutional power (1851 report), 108
& violation of British freedoms, 128
1851 amendments to, 116
betrayal of diggers by Gov't, 114
Capt John Harrison reform activist, 119
early power abuse concerns, 108
fears of abuses of personal liberty, 108
fee collection mode declared anti-British 1851, 114
no British precedent, 108
to delay political progress, 109
Gold movement
& government, 112
Gold resources
& Goldfields Commission, 134
Gold rushes
& evolving goldfield society, 31
& pastoral elite, 28
only 10% successful (Vic) Oct 1851, 125
Gold seekers
& NSW policy, 94
Golden Fleece Hotel
& Ballarat West Council meetings, 209
1st Ballarat West council meeting, 185
1st council elections Jan 1856, 187
Golden Point, 256
1851 water works, 126
Golden Point Lead, 175
Goldfield Commissioners
attitude to mining population, 132
Goldfields
& aversion to Toryism, 201
& Chartism, 129
& employment from 1852, 147
& growing number of townships, 138
& permanent residents, 147
& Peterloo, 78
& steam technology, 147
& Vandemonians, 102
as a separate social political system, 134
as existing outside of civil society, 54
liberal population contained by pastoralists, 95

permanent settlement 1851-1853, 154
private allotments, 136
separated from civil society, 95
Goldfields Commission, 93, 112, 130, 149, 189, 260
& Castlemaine, 53
& civic society, 88, 134
& civic tyranny, 69
& goldfields social change, 79
& haphazard development, 82
& human rights of diggers, 139
& jurisdiction over police, 94
& *laissez faire* management, 88
& local government, 129
& political abandonment of 1851-1855, 136
& problems of centralization. *See* Centralization
& Red Ribbon Movement, 50
& weekly reports, 132
1853 colony-wide building/infrastructure project, 134
1853 infrastructure program, 141
a local Ballarat monopoly, 80
acting as local government by 1854, 133
allegations of waste & mismanagement 1854, 244
as a cause of social division, 55
as a mediating body for Ballarat Township, 136
as a regressive measure, 262
as a separate government, 94
as a social & political step backward, 129
as a temporary arrangement, 135
as the regional government, 93
Ballarat construction of new barracks 1853, 141
Ballarat corruption, 80
Budget 1853-4, 141
call to be disbanded Nov 1854, 148
charter & responsibilities, 113
contrasted with Municipality 1856, 81
demand for immediate removal Nov '54, 155
demise due to new methods & technology, 204

demise expected after Eureka Rebellion, 156
description of, 131
disbanded 1855, 151
early public confidence in, 103
early reports of overbearing methods, 128
employent of unsuitable/inexperienced staff 1851, 127
generic probelms in all locations, 52
informal powers & responsibilities, 114
only Gov't in Western Vic, 113
outrage over overbearing staff, 154
outrage over squandering of revenue, 154
rapid loss of digger support from Oct 1851, 127
removal of, 3
seen as an anacronism, 95
societal role, 114
staffing & personnel, 95
staffing 1853-4, 141
Verdon's criticism of, 68
Goldfields Commission Districts
separate from civic society, 95
Goldfields Commissioners
district appointments, 95
Goldfields Management Act
& Soldiers Hill, 219
Goldrushes
& public fears of, 102
Aust & California compared, 98
early public law & order concerns, 98
early Victorian economic concerns, 103
NSW commencement, 97
NSW police force increased, 99
Victoria - early optimism on Gov't role, 100
Victorian commencement, 100
Goodman, David
& British legal egalitarianism, 261
Government
& concession to diggers 1851-1855, 129
1856 belief in the role of, 153
to be defined by reason & justice in Victoria, 200
Government Camp, 247

under threat from mining 1855, 175
Graham, Mr
opposed to Ballarat West Swamp control, 239
Grant, Bligh, 45
& voluntarism, 48
Gravel Pits lead, 175
& Ballarat South mining, 177
& Ballarat Township 1855, 174
& Ballarat Township boundary, 174
located in Ballarat south 1855, 177
Great Reform Act 1832, 129
exclusion of middle & lower classes, 89
Green, C H
NSW police inspector, 100
Grey, Earl, 106
Guilds
& British local gov't, 83
& local govt, 20
Haines, Acting Governor
& 1855 petition for municipality, 180
Hall, Stuart, 20
Hammond, J E & Barbara, 12
Hanmer's theatre (Ballarat)
riot fatality & injuries Jan 1855, 160
Hardy, J R
& causes of Eureka Rebellion, 56
1st NSW Chief Gold Commissioner, 99
Hardy, J R Chief Commissioner
1st deployed to Ophir XE "Ophir:NSW diggings" diggings May 1851, 100
calls for goldfields reform, 155
NSW goldfields commissioner, 68
Hargreaves, William, 95, 96
Harris, Henry, 159
Harrison, Capt John, 37
& Vic liberal democratic society, 38
Bendigo activist, 119
Harrison, MLA
& unsold land in municipal boundaries, 220
Heathcote, 138
Hennock, E P, 62
Heywood, Abel
& Manchester sanitary construction, 78
Manchester Mayor, 78

Higginbotham, George ham, Attorney General, 207
Hobbes, Thomas, 151
Hogg, James, 12
Holyoake, Henry, 129
  & Ballarat 1855 law & order inquiry, 166
Home, Henry (lord Kames)
  land & commerce, 51
Horne, R H Commissioner
  & Eureka Rebellion, 56
  appeals for local gov't on goldfields, 155
Hotham, Sir Charles, 158
  1854 pledge to reform Goldfields Commission, 157
House of Commons, 32
Howe & Herring, 188
Human Rights
  violation of by 1850s Victorian Gov't, 154
Hume, David
  & land ownership, 51
Humffray, J B, 184, 194, 197, 207, 260, 261, 266
  & Ballarat & regional development, 208
  & Ballarat 1855 law & order committee, 166
  & Ballarat Chamber of Commerce, 196
  & Ballarat municipal govt, 5
  & Ballarat West swamp precinct grant 1857, 238
  & Ballarat West water supply, 243
  & District Roads Board Ballarat, 211
  & initial grant for municipality, 224
  & Lalor rivalry, 1
  & Lalor's constituents, 4
  & liberalism & free trade, 201
  & Main Rd bookshop, 208
  & Soldiers Hill development 1857, 219
  & telegraph connection, 259
  & telegraph to Ballarat West, 197
  & The Bank of Victoria, 192
  behind founding of early Ballarat West Municipality, 50
  future of Ballarat, 1
  his social & political agenda, 70
  obituary, 1
  opposes Lalor on Ballarat Water, 244
  telegraph deemed more pleasing than Eureka Stockade, 259
  threatened by physical force faction, 3
  unheralded contribution to Ballarat, 267
  urges Ballarat to petition for municipality, 167
  water & sewer commission proposal for Ballarat District 1857, 244
Immigrants
  early Port Phillip Chartists, 28
  Port Phillip settlement, 28
Immigration
  & J D Lang, 30
  Australian increase from 1840s, 26
Improvement Commissions, 63, 73, 90
  democratization of, 85
  municipalization of, 85
Industrial Institute
  & James Baker, 205
Industrialization, 11
  & independent trades, 20
  & loss of commons, 14
  emigration as a response to, 24
  population increases due to earlier marriage/more births, 14
Inquiries into Goldfields
  1853, 31
  1853 complaints over Gov't infrastructure expenditure 1853, 143
  1853 Investigation & permanent settlement, 154
  1853, 1854, 129
  Ballarat Gold Diggers list of demands 1853 to Inquiry, 145
Inspector of Nuisances
  Ballarat West, 231
Integration
  & Victorian Miners' Program, 212
Irish
  & Eureka Rebellion, 148
Irving, Terry, 34
Jackson, John, 90
  & Leeds Improvement Commission, 90
Johnstone, Alderman
  & La Trobe on enforcement of license fee 1851, 120

Jubilee
  1906 Ballarat West, 89
Justice of the Peace
  UK pre-reform role, 79
Kemp, Dr
  & Ballarat Gold Diggers Assn, 145
Kirk, Sub-Inspector
  & Ballarat riot Jan 1855, 162
La Trobe Lt Governor, 40, 129
  & creation of Goldfields Commission, 106
  & Goldfields Commission's purpose, 135
  & goldfields policy, 114
  & social political role of Goldfields Commission, 107
  suspends license fee for harvest 1851, 127
Labour surplus 19th century Britain, 21
Lady Kenneway, 106
Laissez-faire
  & goldfields management, 101
  & Manchester, 77
  & miners right, 215
  & Victorian politics 1851, 112
Laissez-faire capitalism
  & modern municipal government, 74
Lalor, Peter, 207
  & Ballarat rail connection 1856, 253
  & Ballarat West municipality petition, 87
  & illiberal values, 1
  & initial grant for municipality, 224
  & Irish independence, 4
  & J B Humffray feud, 1
  & loss of local support to Humffray, 4
  Ballarat West frustration with 1856, 242
  Ballarat West loss of confidence in, 242
  electorate achievements due to Humffray, 5
  loss of Ballarat support 1857, 4
  Member for Nth Grenville, 4
  opposes Humffray on Ballarat Water, 244
Land
  1856 Ballarat West audit, 214
  1856 regional residential, 168
  19th century freehold (UK), 17
  availability in early Colonial Victoria, 27
  Ballarat freehold & leasehold 1855-6, 180
  Ballarat West speculators 1856-7, 215
  funds from sale of public land, 221
  inability to purchase a cause of Eureka Rebellion, 148
  local jurisdiction over unsold, 213
  municipal jurisdiction over unsold lots, 220
  Soldiers Hill speculators, 219
  speculators, 215
  speculators & Ballarat West, 215
Land ownership, 206
  & a fair colonial society, 25
  & British tradition, 59
  & Utilitarianism, 73
  a pillar of British society, 17
  as the basis for the political system, 51
  expansion of in Ballarat West from 1856, 212
  legally restricted in British commercial society, 51
Lang, J D, 26, 30
  & anti-transportation, 30
  & immigration, 26
  & independence from Britain, 35
  1840s Port Phillip administrator, 28, 30
  British independence & Australian nation, 30
  immigration & Aust culture, 19
  sells vision for a better society, 26
Langlands, Henry, 157
  early Victorian manufacturer, 27
Law and order
  fears of breakdown of, 99
Layard M P (UK), 190
Learmonth, Thomas
  Wndouree swamp & local droughts, 243
Lee, Mike
  & Peterloo documentary, 15
Leeds, 85, 90
  & Chartist local gov't candidates, 90
  & freehold land, 17
  industrial revolution & social change, 13
Legislative Assembly, 3, 208

& Ballarat rail connection 1856, 253
1856 Victorian general election, 151
Legislative Council, 139, 140
   & Ballarat West municipality petition, 184
   & district councils, 36
   & municipal grants 1856, 224
   Victoria, 89
Liberalism, 261
   & non-conformists, 16
   19th century Britain, 25
   British, 26
   colonial, 26
   on the goldfields 1856, 207
   taxation, social services & representation, 261
   to define Victorian New Constitution, 200
Liberalism (British)
   & !st Ballarat municipality, 196
Liberalism (colonial), 198, 199, 207
Liberals
   & social & economic potential of gold in 1851, 122
   1854 Vic & local gov't 'revolution', 139
   rise of in UK local politics, 83
Liberty
   & Victorian British population 1850s, 128
   public beliefs & perceptions 1850s Victoria, 128
License fee
   & aliens clause, 107
   & Ballarat Times & Henry Seekamp, 188
   & considered out of step with British law, 121
   & digger protection, 125
   & economic balance, 104
   & La Trobe's opinion of, 106
   & Melbourne Lord Mayor 1851, 120
   & predictions of conflict Aug 1851, 128
   & social engineering, 118
   1852 petition Bendigo & Mt Alexander to lower the fee, 140
   1st incident of resistance to at Ballarat 1851, 123
   'a gross innovation' 1851, 122
   as a violation of human & democratic rights Sept 1851, 124
   as exorbitant Sept 1851, 121
   c/f royalty rent, 110
   campaign against, 40
   considered doomed after Eureka Rebellion, 158
   considered to violate democratic principles (1851), 121
   discouraging Victorian prospecting, 121
   early civic infrastructure concerns, 108
   early compliance 1851, 125
   early resistance to, 107
   fee & method of collection a cause of rebellion, 148
   greatest revenue source 1852, 140
   La Trobe on 'nominal' enforcement 1851, 120
   labelled as tyranny from its creation, 110
   not based on Royal perogative, 124
   not originally enforced at Ballarat 1851, 125
   press report on 1st imposition at Ballarat, 123
   priced to benefit farmers & pastoralists, 107
   reduction to 1853, 129
   trebling of in 1851, 114
   vexatious mode of collection 1851, 114
   Westagarth MLC & reduction & abolition Oct 1851, 126
License to dig
   as social & economic policy, 104
Liverpool
   & post-reform dissenter influence, 62
Local Government
   & Centralization, 45
   & Diggers 1854 Charter, 148
   & technological & economic development, 48
   & voluntarism, 45
   1830s Victoria, 65
   1855 Ballarat movement for, 55
   3 types (Britain), 60
   as harbinger of change, 44
   British Royal Commission 1832, 72
   British, pre-1835, 57
   historiography, 45
   pre-goldrush Australia, 64

Tasmanian, 46
The Age calls for at Ballarat Jan 1855, 158
unincorporated British towns, 57
Vic 1850s compared to present day, 264
Vic 1850s compared to UK, 264
Local Government (British)
  & 19 century dissenter manufacturers, 57
  & autonomy, 63
  & commerce, 58
  & early 19th century manufacturing, 57
  & improvement commissions, 59
  & the church, 57
  adoption of scientific & rational methods, 71
  attraction to 19th century unenfranchied, 90
  consolidation of local bodies after 1835, 71
  existence under centuries of regime changes, 59
  influence of dissenter businessmen, 61
  post-reform 19th century statistics, 62
  pre-reform concept of, 58
  pre-reform utilities as private enterprise, 58
  revenue - pre-reform, 61
  summary of pre-reform, 59
Local Magistrates (Vic), 131
Local water supplies (UK)
  early 19th century legal actions over, 85
Locke, John, 151
London, 17
  & improvement commissions, 59
London Chartered Bank of Australia
  branch est in diggings, 175
London Democratic Society
  affect of factories on independent trades, 20
Lonsdale, Captain William, 65
Lord Grey, 35, 36
Lowe, Robert, 29
Lydiard Street, 176, 185, 213, 240, 254, 255
  & mining, 175
  1855-1858 comparison, 246

Ballarat 1855-7, 169
mining on Southern end 1855-7, 226
Lynch Law, 163
  & California, 97
  at Ballarat, 164
Macclesfield
  1825 advertisement for 5000 workers, 13
Macintyre, Stuart, 199
Mackay, Angus
  Bendigo activist leader, 53
Mackenzie, W J M, 74
  UK local Government historian, 64
Main Road, 208
  & mining 1856, 226
  1855-6 proposal to include in Ballarat West, 181
  1856 extension into Ballarat West, 181
  Ballarat 1854-5, 171
Main Road traders, 213
  & 1855 municipality petition, 178
Mair Street
  & Market Square, 249
  & minning in Ballarat Township 1855, 177
Management of Towns Act (Victoria), 66
  & Ballarat 1852-5, 234
  replacement of 1853-4, 135
Manchester, 76, 77, 78
  & Engels 1840s visit, 14
  & freehold land, 17
  & industrialization, 13
  19th century control from Rolleston Hall, 14
  19th century lawlessness & disorder, 78
  feudal local govt, 15
  Highways, paving & sewerage commitee, 78
  legal action over municipal charter, 84
  local government traditions, 59
Marriage
  occurring earlier with industrialization, 13
Martial law
  at Ballarat 1854-5, 156
Martin & Scott, 246

Ballarat West street contractors 1856, 245
Martin, MLC
& damning 1st goldfields report, 113
1st 6 monthly report (NSW), 108
Marx, Karl, 71
& modernity, 20
&alienation, 19
Masons, 187
Masons, Free and Accepted
Ballarat local branch proposed Jan '55, 159
Mayors
& Vic political activism, 38
as political activists, 41
McMah, John
miner assisted by Commissioner Clow 1853, 133
McNally, David, 10
McNiece, Robert
& Ballarat West land speculators, 215
Mechanical and technical trades
& British emigration to Aust, 26
Mechanics
industrialization & loss of status, 20
Mechanics Institute, 111, 195
Melbourne, 27, 30, 33, 89, 95, 131, 241
& civil government, 154
& increasing goldfields integration 1851-1855, 134
& J P Fawkner a founder of, 30
& municipal council makeup, 87
& need for public utilities fro 1830s, 65
& Select Committee on size & admin, 138
1842 incorporation, 66
1st elected local body 1841, 65
1st local gov't laws passed 1838, 66
1st public markets, 65
a centre of gold rush political activism, 31
absence of monopolies or elites, 27
early history, 52
est of Modern Municipal Gov't, 71
Goldfields Commission head office, 114
incorporation as progress to independence from NSW, 66
Jan 1855 rallies on Eureka Rebellion, 156
land taxes & creation of municipality, 65
Mayor 1850s political avtivist, 30
proximity to Ballarat goldfield, 98
rail to Balarat plan 1856, 253
rallies in support of Ballarat diggers 1854-5, 156
Melbourne Chamber of Commerce
& social & political reform from 1851, 120
Melbourne City Council
& anti-transportation, 106
& rating opposition, 52
Melbourne Lord Mayor, 157
& imposition of license fee 1851, 120
& People's Association, 120
1851 reward offered for gold discovery, 111
Melbourne markets
& Ballarat West, 197
1st representative body in Victoria, 89
Melbourne merchants
& gold discovery, 110
Melbourne Municipal Council
est before Colonial Government, 47
Melbourne Reform Association
list of objectives, 119
Melbourne, Mount Alexander and Murray River Co
railway failure 1855-6, 253
Mercantile system
& monopoly. *see Smith, Adam*
Metcalf, Lord
& colonial Municipal Councils, 140
Methodists
& Ballarat West, 86
Middle-class
civic leaders in UK from 1835, 83
Military
& Aust colonial gov't, 91
& Ballarat crime 1855, 162
& Ballarat local violence 1855, 161
becoming a nuisance at Ballarat 1855, 160
Mill, John Stuart
prominent Benthamite & utilitarian, 74
Miner's Right

& Ballarat West homes scheme, 215
Miner's Right Legislation
   & Ballarat South, 214
Miners Court, 187, 193, 214
   & a new era for mining industry, 204
   & Ballarat South frontage system, 204
   & quartz mining in Ballarat, 251
   1855 elections, 187
   est 1855, 149
Miners Programme.
   & regional Victoria 1856, 212
Miners Protest Committee (Ballarat)
   1853 foiling of gold escort robbery, 133
Miners Right
   1857 case Queen vs Hill, 215
Miners' Charter, 266
Miners' Court
   & frontage system, 6
Mining
   & Ballarat Township, 168
   & Ballarat Township 1855, 171
   & permanent settlement at Ballarat, 186
   & shepherding, 175
   & Steam technology 1855, 174
   & technology 1856, 204
   1856 individual mining, 204
   agitiation by inidividual miners 1856, 206
   mechanization of from 1856, 206
   paused at Ballarat 1855, 175
Mining camps, 132
Mitchell, Sir Thomas
   & NSW gold discovery, 96
Modern municipal government, 75
   & accusations of socialism, 84
   & corporation property rights, 86
   & creation of 19th century urban order, 73
   & historians, 44
   & lack of theoretical clarity, 74
   & local histories, 49
   & social reconciliation, 75
   a transition into modern society, 75
   aristocratic loss of status, 84
   as agent of social progress, 75
   as implementor of modernity, 44
   as lowest level of gov't, 44
   legal fight for legitimacy (UK), 84

   solution for commercial & urbanized society, 81
   solution for urbanization, 76
Modern municipalities
   & social re-organization, 43
Modernity, 20
   & Ballarat 1856, 260
   & British workers, 20
   & emigration, 21
   & local government, 49
   & old institutions as a barrier to, 262
   casualties of, 22
   societal adoption of scientific & rational concepts, 71
   transition to & payment for services, 265
   upper class adaptation, 16
Monarchy, 25
Monopolies, 24
   & J P Fawkner, 30
   aversion to at Ballarat, 206
   Ballarat campaigns against, 206
   British, 206
   British society, 6
   early Ballarat resistance to, 25
   local British arrangements exposed 1830s, 72
   pastoralism & gold discovery, 30
Monopoly
   & free market economics, 9
   aristocratic political & economic, 10
   land, 14
   UK political & economic, 34
Moore and McLaren
   Ballarat West wine & spirit merchants, 228
Moral force
   & Humffray, 4
Moreton Bay, 103
   proposed penal colony, 102
Mount Warrenheip
   & Railway, 252
Mt Alexander
   & Red Ribbon protests 1853, 144
   1852 petition, 140
Muir Brothers
   & local farming, 248
Muir, Robert, 22, 26, 180, 196, 198, 207, 261, 266
   & Agricultural Society, 194
   & Ballarat Chamber of Commerce, 194

& Ballarat Industrial Institute, 194
& Ballarat Swamp capacity project 1856, 238
& Ballarat West water supply, 243
& Carribean sugar estates, 24
& District Roads Board 1856, 194
& District Roads Board election 1856, 211
& failed rating plan 1856, 224
& founding Ballarat West municipality, 50
& goldfields enfranchisement 1855, 193
& law & order inquiry 1855, 165
& Market Square dispute 1856, 250
& Market Square site, 249
& Muir Bros, 182
1856 Ballarat West removal of leaseholders, 180
1st president Ballarat Dist Roads Board, 67
a short bio, 193
action to prevent township mining 1856, 226
an unheralded pioneer of Ballarat West, 267
Ballarat East,West, & rural enterprises, 194
Ballarat West founding councillor, 87
board member Colonial Bank of Aust, 193
chairman of Ballarat law & order committee 1855, 166
proposal to bypass Lalor in Gov't dealings 1856, 242
raised as tenant farmer, 24
resigns all Ballarat positions 1857, 195
Muir, William Patterson
& 1850s Melbourne Chamber of Commerce, 193
Municipal Corporations
& Anti-transportation, 34
pre-reform, 60
UK pre-reform collusion, 79
Municipal Corporations (British)
fight for post 1835 legitimacy, 62
legal actions to establish 1835 reform, 74
Municipal Corporations (Vic)

1st requested for Ballarat in 1853, 146
a solution to goldfields unrest, 139
bringing system & cohesion to goldfields, 140
provisions under 1854 Act, 138
regional localities selected 1854, 138
to end animosity between diggers & Gov't, 140
Municipal Corporations Act (UK) 1882, 64
Municipal Corporations Act (Vic) 1854, 138
Municipal Corporations Act 1854 (Vic)
& colonial development, 139
finalization of Oct 1854, 138
limitations of, 212
Royal Assent Dec 1854, 138
Municipal Councils
& Aust political reform, 35
& early Victorian politics, 30
petitioned by Ballarat diggers Sept 1851 to act for them, 123
Municipal government
& gold rush Victoria, 154
& goldfields progress, 260
& goldfields social integration, 79
& public order, 265
& Select Committee 1853, 138
& social integration, 15
an ancient administrative body, 71
as a vehicle for Ballarat West progress 1856, 265
as the Vic govt before 1856, 7
est through legal action, 265
importance of in Vic before 1856, 33
requested by Ballarat diggers 1853, 32
Municipal Government
& New Vic constitution, 34
as the government in Colonial Vic, 33
est framework of modern local society, 15
Municipal Grants
commencement grants 1855-6, 220
dependent on approved rating/assessment (Vic), 225
Municipal Reform Act (UK) 1835, 64, 66
& non-political interests, 72

a template for Australian colonies, 71
leaders answerable to the public, 83
number of towns & cities affected, 60
Municipalities (modern)
& social re-organization, 43
Municipalities (Vic)
new councils & public works funding, 221
Municipalization
as a solution to goldfields tyranny, 79
Nadin
Manchester overseer, 14
National Library of Australia
& digitized sources, 189
New Constitution
NSW & Vic & municipal Govts, 34
New Constitution (Vic), 37, 89
& committee report Jan 1854, 201
& expectations of social & political progress, 118
& liberals, 200
& Victorian Reform League, 159, 160
New Constitutions
& electoral franchise, 135
New South Wales
pastoral elites, 27
Nicholls, C F, 129, 202
& Ballarat 1855 law & order inquiry, 165
& goldfields enfranchisement 1855, 193
Nicholls, H R
& 1855 municipality petition, 179
& Ballarat 1855 law & order inquiry, 166
& liberty, 129
& White Flat Mining & Drainage Coy 1856, 205
competing petition for Ballarat incorporation, 87
Nicholson, Sub-Inspector
Ballarat police hero arrests bushrangers, 164
Nicholson, William
Melbourne mayor & political reform, 35
Ninteenth Century
revolutionary societal changes, 44

Non-conformists, 16
influence on British liberalism, 16
North Grant, 198
J B Humffray MLA, 207
North Grenville, 198, 243, 253
Peter Lalor MLA, 207
North Star Hotel, 219
NSW
& adoption of UK Municipal Corp Act 1835, 66
NSW Municipalities Act of 1858, 64
O'Neill, Judith, 46
O'Shanassy, John, 193, 201
Oddfellows, 187
Oddie, James, 22, 55, 188, 190, 191, 195, 198, 220, 256, 261
& 1856 6 monthly rating plan, 224
& 1st miners petition 1851, 39
& Ballarat 1855 law & oder inquiry, 165
& Ballarat eight hours movement, 191
& Ballarat Post Office, 170
& Ballarat West streets contract 1856, 246
& crown land sale proceeds, 221
& denial of Ball't East access to water supply, 243
& District Roads Board, 211
& Eureka Rebellion, 51
& goldfields enfranchisement 1855, 193
& housing scheme 1856, 214
& J & T Oddie Auctioneers, 182
1856 support for Peter lalor, 242
1st Ballarat West chairman, 87
British occupation, 23
chairman Ballarat Early Closing Assn, 191
Chairman of Bank of Victoria, 192
Eureka & Ballarat's 1st municipality, 22
Eureka & municipal govt, 23
on miners' campaign against tyranny, 149
part of South Side clique 1857, 255
political afiliation, 23
promotor of Charles Gavan Duffy, 192
resident of Manchester & London, 23

scheme for affordable homes for miners, 192
sworn in as J P Ballarat West, 189
vendetta against J S Carver 1856-7, 256
Old fogeyism, 17
  & Ballarat 1857, 202
  & J B Humffray 1857, 201
Old Post Office Hill, 256
Ophir
  NSW diggings, 100
Orange, 101, 107
  NSW, 98
Ovens Goldfield
  & Fitzroy's 1851 economic stimulus, 104
Owen, Robert, 21, 58
Owenism, 50
Owens, Dr, 52
Paine, Thomas, 21
Panton, Commissioner, 52
Parish, 15
Parkes, Henry, 29, 35
Parliament (British)
  & control of pre-reform local gov't, 79
  & private local Gov't acts from 1660s, 59
Parliament (NSW)
  & working men 1848, 29
Parliament (Vic)
  & expectations of 1850s expansion, 118
Pastoralism
  & creation of Goldfields Commission, 31
  leaseholds & tyranny, 29
  opposition to Victorian democracy, 30
  preservation of political power, 106
Pastoralists
  & Victorian Government, 112
  1850s plan to hold back democracy, 30
  pre-gold rush political control, 91
  Victorian & goldrush Gov't, 101
Pensioners' battalion
  & Ballarat, 142
People's Association, the
  & Capt John Harrison Bendigo, 119
  & Geelong, 37, 119

  & Melbourne & Geelong Municipal Councils, 119
  & T C Riddle of Geelong, 119
  & the 1854 miners' charter, 119
People's Charter, 90
Permanent settlement
  & miners program, 212
Peterloo, 78
  & Eureka, 77
Petition
  1853 miners, 40
  1st against the license fee Sept 1851 (Ballarat), 123
  1st Ballarat miners petition Sept 1851, 39
Petworth Emigration Society, 21
Physical force
  & Irish 1853-4, 148
Place, Francis
  & British local Gov't reform, 72
Police
  & goldfields protection, 265
  & NSW goldfields, 101
  as Goldfields enforcers, 109
  assistance to goldfields population, 132
  at Ballarat 1855, 160
  Ballarat locals urged by Gov't to enrol as special constables June 1855, 168
  Ballarat police to remain under colonial gov't authority, 168
  Ballarat requests police be under local authority April 1855, 167
  corrupted by Vandemonians and criminals, 127
  need for with gold rushes fro 1851, 127
  new goldfields role after Eureka, 151
  official subordination to Goldfields Commission, 134
Political economy
  agricultural as more stable, 10
Political system
  Victorian immigrant vision of, 118
Politics
  & 1856 concept of constitutional liberty, 153
  & anti-transportation campaign, 30
  & ideas of political authority, 153
  & test acts, 153

    & Victorian British diggers & immigrants 1850s, 129
absence of local & colonial franchise a cause of rebellion, 148
British Great Reform Act 1832, 32
British influence & colonial Victoria, 29
British Municipal Reform Act 1835, 32
Conservative drag 1850s, 114
favouritism & factionalism 1851, 116
gold discovery as radical opportunity, 112
goldfield era old guard, 103
Levellers & British political agitation, 153
Liberal Party (British), 62
Mayors as early colonial activists, 30
NSW influence on colonial Victoria, 29
NSW radicals, 29
opposition of Victorian pastoralists to change, 30
Tories, 62
Tories & local Gov't pre-1835, 57
UK middle class enfranchisement, 32
Whigs, 62
Poor laws
    & pre-reform local government, 59
Population
    & goldfields social assimilation, 112
    & goldfields weather, 147
    at Victorian separation 1850, 28
    Ballarat 25,000 Dec 1854, 147
    British growth & problems 19th century, 76
    diggers' fears of increase 1853, 144
    goldfields not considered to be citizens, 146
    Vic regional 1851-1856 without political or civic status, 149
    Victoria 1853, 28
Port Philip Company, 65
Port Phillip
    early land sales & surveys, 65
    est of 1830s Melbourne. *See* Melbourne
    incentives to find local gold, 111
Port Phillip District, 35
Portland, 95

Portland Municipality
    est under 1854 Act, 47
Post Office
    Ballarat, 169
Power, J, 48
Presbyterianism
    & Ballarat West, 86
Press, the
    & commercial society, 83
Preston
    industrial revolution & social change, 13
Primogeniture, 51
Progress, 207
    & 1850s colonial values, 200
    & Ballarat South mining project 1856, 204
    & early colonial Victoria, 29
    & goldfields population 1855-7, 263
    attainable in 1850s Victoria, 261
    social improvement & 1856 miners' program, 212
Progressives
    & Municipal Corporations Act (Vic), 139
Property
    19 century concepts of, 151
Protectionism
    & 1851 pastoral & assoc industry, 115
    1851 Victoria, 116
Protests, 120
Prothero, I J, 20
Public utilities
    & utilitarianism, 63
    municipalization of, 85
Public Works Department, 210, 256
    & local authority, 213
Public, the, 75
    & 19th century corporation property rights, 86
    & convict social panics, 102
    & modern municipal government, 74
    & modern municipal gov't, 84
    19th century aristocratic resistance to, 84
    Adam Smith & monopolies vs public interest, 84
    beneficiaries of 1835 Act, 83
    public opinion on Goldfields Commission, 113

Quaife, G R, 88, 263
   & 1856 general election, 208
   study of 1856 Victorian election, 88
Quartz mining
   1851 prohibition, 114
   1851 tax deemed protectionist, 115
Radical politics
   a response to factory system, 21
Railway terminus
   proposed for Ballarat West only 1856, 181
Rainy, Mr
   Ballarat West lawyer, 191
Ranken & Douglass
   gold brokers, 185
Rankin, A B, 182, 188
Rates, 212, 256
   & est of Ballarat West Municipality, 210
   Ballarat West 1856, 245
   Ballarat West illegal rating plan 1856, 224
   on Ballarat West commencement, 265
   replacement 12 monthly Ballarat assessmts 1856, 225
   resitance to in early NSW, 64
Red Hill Lead, 3, 175
Red Ribbon movement, 50, 52
   & Eureka Rebellion, 124
   & passive resistance, 144
   Gov't & diggers Ballarat collaboration, 133
Rede, Commissioner Robert, 217
   & Ballarat Hospital 1854, 132
   a 1854 member of miners' committee, 132
Redman, William (NSW Solicitor)
   call for goldfields police oversight, 99
Regional towns
   Victoria 1853-4, 135
Religion
   & Ballarat, 202
Revenue
   & miners' protests over fair share, 154
Revolution
   & political aims of diggers, 31
   early goldrush concerns, 102
   fears of & Vandemonians, 102
   fears of with gold rushes, 31

Richmond,
   & J B Humffray, 1
Riddle, T C, 38, 119, 263
   1st landowner at Ballarat 1852, 119
   assists diggers at Ballarat Oct 1851, 126
Rights
   1856 belief in of individuals, 154
Roads boards
   lack of in 1852, 136
Rodier, W B, 197, 208
   Ballarat East Chairman, 242
Roebuck, J A
   & British local government reform, 72
Rootes, Grant, 46
Rowand, Mr
   Central Roads Board Engineer (Ballarat), 210
Royal Commission 1854-5, 56
   & centralization, 212
   & Irish, 148
   & local self-government, 212
   & Miners' Program 1856, 212
   & mining changes, 147
   & social integration of the miners, 212
   3 main causes of Eureka Rebellion, 148
Rule, John, 10, 11, 13
Rural displacement, 13
Rutter v. Chapman
   & Manchester municipal charter 1840s, 84
Ruzicka, E R, 46
   & Tasmanian local govt, 46
Sabbath
   goldfields observance of, 132
Sacramento
   example of goldfields lawlessness, 99
Sandhurst, 52, 53
   municipal candidates 1855, 185
   Sept 1853 diggers' riot, 145
Sanitation, 14
   poor services under old regimes (UK), 84
Schools, 132
Science, 205
   & Ballarat goldfields 1856, 205
Scotland

& rapid commercialization after 1746, 11
decline of pre-commercial culture, 12
Sebastopol, 226
& new mining from 1856, 181
Seekamp, Henry, 188
Select Committee 1853
  failure of Goldfields social & political justice, 147
  on admin of local funds, 136
Self Protection Societies
  Ballarat 1855, 164
Separation
  from NSW, 35, 37
  NSW & Vic, 33
Serle, Geoffrey, 50
  & 1850s morally enlightened elite, 261
  immigration statistics, 24
Service industries, 132
Sheffield
  industrial revolution & social change, 13
Shepherding, 2, 204
Sherrard, Warden, 192
  & Soldiers Hill land, 217
  re Oddie's fair dealing, 191
Slatey Creek, 164
  & Ballarat bush rangers 1855, 163
Smiles, Samuel
  & 'Self Help;, 25
Smith, Adam, 12
  & agricultural political economy, 10
  & goldfields politics, 112
  & ideal society, 10
  & land ownership, 51
  capitalism, monopoly & public interest, 84
  industrial c/f to agricultural society, 9
  on industrialization & urbanization, 9
Smith, J T, 43
  & Tasmanian Convict Dept, 41
  Melbourne Mayor, 33
Smith, Robert, 243
  & Ballarat water supply 1857, 241
  & Market Square, 251
  & road to Ballarat Swamp 1856, 239
Smith, W C, 211, 243, 255
  & Ballarat West water supply, 243

Social change
  & 19th century British municipalization, 86
  & 19th century Scottish philosophers, 9
  & Eureka Rebellion, 79
  & gold discovery, 115
  & industrialization, 13
  & modern municipal government, 44
  & Peterloo 1819, 78
  1850s colonial resistance to, 139
  encouraged by Ballarat leaders 1856, 205
Social instability
  gold & fears of, 106
Social justice
  & early Ballarat West, 22
Social order
  & license fee, 104
Social panics
  & convicts, 95
Social status
  & 1850s immigrants, 23
  loss of with industrialization, 21
  Withers & Ballarat diggers. See Withers, W B
Socialists, 206
Sociology, 19
Soldiers, 101
Soldiers Hill, 181, 218
  & Miners Right 1856-7, 214
  & Railway Station, 252
Sole traders
  commercialization & loss of status, 20
Spirit of the age, 200
Squatters
  & Ballarat West, 210
  & regional Victoria, 118
Sructural inequality
  & Chartism, 261
Star Concert Room, 198
Star Hotel
  & Ballarat law & order investigation, 165
State, the
  & individuals, 151
Steam Power
  & mining 1851, 115
Stewart, Dr James, 180, 182, 188, 192, 220, 261

& Ballarat Water supply 1856, 241
& District Roads Board, 211
original Ballarat West councillor, 209
Stores, 132
Strzelecki, Count, 96
Sturt Street, 176, 182, 213, 248
1856 drainage dispute, 210
Ballarat, 169
Ballarat East water carters terminus 1856, 240
quarrying ordered to cease 1856, 250
Sturt Street North
quarry site for market square 1856, 249
Stutchbury, Mr
NSW Gov't geologist, 96
Surveyor General, 210
Surveyor's Office
Ballarat, 169
Swindells, Herbert
& 1st Vic miners petition 1851, 39
Sydenham, Lord
& colonial Municipal Councils, 140
Syder, Dr Mingay, 38
Sydney Municipal Council
1st election 1842, 34
Sylvester, W, 54
& Ballarat Gold Diggers Assn, 120, 145
1853 miners protest committee, 133
demands local gov't for the diggings 1853, 146
Tait, Joseph
weighbridge operator, 251
Tallow-makers
protection of, 115
Tasmania
& convict 'abomination', 102
Taxation
& local government, 52
& Melbourne City Council, 52
& tyranny, 39
as tyranny without representation, 141
Goldfields taxed when not considered citizens, 146
outrage & protest 1851 on Quartz mining NSW, 115
Taxation without representation
& *Geelong Advertiser* 1851, 121

Taxes
local, 212
Taylor, Mr District Surveyor
cedes premises to Ballarat West Council 1856, 209
Technological improvement
& agriculture, 21
agricultural labour surplus, 21
Technology
& urbanization, 75
Telegraph, 197
& Ballarat West 1856, 177
exchange to be in Ballarat West 1856, 181
Geelong to Ballarat connection 1856, 184
Tenant farmers
& British emigration to Aust, 26
& emigration, 22
Theobald, Marjorie
& History of Castlemaine, 53
Thompson, Dr
Geelong Mayor & leader of People's Assn, 120
Thompson, Dr Alexander
1st Geelong Mayor, 33
Geelong Mayor, 120
Geelong Mayor & political reform, 35
Times and Southern Cross
impressions of 1st Ballarat Municipality, 189
Tories, 72, 77
& Goldfields Commission, 139
& local government, 265
& local govt, 15
& municipal govt, 6
& Peterloo, 77
a leading role in modern local govt, 16
legal opposition to municipal corps, 85
of Sydney, 34
Toryism, 202
& the Goldfields, 201
anti-Toryism, 206
Toulmin-Smith, Joshua, 264
opposed centralization, 63
Town and Country Police Act
Victoria, 136
Town and Country Police Act (Victoria), 66

Town Clerk, 220
Town Hall
  & Thomas Bath, 253
  used as grain exchange 1856, 251
Transportation, 105
  campaign to end, 29
Travelling shows, 132
Tudors
  & land ownership & occupation reform, 10
Tulloch, William, 180, 188, 242
  & Ballarat West water supply, 243
  & rescinding Ballarat East liquor licenses 1856, 228
  action to prevent township mining, 226
Turon
  1st diggers monster protest 1851, 114
Tyranny, 29, 32, 110, 262
  & J P Fawkner, 30
  & separation from NSW, 28
  accusations of Sept 1851 (Ballarat), 39
  aristocratic & monarchical, 261
  as official Gov't goldfields policy, 94
  Goldfields, 69
  system of under Goldfields Commission, 94
Unicorn Hotel, 248
  & telegraph connection, 259
Unincorporated cities, 90
University of Bradford, 74
Urbanization, 16
  & nobility, 14
  & spread of disease, 14
  British 19th century environmental degradation, 73
Urquart, W S, 136
  Ballarat survey 1852, 169
  Victorian district surveyor, 135
Utilitarianism
  & public utilities, 63
  failure to impose centralized sanitation, 75
  happiness quotient, 75
Van Dieman's Land
  early local gov't, 64
Van Diemen's Land, 102
Vandemonians, 102, 164
  & Goldfields Commission, 95
Verdon, Sir George, 54, 67
  & causes of Eureka Rebellion, 55
  & goldfields revenue, 154
  & proceeds from sale of crown land, 221
  civic society as solution to goldfields unrest, 69
  on Gov't response to gold rushes, 68
Victoria
  pre-goldrush regional district councils failure of, 66
  pre-separation industry development, 27
  separation from NSW, 89
Victoria Gold Movement, 111
Victorian Legislative Assembly
  bill for local infrastructure borrowing 1857, 242
Victorian local democracy
  1st form of democracy in Victoria, 89
Victorian local government
  compared with Tas, 47
Victorian parliament
  1857 elections, 207
Victorian Reform League
  & 1855 application of Municipal Institutions Act, 160
  & Ballarat law & order commission of inquiry 1855, 165
  & goldfields enfranchisement 1855, 193
  & importance of local government 1855, 89
  & local government 1855, 55
  & the Crow Club Self-Protection Society, 164
  objectives after Eureka Rebellion, 159
  renewed agitation after Eureka Rebellion, 156
Victorian society
  a fractured society 1851-1855, 55
Vignoles, Captain
  Ballarat local magistrate 1856, 234
Voluntarism
  & 1850s Victorian municipalities, 47
  & Local Gov't response to 19th century modernity, 48
Wakefield, E G
  & emigration as a social solution, 19
  & immigration, 26

Waldie, Thomas
  & dry 1840s Ballarat Swamp, 243
Wall, Dr, 52
Waranga
  1853 license refusal protest, 145
Warrenheip, 242
Waugh, John, 135
Weather
  as a major factor of growth Goldfields population, 147
Webb, Beatrice and Sidney
  British local government historians, 44
  British local Gov't historians, 63
  portrayal of Manchester, 77
Weekes, W C, 165
Wentworth, W C, 100
  & gold licenses, 107
  & transportation, 105
Western District, 253
Westgarth, William MLC, 126
  & goldfields revenue expenditure, 146
  & reduction & abolition of license fee, 126
  & social integration of the diggers, 55
  assists Ballarat diggers with water supply Oct 1851, 126
  early supporter of gold industry, 111
  keen to est good relations with diggers, 126
Whigs, 32, 62
  initiators of 1830s municipal reform, 72
White Flat, 177
Whitehorse and Frenchman's Lead project, 5

Whitehorse Lead, 204
Wigley, Mr
  Ballarat West Council solicitor, 209
Winter, Jock
  Ballarat squatter, 206
Withers, W B, 49
  on goldfields as separate from colonial society, 134
Wool Industry
  protection of, 115
Workhouse, 13
Wright, Chief Commissioner
  & 1853 concerns on viability of Goldfields Commission, 145
  & coercive force, 147
  & growing goldfields employment 1853, 147
  admission of failure of coercive force, 145
  gives seized liquor funds to hospital, 133
  inability to contain 1853 Red Ribbon protests, 145
Wymond & Vasey
  & mining in Ballarat Township 1855, 177
  Ballarat West, 171
Yarrowee River, 177, 178, 205
  & building boom 1855, 171
  & gold claims, 3
  & mining disruption 1856, 226
  1850s mining pollution, 82
  H R Nichols drainage project 1855, 87
Yeomen
  casualties of modernity, 21
Yoke of tyranny
  definition of, 94

APPENDIX

Appendix I

Rated property in Ballarat West 1856[582]

1856 Ballarat Property Summary

Cottage/Land (Behind Store/Shop)	35
Cottage/tent - do – Tenanted	13
Cottage and Buildings	4
Cottage and Buildings – Tenanted	3
Office -	8
Office - Tenanted	16
Office and Buildings	1
House and Land	16
House and Land – Tenanted	4
House/Store and Buildings	7
Store and Land	16
Store and Land – Tenanted	9
Store and Cottage/house/Buildings (let)	5
Government reserve - vacant	2
Government Land - occupied – tent	1
Vacant land	241
Vacant land – tenanted	42
Land and Boarding Hse – Tenanted	3
Vacant Land - not rated	19
Tents and Land	7
Tents/hut and Land- Tenanted	20
Hotel and Land	7
Hotel and Land – Tenanted	4
Shop/Manuf/Dining - Tenanted	28
Shop/Manuf/Dining and Buildings	26
Buildings/Garden	8

---

[582] Public Records *Office Ballarat Rate Assessment Books 1856* – 1857 VPRS 7260/P0002/1 (summary)

Pasture (not rated)	2
Tent /stables- Tentanted	2
Yarding/timber/Stables - horse/cattle	6
Yard (tenant)	5
Cottage and Garden	12
Cottage and Garden - Tenanted	1
Total	573

Owners	392	
Renters		**137**
Commercial		49
Private		88
Vacant land		42
Total Renters		46
Ratio 46/573		**0.08**

Appendix II

Frenchman's & Whitehorse Leads mining 1856

GOLD MINING

ON

SEBASTOPOL HILL, BALLARAT:

WITH

Plans and Sections

SHOWING THE CONTOUR OF THE SURFACE, THE SEVERAL BEDS OF
ROCK, CLAY, AND SAND, AND METHOD OF SURVEY
AND LAYING-OFF OF CLAIMS, WITH
EXPLANATIONS THEREOF;

INDICATING THE PROBABLE COURSE OF THE LEADS.

PREPARED BY ORDER OF THE COMMITTEE OF THE

FRENCHMAN'S AND WHITE HORSE LEADS,

FOR THE BENEFIT OF THE BALLARAT HOSPITAL.

BALLARAT:
PRINTED AT THE STAR OFFICE, MAIN ROAD.
1857.

Gold Mining on Sebastopol Hill,

BALLARAT.

THE history of Ballarat, more than that of any other gold-field in the world perhaps, has shown a succession of engineering difficulties, surmounted only by the miner's physical courage and by indomitable perseverance. Many who had engaged in gold mining had never previously performed any kind of manual labour; but so great was the fascination of the pursuit, that tasks the most arduous were performed under difficulties the most discouraging. Works requiring high mechanical skill were undertaken by men who had not the slightest acquaintance with mechanical appliances; yet the miner worked on undaunted, and, as new difficulties presented themselves, he sought new remedies by which to overcome them. Until with the year just past, however, mining operations were conducted in a very rude and primitive manner; the means available to the miner being exceedingly limited, while the most extravagant prices were demanded for every description of material required in the process of gold seeking on the deep leads.

The digger found gold on the surface first, then he sought beneath the ground, and found the precious metal also at a few feet below the surface. As the gold receded from its apparent source, it still went deeper into the bowels of the earth, whither it had been washed by currents of water that had evidently rushed with great violence; wearing out their own course through the primitive rocks, and forming those channels, long since buried by superincumbent strata of rock and alluvial deposits, and known as the gutters or leads which the miner expends so much time and labour in reaching and ransacking. The waters bore along with them to these gutters fragments of slate, sandstone, quartz, and vegetable matter, tho whole being known to the miner as the auriferous wash-dirt which contains the gold that enticed him to the exploration of these ancient water-courses. The subsequent deposits have accumulated in some instances to a depth of three hundred feet, including layers of drift sand heavily charged with water, and varying in depth from sixteen to twenty feet. These drifts, formed as they frequently are of quicksands, baffled the utmost skill and perseverance of the miner, who, in the early days of gold mining on Ballarat, has been known to continue baling water for six, eight, and even nine months in order to drain the ground. Gradually the miner became accustomed to sinking through the alluvial deposits intervening between the surface and the gutter; and the employment of divers mechanical agencies, including steam-power, and the gin, or horse-whim, as it is called here, helped in the reduction of the water, which has ever been the miner's greatest difficulty. Mining had thus begun to assume a different aspect, when, to the astonishment of the miner, the leads or gutters were found to run under layers of basaltic rock, in some cases fifteen or twenty feet thick. The discovery of this fresh impediment to the conduct of mining operations led to the inauguration of an entirely new era in the pursuit of the precious ore. Men who had the slightest knowledge of blasting were eagerly sought for, and persons quite unaccustomed to that dangerous occupation, in many instances never having seen it performed even, with the usual courage of the Ballarat miner, set to work and sunk shafts through the hard rock. Notwithstanding this new element of danger was introduced, it is worthy of remark that few accidents occurred, although, as has been already observed, many of the men engaged were perfect novices in the practice.

Things were thus progressing, when, to quote a Colonial expression, a "*new rush*" broke out at Magpie Gully, a ravine situated in the southern environs of Ballarat Proper. The lead of gold then discovered proved to be very rich, and, as will be seen upon the map, joined a previously-discovered lead called the Chinaman's. The united leads then took a north-westerly course, and fell into the Frenchman's at the point shown on the chart. After the junction the lead was called the Frenchman's, and it yielded a fine golden harvest to those who were fortunate enough to find its course as above alluded to. Many were the speculations as to the direction the gutter would take; and, while it appeared to tend directly towards a hill that was known to be basaltic, few miners deemed it possible that the lead would be found to continue underneath the hill. Consequently, trial or "prospecting" shafts were sunk in all directions but that which eventually proved to be the right one; until at length the margin of the basaltic rock was struck, as the gutter was traced to a point below the Yarrowee Creek, which will be seen on the map to cross the gutter at right angles. The rock being struck, the problem as to the tendency of the gutter was solved, and it became evident the gutter would be found to run under the plateau beyond the creek, and which rises abruptly to an elevation of nearly one hundred feet above the level of the valley below. The depth of sinking in the valley was then about one hundred and thirty-two feet, and with the extra depth of hard rock to go through on ascending the hill, the prospect, even of the rich gutter beneath, did not look particularly cheering.

About this time the first Local Court was established at Ballarat. This popular institution was one of the results of the Eureka Stockade movement, and was intended to have the management of mining matters; the presumption being that, as its members consisted of practical miners, an improved system of mining legislation would be introduced that should lead to a fuller development of the resources of the gold fields generally. Nearly the first act of the Local Court was the abolition of the practice of "shepherding," or holding claims in reserve and unworked; by which practice one man would mark out as much ground as was apportioned to eight men, which he would keep possession of until the course of the gutter was proved by those who worked instead of shepherding. If the gutter seemed likely to approach the shepherd's claim, a matter which, from the sinuosities of the lead, will at once be seen to be uncertain until the ground had been proved to within a short distance of the claim held in reserve, the shepherd would sell shares in his eight-share claim, and in many instances a good round sum would be obtained without the vulgar interposition of hard work. With the basaltic hill before the miners on Frenchman's, it became a question—how could men afford to sink without a guarantee of the gutter? Under the old system it was known that, for one party who would strike the gutter, twenty might be ruined; and the attention of those interested was given to the matter as one of vital importance to the miner. After several meetings had been held, Mr. Bacon suggested the adoption of a plan which had been mooted previously; but it had met with such vehement opposition, that it had to be relinquished.

This plan was to give a definite length of the gutter to each party, and to mark the claims in parallels across the course of the gutter, instead of the old method of square blocks. Finally the thing was carried in the Local Court by a majority of one, and thus the frontage system of claims became law. The experiment was soon made, but not without opposition; and as one of the first steps taken, Mr. John Wall was appointed surveyor expressly for Frenchman's Lead, such an officer being necessary under the frontage system, and that gentleman being the first who accepted the novel position in the district, as that lead was also the first to which the system was applied.

The new system being fairly introduced, work commenced on the hill west of the Yar-

(5)

rowee, and went briskly on; while the sound of the hammer and drill, and the frequent boom of the blast, showed the miners were in earnest. It should be mentioned that a party of Newcastle men, endowed with more than an ordinary spirit of enterprise, had commenced a shaft on the table-land above the creek, and some forty yards from the brow of the hill. They went to a depth of about one hundred and thirty feet before regular operations had been begun on the hill, and proved beyond a doubt that two distinct layers of rock would be encountered, the second one containing an immense body of water, and thus presenting a new and greater difficulty than any previously met with by the miner. The party did all that unaided human labour could accomplish, and it was unanimously agreed by the miners on the lead that the party should have the first place, and be protected as under the newly-introduced frontage system. The map will show that the line of parallels commences from the ground occupied by the Newcastle party. The frontage system was soon followed by the plan of amalgamation of claims, or the union of several separate claims under one management, and working on the associative principle. The committee that had been appointed to perfect the new system continued to hold office; for it was found that the working required careful supervision, in order to the introduction of such improvements as might be suggested in the practical application of the system to mining operations.

Shortly after the registration of the Frenchman's Lead a trial was made of the White Horse Lead, which had been thought by some to have run out or to contain so small a portion of gold as not to be worth working. The enterprise of some "prospectors" by the creek-side, however, demonstrated the fact that the gutter still yielded gold in paying quantities, and application was forthwith made to have the lead placed under the frontage system. A large number of claims was taken up, companies were formed, and the lead which had been forsaken for nearly two years was again all life and activity. The experience of the miners here showed that the gold has been sometimes carried over steep inclinations of surface and deposited plentifully in the levels beyond; as this lead, which was very poor while running down the declivity shown in the cross section of the map, is now paying good dividends to the miner.

The two leads, Frenchman's and White Horse, being so near each other, it was determined to have one committee for the two, under the name of the amalgamated committee of the two leads; and among the other acts of this committee it was resolved to cause a trigonometrical survey to be made of the leads in the immediate neighbourhood, tracing the leads to their source in the range to the east. One motive to this was the hope of placing in the hands of the miner some data showing the nature of the gold deposits and the geological structure of the district in question; and which should be also a kind of record and *souvenir* of the locality which had been the scene of his anxious labours, his difficulties, privations, and dangers.

The accompanying maps, executed by the surveyor, Mr. John Wall, are the result of the resolution of the committee: the first, or surface-map, showing the source of the leads on the east side of the Yarrowee creek. The range consists of primitive schist, interlaced with veins of gold-bearing quartz, and is evidently the source of the leads, running thence in a westerly and other directions; the washing-stuff of the miner being the *debris* of the primitive rocks, loosened by denudation of the elements, and carried by the agency of water into the channels or gutters previously referred to; the glittering ore being thus transported to a considerable distance from its matrix to form the lead which subsequent accumulations of strata placed at a depth of three hundred feet from the surface of to-day, while recent elemental operations have, from the same source, strewn the present surface with fragments of the precious metal, the search for which led to the discovery of the deeper and more ancient deposits now known as our deep leads. Sinking his shaft through one hundred and sixty feet of basaltic rock, the miner finds under one layer a deposit of very hard sand conglomerate, sometimes twenty feet thick; then comes the second layer of basaltic rock, con-

(6)

taining a heavy body of water, which, defying the efforts of manual labour, necessitates the employment of steam-power to keep the water under in the process of blasting. Under this second layer of rock grey clay is found, then a deposit of black clay, so largely composed of vegetable matter as to resemble coal in appearance and structure. This last deposit always lies over the gutter, and is a sure indication to the miner that he is upon or near to the gutter. From the appearance of this deposit of black clay it is pretty evident that at the time of its deposition, which was prior to the overflow of trap or basaltic rock, the same species of trees existed as now clothe our hills and valleys; specimens of the clay having been found bearing the exact impression of the leaf of the peppermint-tree, one of which specimens is now in the possession of Dr. Kenworthy. As the leads recede from their source the gold becomes finer and is found in much smaller quantities; so that, while the labour and expense become greater, the remuneration is smaller.

The following statistics of mining on the Frenchman's Lead will show that as the workings advanced, without an increase in the area of ground, the operations of the miner became so tedious and expensive as to reduce the margin of profit to a mere nothing, and in some instances to a positive loss.

STATISTICAL TABLE,

Showing the Expences and Nett Produce of the first Twenty-seven Claims on Frenchman's Lead, (under the Frontage System), with other important data:—

Number of Claims.	Depth in feet.	Depth in feet of rock.	Extent in feet of the Drives to the Gutter.	Expenses.	Gross produce.	Wages.	
				£	£	£ s. d.	
1	240	100	170	450	4185	1 6 0	The wages in this Table are for full-sharemen, hence it will appear that in No. 10-12 quarter-sharemen would only get 2s. 6d. per day.
2 — 3	305	170	120	718	6260	0 17 6	
4 — 5	370	225	110	650	3700	0 8 0	
6	335	120	130	700	4050	1 6 0	
7 — 9	380	210	270	700	9000	1 0 6	
10 —12	410	250	90	2000	6500	0 10 0	
13 —14	400	220	50	710	3000	0 11 0	
15 —19	800	430	110	1000	9100	0 9 0	
20 —22	584	331	210	900	9000	0 15 0	
23 —27	912	641	370	3050	15,000	0 9 0	
	4766	2767	1630	10,878	69,795		

Subsequent regulations have, however, allotted a much larger area to each company; a step absolutely necessary to compensate for the increased difficulties and outlay of the miner. In No. 35 claim a third layer of basaltic rock has been found at a depth of two hundred and twenty feet from the surface, and in No. 70 the same layer has been found to be much harder and more difficult than any previously discovered; while in No. 56, a fourth layer of the same rock has just been struck, or what at least appears to be precisely identical with the layers encountered above.

(7)

PLAN SHOWING THE RELATIVE POSITIONS OF THE LEADS & PARALLELS.

This plan shows the relative positions of the several leads, and exhibits at one view the courses of the present and the ancient vallies. The series of eminences whence the Long Gully, Cobbler's, Magpie, Chinaman's, Frenchman's, White Horse, and Terrible Leads take their rise, forms part of a schistose range running north and south; the quartz veins in which are regarded as the matrices whence the gold has been derived, which carried down the watercourses of the ancient valley, forms the treasure for which the gold-miner so laboriously delves. That valley ran in a westerly direction, crossing the course of the present valley at right-angles. The watercourse shown on the plan is called the Yarrowee Creek or River Leigh, and joins the Barwon a few miles north-west of Geelong—the Barwon emptying itself into Corio Bay. It may be mentioned here, that owing to the incessant washing of auriferous earth in the Yarrowee and its tributaries for several miles of its course, the waters of the Barwon were at one time rendered partially unfit for drinking, to the great disgust of the people of Geelong, who forgot not to complain of the detrimental effects of the miners' gold-washing, although at a distance of some fifty miles. The parallels, as laid off under the frontage system, are shown in the plan, the varying widths of parallels indicating the smaller or greater number of claims "amalgamated," or joined together to be worked through one shaft. The locality of Campbell's boring experiment is on the Frenchman's Lead, between Winters' boundary line and the last parallel. The square black marks on the parallels show the distance of the shafts from the gutter, and the course of the drives; when more than one black mark occurs, all those after the first indicate "blind" or "monkey" shafts sunk in the drives; a plan adopted in preference to sinking a new shaft from the surface. At this date (March, 1857) the gutter has been traced as far as the Leviathan parallel on White Horse, and the Redan parallel on Frenchman's; and from the course of the two gutters a confluence is expected near the parallel of the United Miners' Company, on Frenchman's. In anticipation of this junction, registration on both leads was stopped by the Local Court in January of this year.

PLAN OF SECTIONS OF WHITE HORSE AND FRENCHMAN'S LEADS.

The most prominent feature in this plan, as it indicates also one of the greatest obstacles to the miner, is the basaltic rock, or beds of volcanic lava; three separate beds of which, not to mention the discovery of traces of a fourth, have already been found by the miners on these leads. The flow of these deposits of lava appears to have been from the south-west, and the most recent must have taken place at a time in the past so remote as to be only calculated approximatively even by the geologist. This effusion of lava flowed from the volcano over the intervening country, until stopped by the barrier interposed by the range of primitive rocks where the leads shown in the other plan have their origin. The plateau on which the parallels are laid off in that plan, was evidently at one time extended close up to the range; the valley between having been scooped out in the course of ages by the action of water and other agencies. The basaltic mounds shown east of the Yarrowee in the other plan, being remains of the rock which originally crossed the valley on the level of the plateau.

These beds of rock are exceedingly hard, and can only be removed by the process of blasting; their color is dark-slate, and the second bed has been found to be full of fissures holding immense bodies of water: thus containing within itself what is, after all, perhaps, the greatest enemy the miner has to contend against in his operations.

On comparing the contour of the valley of the Leigh, when the passage the latter has worn in the basaltic rock is shown, with that of the ancient vallies worn in the rock

(8)

marked W, by the streams now called the Frenchman's and White Horse gutters, the uniformity of effect produced by analagous causes, is very apparent.

The several layers of clay which make up the whole series of deposits over the gutters, must have taken long periods in their deposition, and their various colors indicate great climatic and meteorologic changes. The red clays, doubtless, owe their color to the oxydisation of mineral substances either mixed with the earth deposited, or held in solution among the waters accompanying the deposition.

The layers of black clay derive their color from the presence of large masses of decomposed vegetable matter. In the black clay, which is almost invariably found immediately over the auriferous deposit of the gutter: trunks of trees and other portions of wood are frequently found, preserving still their form, but so completely decomposed as to crumble to dust when exposed to the air.

The drifts (marked M) are the great dread of the miner, especially the novice; and many a life has been lost, and many a shaft also "lost" or ruined while sinking through those beds of sand. The danger and difficulty consists in the combat with a deposit of sand, oftentimes exceedingly fine, and charged with an apparently exhaustless flow of water; the want of cohesion among the particles of sand, added to the weight of water, rendering it a matter of the most extreme difficulty to fix the shaft timber in its place, so as to preserve the labor of, it may be months, from total destruction by the sudden rushing down of the drift, sand, and water, and consequent falling in of the walls of the shaft. In some cases when the source of water in these drift-beds has been higher than the point struck in sinking the shaft, the rush of water has been so great and rapid that the miner has not been able to escape; and before his mates could haul him up from below, the water has risen above his head and drowned him.

"The reef" is a term in constant use among the miners, and is the name given to the bottom or primitive rock, upon which all the alluvial, diluvial, and volcanic deposits rest; including, of course, the lowest of all, and best of all, the auriferous bottom of the gutter. In the lower portion of the plan, showing the cross section of the Frenchman's and White Horse Leads, the "reef" is seen to rise between the two leads in the form of a cone; the gutters, or old water-courses, having been filled up by a series of depositions that have not only covered over the ancient creeks, and filled the valley up to the top of the hills of those days—or reefs, as they are now called by the miner; but layer upon layer continued for nearly two hundred feet higher still. Thus, should "chaos come again," and the present valley of the Leigh, as seen in the upper portion of the plan, be filled up, and miners of the year 20,000, or somewhat later, perchance, essay to find the gutter of the Leigh—"reefers," instead of landing upon "micaceous sandstone," would, of course, bottom upon the dark-basalt, marked B, and shown on both sides of the creek rising in precisely the same manner as did the old rock from the sides of the ancient creeks now known as Frenchman's and White Horse gutters.

Printed at the *Star* Office, Ballarat.

Appendix III

April 1855 Public rally on Law & Order

The Age (Melbourne, Vic.: 1854 - 1954), Tuesday 17 April 1855, page 5

Ballarat should be in the disorderly condition it not was, and secondly, he regretted that we were under a government which could not fulfil the first duty of government, namely, the protection of life and property. Nothing shewed more plainly the inefficiency of a government than the feeble administration of justice, and, certainly, from the specimens he had seen, he should say that colonial justice resembled very much the justice spoken of by Butler,—

Which winks at crimes,
But stumbles on innocence sometimes.

However, they had not met there to argue, but to act. They had not met there to discuss political questions, but to redress social grievances. They all knew the facts. Outrages were perpetrated in the very midst of them, and the police were totally inefficient. "Necessity had no law." If the government would not give them protection they must protect themselves. The number of police now on the diggings was totally inadequate to the duties they were required to perform. It was true there were ninety soldiers on the camp, who, he believed, were principally occupied in the arduous duty of polishing their bayonets and pipeclaying their belts. He would suggest that, as the soldiers were quite unnecessary, they should be sent away, and an efficient police force sent in their place. The speaker then called upon the meeting as inhabitants of Ballarat, to vindicate the district in which they lived, and shew, whilst they valued their political rights, and were determined to work for them, they were not inclined to allow a few organised ruffians to make this gold-field notorious for outrages committed upon it. He concluded by moving the following resolution:—

2. That as outrages on person and property are sure to be more numerous as the winter advances, this meeting is of opinion that a committee should be formed to organise volunteers for the protection of life and property.

Mr. C. F. NICHOLLS seconded the resolution. He said that this was not a question on which to make speeches, but to act determinedly. He, for one could not understand why Ballarat should not be as well protected as Melbourne or Geelong. The amount of property on the gold fields was very large and the owners of it had a right to protection from the Government. The miners and storekeepers were taxed for the ostensible purpose of supporting an efficient police, but if the Government still continue to neglect this important matter, he considered that they were obtaining money under false pretences What they had to do at present was to see after their own safety. A memorial to the Governor would of necessity not receive an answer for some time, but the danger was imminent. It had been said that those who took part in this meeting would be marked. He for one felt perfectly indifferent to any threats of that kind, for he was able and willing to defend himself, if he should be compelled to do so After quoting some facts relative to the present inefficiency of the police, the speaker concluded by calling on the meeting to act with energy and unanimity in this matter.

The resolution was put in the usual manner, and carried.

Mr. BINNEY, of the firm of Binney and Gillot moved, and Mr. Allen, a miner, seconded the third resolution, with some useful and practical remarks.

3rd. That the following gentlemen form the Committee for the protection of life and property, with power to add to their number:—

Mr. Robert Muir   Mr. H. R. Nicholls

Mr. Robert Muir   Mr. H. R. Nicholls
Rolf   Lester
Oddie   Norman
Wilson   C F. Nicholls
Abrahams   W. C. Weeks

The resolution was put and carried unanimously.

Mr WEEKES next presented himself, and proceeded to read the form of memorial to His Excellency, as follows:—

To His Excellency Sir Charles Hotham, K.C.B., &c.—
The Memorial of the Storekeepers and Miners of Ballarat, in public meeting assembled.

Shaweth—That for some time past outrages on persons and property have been extremely prevalent on Ballarat.

That the evidence of storekeepers and miners, taken before a Sub-Committee of the Victorian Reform League proves that the police are totally inefficient in affording protection to your memorialists, and that outrages on person and property are becoming more numerous and audacious every day.

Your memorialists therefore pray that your Excellency will take immediate steps for providing a sufficient force of police to supply protection to the inhabitants of Ballarat, and thereby to save your memorialists the inconvenience of organising themselves for mutual protection.

And your memorialists will ever pray.

Mr Weekes in conclusion observed, that this was a measure of the highest importance. He wished always to act constitutionally. The Government had a right to give the people protection. There could be no doubt as to the facts; the present dangerous condition of the diggings was patent to all the world. But if the Government did not protect them they must protect themselves. He wished that the Governor would see the importance of this matter and take immediate steps to remedy the present defective condition of the police on Ballarat.

Mr ROLFE seconded the adoption of the memorial. He said he regarded the meeting as highly useful and necessary. He had been "stuck up" several times and even then was suffering from illness caused by exposure in guarding against depredations. He thought it was high time that some energetic measures were taken. If the Government would not and could not protect them there was only one course. The speaker concluded his very pertinent observations by stating, that he trusted something would be done at once to remedy the present bad state of affairs here.

The memorial was adopted by the meeting for presentation to the Governor, amidst loud applause.

Mr H. T. HOLYOAKE moved that a subscription be made to defray expenses of meeting, printing report, &c., which being carried, a vote of thanks was passed to the chairman, and the meeting separated.

It was noticed that several of the "rowdy" mob were in attendance, and inclined to be boisterous. The greater portion of the meeting seemed anxious that immediate and active steps should be taken to crush this dangerous evil. The committee appointed at the meeting meet on Monday evening to arrange matters for further organisation.

April 14th.

During the week a portion of the gang whose malpractices have of late annoyed us, have been captured. Messrs. Commissioner Daly, Sub-Inspector Nicholson, and Lieutenant Stoney, with a body of mounted troopers succeeded in doing this near Slaty Creek, where these worthies had made a regular settlement, and while nominally carrying on a lawful business, managed to obtain a living in a more questionable way. A large quantity of goods and a considerable sum of money are reported to have been found on way. A large quantity of goods and a considerable sum of money are reported to have been found on the premises, and as the men (six in number) have been remanded at the police-office for eight days, it is to be hoped that most of the property may be identified. I understand that, among the other things which have been come at, is a dog belonging to Mr. Daly. It was a rather singular greeting for this gentleman to find his own dog fawning upon him in the head quarters of such a party. It is said that a horse which was found in their possession had the brand on his shoulder, and a mark on his forehead, cut out, lest he might be recognised by his owner. One of the six was up at the last sessions here, but was acquitted. He stands a fair chance of again being honored by Mr. Crown Prosecutor Stawell's attention on the 20th instant. It is well that the affair has been nipped in the bud so far; it would be still better could the whole system be upset. There is one consolation that they are now in the hands of one of the most active of our police officers, Nicholson, who will try hard, now that he has got the game a foot, to see the chase well concluded.

To add to our state of fear, we have had a new source of terror added to that under which we have been for some time laboring. It is this:—Some soldiers who had been out carousing felt annoyed that they had not been included in a "shout" in a grog tent. They left, and on the way to the camp insulted and assaulted all who came in their way, until at last a large party of miners coming up, the soldiers were compelled to "shout" police, and fly to the camp. Up till this time there had been four of them. Information was given to the officer on guard. He coolly said, if they were out they would be missed at eleven o'clock, and then, he said, they would be punished, if you call to-morrow.

In about half an hour after this, two of the four referred to left the camp, armed with their muskets, and paraded along the main road, subjecting the passers by to a strict inspection, asking them what they were doing there at that hour, and in one well-established case, presenting their pieces at the men who would not be "stuck up." Information was again conveyed to the officer on guard, and as the report was confirmed by the arrival of an officer of police, the guard and a constable, after nearly an hour's delay, turned out to see what was going on. The delinquents were not found, as they had again gone to the camp in the meantime, and turned in; but it has since been discovered that one gun was loaded and another bore marks of having been lately fired off, or had the charge drawn, and one of the pouches had two rounds missing. This matter should be thoroughly investigated. Such pranks should not be permitted, on Ballarat especially. A repetition of the lark might, nay, would certainly lead to lamentable consequences.

Appendix IV

The Municipality Petitions 1855

VICTORIA
GOVERNMENT GAZETTE.

Published by Authority.

No. 97.]   TUESDAY, OCTOBER 2.   [1855.

Colonial Secretary's Office,
Melbourne, 4th September, 1855.

PETITION FOR MUNICIPAL INSTITUTIONS.

BALLAARAT.

IN pursuance of the Act of Council, 18 Victoria, No. 15, His Excellency the Governor, with the advice of the Executive Council, has been pleased to direct the publication of the substance and prayer of a Petition to His Excellency, signed by Two hundred and ninety-two householders, resident in the township of Ballaarat, as follows :—

The Petitioners state that they are resident within the township of Ballaarat, which contains a population of more than three hundred householders, within an area not exceeding nine square miles, no point of which is distant more than six miles from any other point.

They further state that they are desirous of availing themselves of the operation of the said Act of Council, and that the township of Ballaarat may be proclaimed a Municipal District by the name of "The Municipality of Ballaarat," and that the boundaries may be regulated in accordance with the said Act of Council.

And the Petitioners pray as follows :—

"Your Petitioners therefore humbly pray that Your Excellency may be pleased to cause the said township of Ballaarat to be proclaimed in due form a Municipal District, and also that the boundaries of the said Municipal District may be regulated pursuant to the provisions of the said Act of Council."

By His Excellency's Command,
P.10587.   WILLIAM C. HAINES.

Colonial Secretary's Office,
Melbourne, 4th September, 1855.

PETITION FOR MUNICIPAL INSTITUTIONS.

BALLAARAT.

IN pursuance of the Act of Council, 18 Victoria, No. 15, His Excellency the Governor, with the advice of the Executive Council, has been pleased to direct the publication of the substance and prayer of a Petition to His Excellency, signed by Two hundred and ninety-two house-holders, resident in the township of Ballaarat, as follows :—

The Petitioners state that they are resident within the township of Ballaarat, which contains a population of more than three hundred house-holders, within an area not exceeding nine square miles, no point of which is distant more than six miles from any other point.

They further state that they are desirous of availing themselves of the operation of the said Act of Council, and that the township of Ballaarat may be proclaimed a Municipal District by the name of "The Municipality of Ballaarat," and that the boundaries may be regulated in accordance with the said Act of Council.

And the Petitioners pray as follows :—

"Your Petitioners therefore humbly pray that Your Excellency may be pleased to cause the said township of Ballaarat to be proclaimed in due form a Municipal District, and also that the boundaries of the said Municipal District may be regulated pursuant to the provisions of the said Act of Council."

By His Excellency's Command,

P.10587.   WILLIAM C. HAINES.

Appendix V

Petition Proclamation

VICTORIA
GOVERNMENT GAZETTE.

Published by Authority.

No. 127.]　　TUESDAY, DECEMBER 18.　　[1855.

3275

LOCAL COURT DISTRICT OF STEIGLITZ.

PROCLAMATION

By His Excellency Sir CHARLES HOTHAM, Knight Commander of the Most Honourable Military Order of the Bath, Captain-General and Governor-in-Chief of the Colony of Victoria, and Vice-Admiral of the same, &c., &c., &c.

WHEREAS by an Act of the Governor and Legislative Council of the Colony of Victoria, passed in the eighteenth year of the Reign of Her present Majesty, initituled, "*An Act to amend the Laws relating to the Gold Fields*," it was amongst other things enacted that it should be lawful for the Governor, with the advice of the Executive Council, by Proclamation from time to time, to declare any Gold Field to be a District for the purpose of forming a Local Court, with the powers and authorities thereinafter described, and to declare the name of such District, and define the limits thereof, and after the publication of any such Proclamation the locality so described should be and become a District for the purposes of the said Act : Now therefore I, the Governor of the said Colony, do by this my Proclamation, in pursuance of the provisions of the said Act, and with the advice of the Executive Council, declare that the District hereinafter described and named shall be a District for the purpose of forming a Local Court within the meaning of the said Act, that is to say :—

DISTRICT OF STEIGLITZ.

Commencing at the north-west angle of the parish of Darriwil, thence by the northern boundary of that parish three miles and forty-four chains, thence by a line bearing north nine miles and forty chains, thence by a line bearing west six miles and twenty chains to the River Moorarbool, thence by the River Moorarbool to the north-west angle of the parish of Darriwil the commencing point aforesaid, and the said District shall be called "The Local Court District of Steiglitz."

Given under my Hand and the Seal of the Colony, at Melbourne, this seventeenth day of December, in the year of Our Lord One thousand eight hundred and fifty five, and in the nineteenth year of Her Majesty's Reign.

(L.S.)　　CHA^s. HOTHAM.
By His Excellency's Command,
WILLIAM C. HAINES.

GOD SAVE THE QUEEN!

MUNICIPAL DISTRICTS OF BALLAARAT AND PORTLAND.

PROCLAMATION

By His Excellency Sir CHARLES HOTHAM, Knight Commander of the Most Honourable Military Order of the Bath, Captain-General and Governor-in-Chief of the Colony of Victoria, and Vice-Admiral of the same, &c., &c., &c.

WHEREAS by an Act of the Lieutenant Governor and Legislative Council of the Colony of Victoria, passed in the eighteenth year of the Reign of Her present Majesty, initituled, "*An Act for the establishment of Municipal Institutions in Victoria*," it is amongst other things enacted, that any district of the Colony of Victoria, the area whereof shall not exceed nine square miles, and which shall contain a population of householders not less than three hundred, may, subject to the provisions of the said Act, be constituted a Municipal District as thereinafter mentioned, provided that no one point in any such area shall be distant more than six miles from any other point ; and it is further enacted that it shall be lawful for the Lieutenant Governor, with the advice of the Executive Council, on the receipt of a petition signed by not less than one hundred and fifty house-

trict under the said Act, to cause the substance and prayer of such petition to be published in the *Government Gazette*, and (if no counter petition, signed by an equal or greater number of householders resident within such locality shall have been delivered at the Office of the Colonial Secretary within one month from the date of such publication) the Lieutenant Governor, with the advice aforesaid, may, if he think fit, declare by Proclamation such locality a Municipal District by a name to be mentioned in such Proclamation, and also by the same or any other Proclamation may define the limits and boundaries of such Municipal District, and such limits and boundaries as any time thereafter in the same manner on receipt of a similar petition may vary and alter, but so as in no case, save as thereinafter mentioned, to include within the limits or boundaries of such Municipal District an area of more than nine square miles, and upon the publication of any such Proclamation in the *Government Gazette*, such locality so defined shall be deemed and taken to be a Municipal District within the meaning of the said Act ; And whereas petitions have been presented to the Governor by the householders resident within the respective Towns of Ballaarat and Portland, the substance and prayer of which petitions have been published, as directed by the said Act, but no counter petitions have been delivered in opposition thereto : Now therefore I, the Governor of the said Colony, do by this my Proclamation, in pursuance of the provisions of the said Act, with the advice of the Executive Council, declare that the districts hereinafter described and named shall be Municipal Districts within the meaning of the said Act : that is to say,—

MUNICIPAL DISTRICT OF BALLAARAT.—Commencing at the north-east angle of allotment 1 of section A, Parish of Ballaarat, thence by a line bearing east one mile twenty-two chains and eight links to a marked post; thence by a line bearing south to the River Yarrowee ; thence by the River Yarrowee to the southern boundary of the Township of Ballaarat ; thence by the said southern boundary and a line bearing west one mile and ten chains to a marked post ; thence by a line bearing north one mile four chains and forty links to the western boundary of the Police Paddock ; thence by the western and northern boundary lines of the said Police Paddock to the north-west angle of allotment 2 of section C, in the Parish of Ballaarat aforesaid ; and thence by a line bearing east, being the south side of a Government road, to the commencing point aforesaid.

And I do hereby, with the advice aforesaid, direct that the Council of the said Municipal District of Ballaarat shall be called by the name and style of "The Municipal Council of the District of Ballaarat."

MUNICIPAL DISTRICT OF PORTLAND.—Commencing at a point on the beach bearing east eight chains from the north angle of allotment 31 of northern suburbans, and bounded on the north by a line bearing west seventy-two chains ; on the west by a line bearing south two hundred and thirty-three chains and thirty-four links, more or less ; on the south by a line bearing east to the sea coast, and by the sea coast northerly to the point of commencement.

And I do hereby, with the advice aforesaid, direct that the Council of the said Municipal District of Portland shall be called by the name and style of "The Municipal Council of the District of Portland."

Given under my Hand and the Seal of the Colony, at Melbourne, this seventeenth day of December, in the year of Our Lord One thousand eight hundred and fifty-five, and in the nineteenth year of Her Majesty's Reign.

(L.S.)　　CHA^s. HOTHAM.
By His Excellency's Command,

Appendix VI

List of Petitioners
Ballarat (Vic.). Council. *City Council of Ballarat: the mayor's special report, 25th anniversary, 1881* Ballarat 1881

Copy of Petition of Householders of Ballaarat, praying for incorporation under the "Act for the Establishment of Municipal Institutions in Victoria," presented to His Excellency Sir Charles Hotham, &c.

To His Excellency Sir Charles Hotham, Knight of the most Honorable Military Order of the Bath, Captain General and Governor-in-Chief of the Colony of Victoria, and Vice-Admiral of the same, &c., &c., &c.

The humble Petition of the undersigned householders resident in the Township of Ballaarat, in the Colony of Victoria, SHEWETH—

THAT your Petitioners are resident within the Township of Ballaarat, in the Colony of Victoria.

THAT such township contains a population of more than Three hundred householders.

THAT the area of the township of Ballaarat does not exceed nine square miles, and that no one point in any such area is distant more than six miles from any other point.

THAT your Petitioners are desirous of availing themselves of the operations of the Act of Council 18th Vict., No. 15, entitled "An Act for the establishment of Municipal Institutions in Victoria," and they are desirous that the township of Ballaarat may be proclaimed in due course of law a Municipal District by the name of the Municipality of Ballaarat; and also that the boundaries of the said Municipal District may be regulated in accordance with the provisions of the said Act of Council.

Your Petitioners therefore humbly pray that your Excellency may be pleased to cause the said township of Ballaarat to be proclaimed in due form a Municipal District, and also that the boundaries of the said Municipal District may be regulated pursuant to the provisions of the said Act of Council. And your Petitioners:—

Wm. Henry Surplice, householder
★Muir Brothers & Co., householders
Adam Loftus Lynn, householder
★Thomas Comb, householder
Alex. McLaren, householder
★Wm. Tulloch, householder
W. E. Pierce, landowner
John T. F. Bowker, householder
William Craven, householder
James Bourchier, householder
Thomas Jones, householder
Joseph Dixie, householder
Thos. P. Genard, householder
Davies & Son, householders
Thomas Brown, householder
William Brown, householder

Charles Potts, householder
G. F. Potts, householder
R. Potts & Co., householders
Thos. Randall Solicitor, householder
★J. H. Harris Solicitor, householder
J. E. M. Wigley, Solicitor, householder
Henry Harris, householder
Samuel Irwin, landowner
John Gibbs, householder
H. J. McMillan, householder
Alex. Fraser, householder
George Redman, householder
J. H. F. Spanhake, householder
George Roberts, landholder
★A. B. Ranken, house and landowner
J. W. T. Cairns, house and landowner

II.

Francis Herring, house and landowner
George Howe, hotel-keeper
Geo. H. Gibson, surgeon
Thomas Cowan, householder
James W. R. Pringle, householder
Wm. Richards, householder
M. H. Cobea, house and landowner
Fred. Hitchins, landowner
H. L. Wortle, householder
Charles Brazier, householder
Joseph Southward, householder
George Anderson, publican
Craser & Co., house and landowners
H. M. Morris, householder
John Stewart, householder
Robert Dent, householder
Silas E. Craine, householder
Hauer Jusmond, householder
Thomas Lang, householder
Edward John Lewis, Solicitor, householder
Richard Clark, householder and Solicitor
Thomas Bath, householder and landowner
J. H. Alley, householder and landowner
H. George Wm. Cooper, householder and landowner
Moore & Dunn, householders and landowners
John Allen, householder and landowner
George Hunt, householder and landowner
Charles R. Williams, householder and landowner
Thomas White
S. C. Fraser
James R. H. Thackeray, M.A., P.L.D., householder and landowner
Augustus Dimock, M.D.
Benjamin Brokenshire, householder & landowner
Helpling & Greig, householders and landowners
Wm. Gibson, for self and partners (King, Gibson & Brown), storekeeper
Edward Hillson, householder
Lawrence Gibson
J. H. Bruce
Francis Brophy
H. Seekamp, householder and landowner
William Wills, householder and landowner
John Campbell, householder
Frederick D. Reed, householder
James Tappin, householder and landowner
Robert Reeves, merchant, Mair-st.
Benjamin Ward, Pimlico Store
Fletcher & Evans, printers
Arthur Crisp, householder
Jeremiah Blade, butcher
Wright & Evans, Auctioneers
C. Tarrant, householder
C. Simpson, householder
Crossley & Co.,
Robinson & Cole, Chemists, etc.

Biggs & Shoppee, storekeepers
John Watts
Williamson & Hart, storekeepers
Gibson & Stewart, storekeepers
T. and J. Bray, storekeepers
Gerrard & Co., storekeepers
J. W. Isaacs, Q.P.S., householder
Henry Paul Leman, surgeon, etc., householder
Oliver Brothers, householders
J. R. Grundy & Co., householders
Williams & May, householders
Joseph Willis, householder
Andrew McEmison, householder
A. E. & R. Alexander, merchants, householders
C. Stewart, householder
Robert Dickson, householder
Robert McNiece, timber merchant, householder
Henry Col, householder
Wm. Robertson, Manager Bank of Victoria, Ballarat
W. B. Chilwell, Manager Bank N. S. W.
Daniel Sweeney, auctioneer and landowner
M. Elliot, Manager Bank of Australasia, Ballarat
James Gray, householder
Hermand Berged, chemist
Gougon & Herring, storekeeper
Wm. McNee, Crow Dining Rooms
James Cummins, timber merchant
B. Bibanfold, storekeeper
Reynolds & English, storekeepers
E. Peril, storekeeper
Wm. Walker, storekeeper
Bradshaw & Salmon, storekeepers
Eyres Bros. & Newman, storekeepers
S. Solman
James D. Macartney, watchmaker
Chambers Brothers & Co., storekeepers
H. V. Freestone, storekeeper
H. Levinson, watchmaker
W. M. Letcher, gold broker
Alfred D'Bracy Brook, apothecary
Charles King, storekeeper
Adolph Pohl, merchant
James Mulholland, Innkeeper
William Wright, billiard-tablekeeper
Robert Walsh, Barrister-at-Law
W. C. Smith, auctioneer
Henry Thurston Evans, gold broker
B. J. Harris, householder
A. P. Bowes, auctioneer
W. Hood, landholder
William Bradshaw, landholder
Adam Beveridge, landholder
Edward Agar Wynne, landholder
Emil Pohl, wine merchant
Edward Hancock, Professor of Music
F. Lewers, landholder

III.

Samuel Walford, householder
R. A. Burton, solicitor
Joseph Tait, householder
Alfred A. Surplice, householder
William Surplice, householder
William Duncan, householder
James A. Douglas, householder
William Jackson, house and landholder
G. Butchart, Manager London Chartered Bank
J. W. Wilis, merchant, Ballarat
T. Conks
E. G. Emery
Robert Smith, house and landowner
George Heather, builder
A. & H. B. Chalmers, storekeeper
James Stewart, M.D.
Symons Oasey, land and householder
William Bramwell Robinson, chemist
Samuel M. Walker, householder
Charles Brown
Hilfling & Greig
Wm. Morrison, Township, merchant
John Allen, merchant
John Wilson, Township
Thomas Patti, Township, publican
Peter D. Murphy, Main Road, storekeeper
J. P. Jamieson, Main Road, merchant
Spencer Wilson & Co., Main Road, storekeepers
J. F. Grayling, Main Road, storekeeper
E. S. Woodin, Main Road, storekeeper
Hemmingway & Jones, Main Road, storekeepers
Morris Colman, Main Road, storekeeper
Thos. W. Brammer, Main Road, storekeeper
Swan & Co., Main Road, storekeepers
John Moore, Main Road, storekeeper
M. Walker, Main Road, storekeeper
George Fields, Bakery Hill, storekeeper
Reuben Marks, Bakery Hill, storekeeper
Edward Galastin, Bakery Hill, storekeeper
Robert McLister, Ballarat, storekeeper
Ansen P. Morris, Ballarat, storekeeper
Alex. Fraser, Black Hill, Union Hotel
Mr. F. Tyree, Ballarat, His Lordship Larder
G. B. Evans, Ballarat, labor mart
John C. McMamny, Golden Point, storekeeper
John English, Golden Point, storekeeper
Joseph Furlong, Golden Point, storekeeper
James Meagher, Golden Point, storekeeper
John Wildredge, Poverty Point, storekeeper
John Mildridge, Main Road, storekeeper
Henry Thos. Holyooke, Mechanics' Institute, storekeeper
Andrew Morrison, Red Streak, storekeeper
Brunery & Gillott, Red Streak, storekeeper
John Campbell, Main Road, "Age" Agent
Pole & Co., Main Road, storekeepers
Jeremiah Blann, Main Road, butcher

Hogg & Norris, Main Road, storekeepers
Peter Humble, Main Road, butcher
Charles Spencer, Main Road, storekeeper
Wicks & Herring, Main Road, storekeeper
J. R. Grundy & Co., Main Road, storekeepers
S. Braham, Main Road, storekeeper
E. Dight, storekeeper, Ballarat
M. E. Cooney, Main Road, storekeeper
W. Fletcher, Main Road, gold broker
J. H. Walters, Main Road, butcher
John Moon, thistle store, Main Road
Howell & Sherlock, caps tin shop, Main Road
Kean & Neilson, auctioneers, Main Road
Hyman Levinson, watchmaker, Main Road
Arthur H. Bayley, agent, Main Road
Henry Carpenter, ironmonger, Main Road
Joseph Whiat, storekeeper, Main Road
J. W. Green, "Argus" Agent
L. Sutton, musical instrument repairer, Bakery Hill
George M'Intosh, baker, Bakery Hill
P. Philp, Gravel Pit Flat
Thos. E. Young, storekeeper, Bakery Hill
Joseph Hull, bootmaker, Bakery Hill
Alexander Keens, watchmaker, Bakery Hill
Robert Bucten, storekeeper, Bakery Hill
Geo. Copley, coachmaker, Bakery Hill
T. H. Butler, physician, Red Hill
Chas. Wright, digger, Bakery Hill
David Alledsen, Milbugett
J. O. Veauzery, carpenter, Bakery Hill
John Harris, butcher, Bakery Hill
Augustus Beyer, blacksmith, Bakery Hill
R. A. Morrison, storekeeper, Bakery Hill
Mitchison Bros., auctioneers, Bakery Hill
Campbell & Davidson, bakers, Bakery Hill
A. Aussell, storekeeper, Bakery Hill
Hermansons, storekeeper, Bakery Hill
P. Cullen, Surgeon, Bakery Hill
D. Weigert, tobacconist, Bakery Hill
James Davis, druggist, Golden Point
Smith & Linklater, storekeepers, White Flat
C. W. Thompson, druggist, Golden Point
George Wilson, butcher, Golden Point
Thos. Michel, butcher, Golden Point
J. Kane, butcher, Golden Point
Herman, & Co., chemists, &c., Old Post Office Hill
Wilson & Co., storekeepers, Red Hill
B. D. McGill, jeweller, Red Hill
John Godfrey, watchmaker, &c., Red Hill Flat
William Gyland, watchmaker, &c., Main Road, Ballarat
S. & M. Joel, gold brokers, Red Hill Flat
Hobson & Warner, surgeons, &c., Main Road
S. Bielefeld, merchant, Ballarat Flat
H. Block & Co., storekeepers, Red Hill Flat

IV.

W. B. Rodier, storekeeper, Red Hill Flat
D. W. Callum, storekeeper, Specimen Hill
H. Boulter & Co., storekeeper, Specimen Hill
Wm. S. M. Fox, miner, Black Hill Flat
William McCullough, tailor, Township
H. P. R. Nicholls, miner, Township
C. F. Nicholls, miner, Township
Wm. S. Madden, miner, Bakery Hill
Alfred C. Hadral, miner, Gum Tree Flat
E. G. Tyree, builder, Gum Tree Flat
Robert Dunn, Township, merchant
Dixie & Partlin, Township, gold brokers
W. Surplice & Sons, Township, gold brokers
W. B. Ochiltree, Township, Manager Bank of New South Wales
T. Jones, Township, bootmaker
G. Roberts, Township, grocer
David McCallum, Township, storekeeper
Howe & Herring, Township, storekeepers
Davis & Son, Township, saddlers, &c.
Thos. & Wm. Brown, Township, stationers
William Dunkin, Township, blacksmith
H. H. McMillan, Township, Commission Agent
Edward Owpun, Main Road, mechanic
Alfred Lester, Free Trade Hotel, Eureka
Thomas Horne, Township, baker
Samuel C. Fraser, Township, merchant
John G. Strachan, Suburbs
Issachau Marks, Main Road, storekeeper
Tryree Green & Co., Main Road, auctioneers
Henry Jackson, Main Road, butcher
William Wasley, Red Hill, butcher
Binney & Gillott, Golden Point, storekeeper
Charles Evans, Ballarat, printer
Charles Norman, Main Road, pastry cook
Charles Wood, Golden Point, storekeeper
William Cameron, Golden Point, storekeeper
Fred. Young, Golden Point, chemist & druggist
Neill & Lang, Golden Point, bakers
James Wright, Golden Point, baker
William Fryer, Golden Point, householder

Appendix VII

Offer of Land by Government Surveyor

VPRS 2500 P0000/1 *Ballarat Municipal Council Letters Inward January December 1856-1857*

> Ballaarat 29th January 1856
>
> Dear Sir   Ballaarat Municipality
>
> In compliance with the request conveyed in yours of 28th inst. I beg to enclose the original letter received by me from the Surveyor General, informing me that His Excellency in Council has been pleased to approve of the portion of Land Allotment 2 of Section 1 Town of Ballaarat being appropriated for the use of the Municipal Council.
>
> At the same time I have to ask that the Council will direct its production in the event of my requiring reference to it hereafter, inasmuch as it forms a portion of a correspondence undertaken by myself on the suggestion of the Committee for obtaining the Municipality.
>
> I beg to inform the Council that the Land in question was some time since applied for by Mr Taylor the Government Surveyor at Ballaarat, but that he consented to waive his claim for the benefit of the Municipality, provided a sufficient portion of the Land for Government Survey Offices was reserved to the

Government. I was upon this understanding that he recommended to the Government on being applied to for the subject my application that the Grant should be made for a Town Hall &c. —

And though from a verbal communication from him I have reason to believe he is prepared to give up all claim to any part of the Land, yet I think it right to put you in possession of the circumstances affecting the proposed Grant of Land

I have the honor to be
Sir
Your obedt Servt

J. M. Wigley

To
The Chairman of the Ballaarat Municipality

Appendix VIII

Valuator's First Report:

VPRS 2500 P0000/1 *Ballarat Municipal Council Letters Inward January – December 1856-1857*

Abstract of Assessment

#	Street	Assessments	£
1	Sturt Street	44 assessments	3,605
2	Mair Street	44 do.	3,936
3	Dana Street	51 do.	2,040
4	Eyre Street	33 do.	730
5	Urquhart Street	" do.	"
6	South Street	" do.	"
7	Drummond Street	18 do.	256
8	Errard Street	36 do.	758
9	Raglan Street	30 do.	853
10	Lyons Street	26 do.	870
11	Dawson Street	30 do.	947
12	Doveton Street	43 do.	2,247
13	Armstrong Street	54 do.	5,998
14	Lydiard Street	57 do.	15,225
15	Eureka Street	9 do.	195
	Suburban Lands Facing Swamp	20 do.	2,348
	Drummond St North of Mair St	28 do.	2,089
Suburban Lands	Gov'n Road North & Main Street	25 do.	4,777
	Great Main Road and Market Place	57 do.	3,747
	North East of Swamp	1 do.	187
	Burnbank road and Facing north of Swamp	9 do.	540
		595 assessments	£48,328

www.ingramcontent.com/pod-product-compliance
Lightning Source LLC
Chambersburg PA
CBHW051418290426
44109CB00016B/1342